Advising Clients with HIV and AIDS

Advising Clients with HIV and AIDS

General Editors

Isabel Manley
BA; LlM; Solicitor, formerly with Immunity Legal Centre; part-time Chairman of Employment Tribunals

Avrom Sherr
Woolf Professor of Legal Education, Institute of Advanced Legal Studies

Contributors

Geoffrey Bindman
Solicitor, Bindman & Partners; Visiting Professor of Law, University College London; Honorary President of Discrimination Law Association

Alison Burt
Solicitor, Bindman & Partners

Luke Clements
MSc; Solicitor, Thorpes; Research Fellow, University of Wales, Cardiff

Stephen Deutz
Solicitor, Terrence Higgins Trust

Terrence Donovan
BA (Hons, History); Solicitor, Bindman & Partners

Wesley Gryk
BA (Harvard); JD (Harvard); Fulbright Fellow, Warsaw University; Member of the Bar of New York; Solicitor, Wesley Gryk Solicitors

Angus Hamilton
Solicitor, Hamiltons

Ivan Massow
Financial Adviser, Massows

Lorraine Sherr
Doctor, Reader in Health Psychology at the Royal Free Hospital Medical School

Julia Thackray
Solicitor, Bindman & Partners

Butterworths

United Kingdom	Butterworths, a Division of Reed Elsevier (UK) Ltd, Halsbury House, 35 Chancery Lane, LONDON WC2A 1EL and 4 Hill Street, EDINBURGH EH2 3JZ
Australia	Butterworths, a Division of Reed International Books Australia Pty Ltd, CHATSWOOD, New South Wales
Canada	Butterworths Canada Ltd, MARKHAM, Ontario
Hong Kong	Butterworths Asia (Hong Kong), HONG KONG
India	Butterworths India, NEW DELHI
Ireland	Butterworth (Ireland) Ltd, DUBLIN
Malaysia	Malayan Law Journal Sdn Bhd, KUALA LUMPUR
New Zealand	Butterworths of New Zealand Ltd, WELLINGTON
Singapore	Butterworths Asia, SINGAPORE
South Africa	Butterworths Publishers (Pty) Ltd, DURBAN
USA	Lexis Law Publishing, CHARLOTTESVILLE, Virginia

A CIP Catalogue record for this book is available from the British Library.

ISBN 0406 903034

ISBN 0-406-90303-4

9 780406 903037

Printed by Redwood Books, Trowbridge

Foreword

This book is a valuable addition to Butterworths' publications in important areas of medical law and practice and the effective protection of human rights. It explains in clear and practical terms the complex areas of law and practice that need to be understood by everyone who advises clients suffering from HIV and AIDS. It deals sensitively with a very wide range of difficult legal and social problems.

The reader is skilfully led through the tangled thickets of discrimination law. The book explains the duties and responsibilities of social services providers and the knotty problems about consent and liability for medical treatment. It examines issues concerning children and the family, immigration and the right to travel, the criminal process and imprisonment, organising the client's financial affairs and preparing for death.

Like the companion work, *Advising Gay and Lesbian Clients*, its authors combine impressive professional skills with a wealth of practical experience acquired in working to protect the interests of this and other minorities.

It is a handbook that needs to be in the libraries not only of specialist lawyers who are advising this group of clients, but also of health professionals, local authorities and advice agencies, to guide them in their daily work.

Lord Lester of Herne Hill QC

Contents

Chapter 6 Immigration and the right to travel

Wesley Gryk

Chapter 7 HIV and criminal law

Angus Hamilton

Chapter 8 Personal finance and HIV

Ivan Massow

Chapter 9 Preparing for death *Steve Deutz*

Appendix I

Appendix II

Appendix III

Appendix IV

Afterword

Table of statutes

References in this Table are to paragraph number.

Table of statutory instruments

Table of cases

A

B

S

Chapter 1

The client affected by HIV and AIDS

Isabel Manley

A INTRODUCTION

1.01 In the normal course of events, a lawyer or adviser will, of course, see a range of clients with a variety of legal problems. Some may present a number of different issues, not all of which will be easy to resolve in terms of any legal remedy. Many of them may already be vulnerable individuals from a disadvantaged group. In the case of clients with HIV or AIDS, there are often a multitude of problems to add to the extra difficulties of ill-health and the knowledge that they have a terminal condition. Advisers may be seeing the client at a particularly stressful time of their life, possibly when they have just been diagnosed or when they have become ill with an AIDS-related condition. They may even be facing the prospect of imminent death. Add to this any legal problem and the adviser has a highly vulnerable client and one for whom particular sensitivity should be shown.

1.02 It is often the case that the adviser may first speak to a partner, family member or professional health care or social care worker. In some cases, the client will not be the person with the virus, but someone 'affected' by it, a bereaved child or partner for instance. All these factors mean that advisers should be particularly aware of the special needs of this client group and this chapter aims to establish some of the ways in which these needs might begin to be met.

1.03 In many ways there is nothing about a client affected by HIV and AIDS that is different from any other client[1]. All are entitled to a first class service where their individual needs are met, where standards are high, where systems ensure confidentiality and that the best possible outcome is achieved. In many ways, the suggestions made in this chapter are a reminder of what best practice is in any legal service and they are only contained within this book because failure to abide by them may have greater consequences for clients already in a difficult situation.

1 See Sherr, A, *Client Care for Lawyers* (1999). But see also Afterword:The legal needs of people

1.04 Many of those affected by the virus in the UK are gay men. Advisers should be aware of this and ensure that they do not make assumptions based on society's predominant heterosexual partnering. However, advisers should be similarly aware that many heterosexual men are HIV positive and not make incorrect assumptions here either. It will usually be irrelevant to have details of sexual history or to guess how the person became infected, unless that is the issue which the client wishes to address.

1.05 Another large group of people with HIV are those from countries other than the UK, particularly Africa. These clients may have a number of legal problems and may well have lost more than one family member to the disease. They may also not have English as their first language and will therefore need an interpreter. It is necessary to use recognised independent interpreters and to be extra vigilant about confidentiality. It will be essential to respect religious and cultural views and traditions and, again, not to make any assumptions.

1.06 Intravenous drug users are another group of those who have become infected with HIV. An adviser will not necessarily know this but, if it does emerge as an issue, it should not be allowed to colour the judgment of the case. Finally, a number of haemophiliacs became infected through transfusion of blood products, a situation which should no longer occur as all donated blood has been routinely screened since the mid-1980s. A settlement between the government and haemophiliacs was reached some years ago but they may well present with other legal problems.

B THE HEALTH BACKGROUND

1.07 In the UK there have been a total of 32,000 HIV infections diagnosed with 15,500 of those having progressed to AIDS. There have been 12,800 AIDS- or HIV-related deaths[1]. HIV (Human Immunodeficiency Virus) is a virus that attacks the body's immune system. After infection the body's defences will continue to work for some time, maybe for many years and the person can remain well. However, in the majority of cases, the immune system does begin to break down and the person may succumb to minor or major infections. AIDS (Acquired Immune Deficiency Syndrome) is the term which has been used for the later stages or more serious infections of someone who is HIV positive. The use of these terms has changed over the years and they may be differently defined in the UK from other countries. Advisers should avoid using the term AIDS unless it is of benefit to the client, for instance, in mitigation in a criminal matter of for support where the exercise of discretion is being sought. A dramatic reduction in the numbers progressing to clinical illness (AIDS) has been observed since 1997, due in the most part to the new combination of highly active anti-retroviral therapy (HAART).

1 Public Health Laboratory Service (PHLS), June 1999.

1.08 A person becomes infected when a significant amount of the virus enters the bloodstream. Only some bodily fluids potentially have sufficient amounts of the virus. These are blood, sperm and seminal fluid, vaginal fluids and breast milk. In the UK the two most affected groups are gay men through unprotected anal sex and heterosexuals, with high concentrations among people from countries where HIV is endemic. The virus attacks the immune system by infecting white blood cells known as CD4 (or T cells or helper cells). As the numbers of CD4 cells decline the body has increasing difficulties in fighting off infection. One of the ways in which the health of a person with HIV will be measured is by reference to the CD4 count. The range for someone without the virus is between 800–1500. Those who are HIV positive may have drug therapy suggested to them if their CD4 count is below 500 but there are those with low CD4 counts who may still be 'healthy'. The risk is that they are prone to life threatening or 'opportunistic' infections such as:

(a) pneumocystis carinii pneumonia (PCP)—a form of pneumonia;
(b) cytomegalovirus (CMV)—which can cause blindness and serious brain and lung problems;
(c) karposi's sarcoma (KS)—a rare cancer; and
(d) tuberculosis (TB) and lymphomas.

1.09 A person living with HIV in the UK will have access, especially in London, to some excellent treatment centres where their CD4 and viral load will be monitored. Within the last few years drugs have been developed that have dramatically improved the health and prognosis for many living with the virus (HAART). These are known as combination or triple therapy. However, it is not a cure and it involves a large number of drugs with some unpleasant side effects. It has been found that the drugs are not effective for everyone who might benefit from them. Rigid adherence is demanded and resistant strains create a problem.

1.10 It will very much depend what the client's legal problem is as to how much of their health background the adviser will need to know. It is always advisable to have some idea of prognosis in case the client's life expectancy is very limited and needs processing urgently. Otherwise it will be particularly relevant for immigration cases where the Secretary of State is being asked to exercise discretion on compassionate grounds, for cases involving children and mental capacity.

1.11 The best sources of information on all the health issues are the National AIDS Manual (NAM) Reference Manual and NAM Treatments Manual. As far as the individual client is concerned, his or her doctor, either at the clinic or in General Practice, should be approached. Written consent will be needed, of course and advisers should be careful to ask just for the information they need.

C CONFIDENTIALITY

1.12 There is no right to privacy in the UK. However, a person who believes that information has been unlawfully disclosed may bring a civil action for breach of confidentiality. It is possible that an injunction may be granted if a breach is about to occur and damages or a declaration are other possible remedies. Confidentiality was defined in *A-G v Guardian Newspapers (No 2)*[1] in the following way:

> 'A duty of confidence arises when the confidential information comes to the knowledge of a person (the confidant) in circumstances where s/he ... to have agreed, that the information is confidential, ... circumstances that

This rule does not give absolute protection and must be weighed in the public interest. This was examined in the case of *X v Y*[2] where a newspaper wanted to disclose the identity of two HIV positive doctors. A permanent injunction to prevent the paper from doing so was granted. See also the case explored below at para **1.17**.

1 [1988] 3 All ER 545.
2 [1988] 2 All ER 648.

1.13 Solicitors and barristers, in their professional lives, are bound by their respective codes of conduct in respect to keeping clients' affairs confidential[1]. This obviously applies to all clients except those who have waived their right to confidentiality for any reason. This may seem to be an obvious thing to say but most practitioners will be aware that client confidentiality is routinely broken by advisers who do not think things through carefully enough. For instance, how many times do lawyers ring to speak to a client who is not there and then leave a message saying who has called, often with a complete stranger? How many solicitors' offices can you walk into where you can see files with clients' names clearly visible upon them? How many dinner parties have you been to where another lawyer has discussed their interesting case where all the parties are easily identifiable?

1 The Law Society's Guide to the Professional Conduct of Solicitors (8th edn, 1999), ch 16 and The Code of Conduct of the Bar of England and Wales, para 603.

1.14 It is vital for anyone doing work with those affected by HIV and AIDS to have a clear and effective confidentiality policy. Immunity Legal Centre, which closed in March 1998, had a policy as does the Advice Centre at the Terrence Higgins Trust. Although these policies have the particular vulnerability of people living with HIV and AIDS in mind, there is no reason why they should not apply to all legal services. Why they are of such importance to people with HIV or AIDS is primarily because the media, or more specifically, one or two newspapers, have chosen to use stories about people living with the virus as a means of scaremongering and as further ways to attack groups already vilified by the press. It is not always possible to ensure that the press does not get hold of information, especially if the matter goes to court (see paras **1.17**ff on anonymity), but it is essential to ensure that leaks do not occur from the adviser's own offices.

D ANONYMITY ORDERS IN COURT PROCEEDINGS

1.15 Anyone who is advising a client on whether to choose litigation as a way of resolving a dispute should always bear in mind the possible adverse publicity which may result. For a person with the virus it is often of concern for a number of reasons. Many clients affected by HIV and AIDS come from groups which already bear the brunt of attacks by critical media. They may be gay men or asylum seekers for instance. They may be neither but understand that the common perception of someone who is HIV positive may suggest that they come from one of those groups. Some but by no means all, have told their friends and family of their HIV status, but may not want their employer or neighbours to know. For these reasons it is vital that the publicity aspect is discussed realistically and in detail. It may be that the client neither minds nor cares who knows that they are HIV positive and may even wish to litigate to raise awareness about a particular issue. As long as they are reminded about the distortions and innuendoes which could occur, there is no reason why they should not exercise their right to litigate for the fear of publicity alone.

1.16 For others, it will be a real and genuine fear and much thought will need to be given as to how to assist them exercise their right to litigate whilst protecting them, as far as possible, from publicity. Most hearings (with the exception of cases involving children) before courts and tribunals in England and Wales are held in public. The principle of justice being seen to be done is one which is fundamental to the rule of law in the UK and, rightly or wrongly, does not seem to be capable of amendment at the present time. The best way to protect the client is to secure an anonymity order in court proceedings.

1.17 This was most recently explored in the case of *Re D*[1]. This case concerned a Brazilian overstayer who had applied for assistance to Brent Council under the National Assistance Act 1948. When he was refused, he applied for leave to move for judicial review and, at the same time, applied for an order protecting him from being identified. The court granted leave and made the anonymity order under the Contempt of Court Act 1981. There had already been some publicity about the case and the *Evening Standard* applied to the court for the anonymity order to be rescinded. The judge considered a number of cases, including *R v Westminster City Council, ex p Castelli and Tristan-Garcia*[2] which also involved plaintiffs who were HIV positive. In the earlier case, the court had refused to make an order mainly on the grounds that there had been substantial publicity as a result of the leave application. The names of the plaintiffs were already in the public domain. In *Re D* this was not the case and the judge made the order. The test is whether the applicant would reasonably be deterred from seeking justice at the hands of the court.

1 (1997) 45 BMLR 191, QBD, CCLR 1998 Legal Action Group.
2 [1996] 3 FCR 49, QBD.

1.18 In Employment Tribunals there is no right to seek an anonymity order but there are two ways that publicity might be avoided. If the case is one under the Disability Discrimination Act 1995, an application can be made under the Employment (Constitution etc) Regulations 1993, reg 14[1] for a restricted reporting order. This will prevent the party in respect of whom the order is made from being identified, but only whilst the case is progressing. Once a decision is promulgated it becomes a public document and the names must be given.

1 SI 1993/2687.

1.19 Under the rules of procedure, an employment tribunal chairman has some discretion as to how the hearing proceeds and it will often be worthwhile to ask not to disclose addresses in public or refer to the nature of the illness unless necessary. This should be discussed with the client and a letter to the tribunal explaining the circumstances may mean that no information is disclosed other than that which is strictly necessary.

E BEYOND THE INDIVIDUAL CASE

... may be called upon to represent the views and interests ... of government, local

1.21 The case of the mother and baby in *Re C*[1] involved lawyers and others on behalf to the hospital, the parents and the local authority, all with quite different standpoints on the best interests of the baby and its parents. Issues of testing in general and pregnant women and mothers in particular, present great conundrums in relation to individual liberty and public health, which may need legal assistance to pull apart and identify with clarity.

1 [1999] 3 FCR 289.

1.22 Groups who work on behalf of those with HIV and AIDS often also lend assistance to hone their views or transmit a useful expression of those views. Legal advice can be essential to finding a current position. Legal skills may also be useful in surveying the onus of rights and discrimination more generally in order to develop the law and policy which affects people with HIV and AIDS and all those who are affected by the disease.

F THE HUMAN RIGHTS ACT 1998

1.23 This was given Royal Assent in November 1998 and comes into force in October 2000. Essentially the Act is an attempt to incorporate the European Convention on Human Rights (ECHR) into UK law. A number of articles of the Convention may be of relevance to people with HIV or AIDS and advisers should consider the ECHR with a view to arguing their persuasive elements to the court. In particular, consider the following:

(a) art 2 Right to life (withdrawal of drug treatment);
(b) art 3 Right to respect for private and family life (separated families or same-sex couples); and
(c) art 14 Prohibition of discrimination (only when attached to another right).

This introductory chapter has only touched the surface of some of the many legal issues that concern people affected by the virus. Above all, all clients should be treated with respect and, in the best traditions of the law, given a high standard of non-judgmental legal help.

Chapter 2

Discrimination

Geoffrey Bindman

A INTRODUCTION

2.01 There are many people from a range of backgrounds who face discrimination in many areas of their lives. It is acknowledged that, for example, women, children and the elderly, people from ethnic minority backgrounds, those whose lifestyle may be different from the common perception of what is acceptable and many others often are treated less favourably than others.

2.02 Discrimination fails to treat people as individuals by concentrating on stereotypical assumptions. Anti-discrimination measures have tried to deal with this problem by introducing the concept that these assumptions should not lead to unfair treatment in particular areas of life. The campaign for equal treatment has been a long one and is continuing. The law has only managed to deal with a few narrow issues affecting certain groups, thereby leaving discriminatory treatment against some groups completely unprotected.

2.03 People affected by HIV and AIDS have found themselves the victims of discrimination. Some people affected by the virus already face discrimination on other grounds, for instance gay men, refugees and asylum seekers or intravenous drug users. The aim of this chapter is to focus on what might be unlawful and therefore actionable discrimination. It should be stressed that, however reprehensible it may be, not all unjustified discrimination will also be potentially unlawful.

2.04 On specified grounds and within important limits, discrimination in the employment context and in the provision of goods and services has been a civil wrong since 1968 when the second Race Relations Act came into force in the UK. Since then the law against racial discrimination has been strengthened as the Sex Discrimination Act 1975 prohibited discrimination on the grounds of sex or marital status and the Disability Discrimination Act 1995 has attempted to address the difficulties of those living with disabilities. The Protection from Harassment Act 1997 introduced both civil and criminal sanctions to assist victims of discrimination.

2.05 The United Kingdom, as a member of the European Community and [illegible] in that regard. Specifically, the and, following the Amsterdam Treaty, discrimination on other grounds will be addressed. Finally, the Human Rights Act 1998 will incorporate the European Convention on Human Rights into UK law and will almost certainly impact on the area of anti-discrimination. It is to be expected that there will be challenges that seek to extend protection to people including those who otherwise fall outside of the remit of the aforementioned legislation.

People affected by HIV and AIDS

2.06 Discrimination against a person with HIV is not, of itself, unlawful unless the person is within the definition of a person with a disability under the Disability Discrimination Act 1995 or, where arguments could be raised under the other anti-discrimination statutes outlined in para **2.05**. However there are a number of ways in which unequal treatment can be challenged some of them requiring some imagination and advisers will be directed towards them in the relevant instance.

2.07 The possibilities will be considered by area: first, discrimination in employment and then in other areas, including in the provision of goods and services and in education. There are also a number of instances of discrimination in insurance that affect people with HIV and AIDS which will be considered separately (see also Ch 8).

B DISCRIMINATION IN EMPLOYMENT

2.08 Most employment rights, such as the right not to be unfairly dismissed and the right to a minimum notice period, do not come into effect until after employment has started. Some further rights may take up to two years to come into effect and may depend on whether the person concerned is an 'employee'. However, anti-discrimination legislation can be effective regardless of the period of employment and can also cover the recruitment process and a wider range of workers than those defined as 'employees'. In discussing the Disability Discrimination Act 1995 and other anti-discrimination legislation it should be remembered that a person who is HIV positive may be able to use the limited protection of that Act if they consider that they have been discriminated against in not being offered a job in addition to experiencing discrimination once employment has started.

1 Disability Discrimination Act 1995

2.09 This is probably the best starting place when someone who is HIV positive complains of discriminatory treatment in employment. The employment provisions of the Disability Discrimination Act 1995 came into force in December 1996 so at the time of writing there are few reported cases and it is taking some time for a clear picture to emerge of its effectiveness. It has important differences from the Sex Discrimination Act 1975 and the Race Relations Act 1976 including a small employer exemption which, since December 1998, has meant that employers with less than 15 employees are not covered, although this limit is subject to review[1]. There are also a number of occupation groups which are excluded, including prison officers and the armed forces.

1 Disability Discrimination Act 1995, s 7.

2 Definition of disability

2.10 Only those whose disability falls within the definition contained in the Act can rely on its provisions: which is a particular difficulty for clients affected by HIV. The Act covers disabled people and people with past disabilities. The primary definition is as follows:

> '...a person has a disability for the purposes of this Act if he has a physical or mental impairment which has a substantial and long-term adverse effect on his ability to carry out normal day-to-day activities.'[1]

1 Disability Discrimination Act 1995, s 1.

2.11 This provision is supplemented by Sch 1 to the Act where the meanings of the component parts such as 'impairment', 'long-term adverse effect', 'normal day-to-day activities' and 'substantial...adverse effect' are further defined. There are also regulations in respect of the definition but these are not particularly relevant to someone with HIV. However para 8 of Sch 1 is of significance. This deals with progressive conditions:

> 'Where—
> (a) a person has a progressive condition (such as cancer, multiple sclerosis or muscular dystrophy or infection by the human immunodeficiency virus);
> (b) as a result of that condition, he has an impairment which has (or had) an effect on his ability to carry out normal day-to-day activities; but
> (c) that effect is not (or was not) a substantial effect;
> he shall be taken to have an impairment which has such a substantial adverse effect if the condition is likely to result in his having such an impairment.'

2.12 What this means in practice is that someone who is HIV positive need not show that they have had the condition for a year or that it has a substantial adverse effect, only that it has some effect on their ability to carry out day-to-day activities. This is thought to indicate that those who have been diagnosed with an AIDS-related condition or are HIV symptomatic would be covered, but not someone with no symptoms. This is problematic because the definitions of those conditions can be flexible and still depends on the applicant being able to prove that day-to-day activities are affected.

2.13 Help can be sought from the Code of Practice and the Guidance which were published to support the Disability Discrimination Act 1995 and which will be taken into account by tribunals. There are also a number of cases on this initial point of definition.

2.14 But, if the condition of the person fits into the definition or it is arguable that they will, when will discrimination be prohibited by the Disability Discrimination Act 1995? First, considering the position of a job applicant, the Disability Discrimination Act 1995 makes it unlawful for an employer to discriminate against a disabled person:

> '(a) in the arrangements which he makes for the purpose of determining to whom he should offer employment;
> (b) in the terms on which he offers that person employment; or
> ... him employment.'[1]

2.15 Section 5 of the Disability Discrimination Act 1995 makes it clear that discrimination exists where there is less favourable treatment and that treatment cannot be justified. A further duty is placed on a potential employer under s 6:

> '(1) Where—
> (a) any arrangement made by or on behalf of an employer; or
> (b) any physical feature of premises occupied by the employer;
> place the disabled person at a substantial disadvantage in comparison with persons who are not disabled, it is the duty of the employer to take such steps as it is reasonable, in all the circumstances of the case, for him to take in order to prevent the arrangements or feature having that effect.'

There follows an explanation of when this duty arises, examples of steps that might be taken and what might be taken into account in deciding what is reasonable.

2.16 A disabled person includes an applicant for employment, or someone who has notified the employer that they may be an applicant, who has a disability[1]. There are a number of possible instances of discrimination that arise for people before employment. The first is that a potential employer may ask all applicants or interviewees to have an HIV test. As mentioned in Ch 4, anyone asked to take an HIV test must give informed consent and the results of that test are confidential to the medical practitioner and the 'patient'. The reality is that people may feel they have no alternative but to consent in order to be considered for employment. In the writers' experience there are only two large employers who ask for such a test and then in limited circumstances. Is such a request a breach of the Disability Discrimination Act 1995? This would seem to be arguable although there are no reported cases. Of course, it would depend on whether the person had taken the test and what the result was. This is a problem that runs through the Act, that it only protects those who have a disability according to the definition in s 1. This difficulty will be discussed in more detail later when looking at the limited help the Act may give. Suffice it to say that, currently, someone who refuses to take the test or has a positive test result but who is asymptomatic, may well not have a remedy. However, advisers should consider carefully whether, even though the person believes they are aysmptomatic, there might be sufficient ill-health to bring them within the definition of s 1. Clients may be inclined to underestimate their symptoms and a medical report may indicate some effects that are not immediately obvious. It is also possible that the employer will consider settling a possible discrimination case rather than risking adverse publicity and the cost of litigation.

1 Disability Discrimination Act 1995, ss 5, 6.

2.17 What of other barriers to recruitment? Again, anyone seeking to use the protection of the Disability Discrimination Act 1995 must fit within the definition of disability in s 1. If they do, they may be able to indicate discriminatory treatment if they fail to be offered a post or argue that reasonable adjustments were not made to enable them to succeed. In the first instance 'less favourable treatment' under s 5 will have to be demonstrated, which means finding a 'comparator'. Identifying the correct comparator has often been harder than it ought to be in anti-discrimination legislation. The question has recently been clarified by the Court of Appeal in the case of *Clark v Novacold Ltd*[1] in which it was decided that a disabled person would need to show that the correct comparator would be someone to whom the reason for that less favourable treatment does not apply. In the case of someone who has symptoms as a result of HIV, there might be a situation where the arrangements for the interview or the failure to make a job offer may be for such a reason—for example, the need to eat regularly or facilities to take medication—that would not apply to another person. In the case of job interviews, one reported case is not of a great deal of assistance. Where a disabled person is not offered the job, there are a number of possibilities of discrimination and it will depend very much on the level of the necessary adjustment, the cost and the size of the employer. In one case the Employment Appeal Tribunal decided that whilst it would be reasonable to make physical adjustments to provide disabled access to the toilets, the employer did not have a duty to provide a carer[2]. One of the most useful ways of considering whether a person who has not succeeded in securing a job because of their need for an adjustment is to consider the Code of Practice and the Guidance to the Disability Discrimination Act 1995 which give useful examples of what might be reasonable adjustments and those which tribunals have indicated should be considered. On a practical and negotiating level, employers should be reminded that the Department for Education and Employment through PACT (Placing, Assessment and Counselling Team) under the Access to Work Scheme have funds and advisers available to assist employers in this respect.

1 *Clark v Novacold Ltd* [1999] 2 All ER 977, [1999] ICR 951, CA.
2 *Kenny v Hampshire Constabulary* [1999] ICR 27, [1999] IRLR 76.

2.18 A person may already be an employee who has encountered discrimination, including dismissal, when he or she seeks advice. The Disability Discrimination Act 1995 states:

> '(2) It is unlawful for an employer to discriminate against a disabled person whom he employs—
> (a) in the terms of employment which he affords him;
> (b) in the opportunities which he affords him for promotion, a transfer, training or receiving any other benefit;
> (c) by refusing to afford him, or deliberately not affording him, any such opportunity; or
> (d) by dismissing him, or subjecting him to any other detriment.'

2.19 The duty under s 6 to make reasonable adjustments also extends to employees. The circumstance where it is most likely to occur is when people are facing action under the disciplinary or capability procedure and dismissal may be contemplated. Reliance on the Disability Discrimination Act 1995 may be useful for existing employees when they have been on long-term sick leave or are newly diagnosed and feel unable to continue working on a full-time basis.

2.20 Advisers should remember that the s 6 duty will only be relevant where the employer knows or ought to know about the disability. Guidance is given on this in the Code of Practice which states:

> 'The Act does not prevent a disabled person keeping a disability confidential from an employer. But it is likely that unless the employer could reasonably be expected to know about the person's disability anyway, the employer will not be under a duty to make a reasonable

case may be, someone acting on the employer's behalf—with sufficient information to carry out that adjustment.

An employee has symptomatic HIV. He prefers not to tell his employer of the condition. However, as the condition progresses, he finds it difficult to work the required number of hours in a week. Until he tells his employer of his condition—or the employer becomes or could reasonably be expected to be aware of it—he cannot require the employer to change his working hours to overcome the difficulty. However, once the employer is informed he may then have to make a reasonable adjustment.'[1]

1 Code of Practice for the Elimination of Discrimination in the Field of Employment Against Disabled Persons or Persons who have had a Disability (1996).

2.21 This extract suggests that an adjustment to part-time working is one which would be expected to take place, bearing in mind that any failure to make such an adjustment could be justified by reference to the size of the business, cost and efficiency and so on.

2.22 However, the extract also hints that many people who are infected with HIV may not want their employer to know. Confidentiality is dealt with in more detail in Chapter 1 but it is important for employees who want to ask for adjustments to realise that it will necessitate some information being passed on, albeit that it should be possible to limit the extent of the information to certain key people in the organisation. Case law has indicated that, where the employee had ME or chronic fatigue syndrome, as the Code suggests, there will be no duty without some knowledge on the part of the employer of a disability[1].

1 *O'Neill v Symm & Co Ltd* [1998] ICR 481.

3 Other rights under discrimination legislation

2.23 It may be forgotten in the concentration on new rights under the Disability Discrimination Act 1995 that the person may have other claims arising out of discriminatory treatment. Advisers should remember that many people who are HIV positive may be discriminated on the grounds of their sex or race. We will deal with these together for the purposes of explaining the basic concepts that apply in these two areas. Both the Sex Discrimination Act 1975 and the Race Relations Act 1976 cover 'direct'[1] and 'indirect'[1] discrimination.

1 Sex Discrimination Act 1975, s 1(1)(a) and Race Relations Act 1976, s 1(1)(a).

2.24 Direct discrimination covers the situation where a person is treated less favourably than a person of a different sex, marital status, race, nationality etc on the grounds of that difference. There is, therefore, a need in these circumstances for the person complaining to find a comparator. This comparator (a man, a white person, for example) does not in fact necessarily need to exist. It can be a hypothetical person, although it is obviously more difficult to prove such less favourable treatment as it depends on supposition and the tribunal drawing inferences. Once direct discrimination is proved it cannot be excused by any justification. This should be compared to the indirect discrimination provisions and the Disability Discrimination Act 1995.

2.25 There would seem to be no circumstances in which someone who is HIV positive or has AIDS can claim direct discrimination under the Sex Discrimination Act 1975 or the Race Relations Act 1976. However, advisers should consider whether there are any claims that could arise out of their other characteristics, if they are from an ethnic minority or a woman, for example. Take, for instance, a woman who finds out she is HIV positive when she is pregnant, which is sometimes the case. She will be protected by the maternity provisions of the Employment Rights Act 1996, sex discrimination law (both under the Disability Discrimination Act 1995 and European case law), possibly other provisions of the Disability Discrimination Act 1995 and, depending on her length of service, other rights contained in the Employment Rights Act 1996 and elsewhere.

2.26 Indirect discrimination would include the situation in which an employer imposes an apparently neutral requirement (for employment, promotion or other benefit) which disproportionately affects one group over another. In order to establish such a claim it must be established that:

(a) there is a requirement or condition applied equally to men and women (or people of all races, ethnic groups etc);
(b) the proportion of the complainant's group who can comply with the requirement or condition is considerably smaller than the proportion of persons of the other group, sex or race etc;
(c) there is a detriment caused by the inability to comply; and
(d) there is no justification for the disproportionate impact.

2.27 For example, an employer decides that he will make all part-time workers redundant. The requirement or condition is that workers must work full-time. This is applied equally to men and women but it disproportionately affects women as they are the majority of part-time workers. It is obviously to their detriment to lose their jobs and there would seem to be no justification[1]. Similar examples could be given in the race context. For instance a requirement that someone holds a degree from a UK university would be to indirectly discriminate against members of ethnic minorities whose degrees have been gained outside the UK.

1 *Clarke v Eley (IMI) Kynoch Ltd* [1983] ICR 165.

2.28 One of the main problems in pursuing indirect discrimination claims is that they rely heavily on choosing the right pool for comparison and on the production of reliable and useful statistics which are not always available. Specialist discrimination practitioner advice is likely to be needed as these cases are complex.

2.29 In the particular context of a person with HIV or AIDS in the UK there is a possibility of an indirect sex discrimination claim. This is due to the current estimate that out of all HIV positive people in the UK, 85% are male and 15% are female. A requirement not to be HIV positive could therefore disproportionately impact on men and might have to be justified, which it could be only in very limited circumstances. However, the number of affected people in the UK—currently around 30,000 out of a population of 56 million—could mean that it would be difficult to prove that the proportion of men who can comply is considerably smaller than the proportion of women. The case of *R v Secretary of State for Employment, ex p Seymour-Smith*[1] is helpful in part but is now awaiting a return to the House of Lords from the European Court detriment because he is HIV positive may be indirect sex discrimination and, to the author's knowledge, a number of proceedings have proceeded with this claim but they have all been settled without any tribunal decisions on the point. It may be advisable to raise it as an issue, not least because it increases the chances of a good settlement.

1 [1995] ICR 889, CA; [1997] ICR 371, HL and [1999] ICR 447, ECJ.

2.30 Finally, in the context of discrimination it is worth looking briefly at the possibility of a claim based on the person's sexual orientation. As a substantial proportion of those who are HIV positive are gay men, this is an area where they can face discrimination. However, at the time of writing, it seems that their opportunity to pursue any legal remedy in respect of that discrimination is limited. Campaigners were initially hopeful that the cases of *Grant v South-West Trains Ltd*[1] and *R v Secretary of State for Defence, ex p Perkins (No 2)*[2] offered hope in the clarifying the application of sex discrimination to sexual orientation. Unfortunately the European Court of Justice has not interpreted the Treaty of Rome, the Sex Discrimination Act 1975 or the Equal Treatment Directive in that way and discrimination against people on those grounds therefore remains lawful.

1 [1998] All ER (EC) 193, [1998] ICR 449.
2 [1998] 2 CMLR 1116, [1998] IRLR 508.

2.31 Gender re-assignment discrimination has been dealt with by the ECJ and the Sex Discrimination (Gender Reassignment Regulations 1999[1] and is unlawful following *P v S and Somerset County Council*[2] but that may be of little application to an HIV positive person. There remains the possibility of a claim connected to the UK's obligations under the European Convention of Human Rights. Additionally, *R v Ministry of Defence, ex p Smith*[3] awaits a determination of a claim by former members of the armed forces forced to leave because of their sexual orientation. For the future, the incorporation of the European Convention on Human Rights through the Human Rights Act 1998 and the proposal to make art 14, the anti-discrimination article, a free-standing right and amendments to the Treaty of Rome following ratification of the Treaty of Amsterdam make it likely that there will be legislation in this area within the next few years[4].

1 SI 1999/1102.
2 [1996] ECR I-2143, [1996] ICR 795.
3 [1996] QB 517, [1996] ICR 740.
4 For further information see Barlow et al *Advising Gay and Lesbian Clients* (1999) Butterworths.

4 Checklist of employment rights

2.32 There are, of course, a whole range of rights at work that are not covered by anti-discrimination legislation but which advisers should not overlook. A brief reminder and checklist of rights follows.

2.33 The right not to be unfairly dismissed The qualifying period for the right not to be unfairly dismissed as in the Employment Rights Act 1996, s 94 is currently two years of employment but is expected to be reduced to one year. It would almost certainly be unfair to dismiss someone simply on the grounds that they are HIV positive except in a very limited number of occupations in the healthcare field. The other possibility is that there may be a dismissal because of long-term sickness. The usual tests of fairness in relation to getting independent medical reports and so on should be followed by employers.

2.34 The right to a redundancy payment Again the qualifying period of two years' employment as under the Employment Rights Act 1996, s 135 is likely to be reduced to one year as in para **2.33**.

2.35 The right not to suffer unauthorised deductions Under the Employment Rights Act 1996, this right includes unpaid wages, holidays and applies from the first day of employment.

2.36 The right to a statement of initial employment particulars Under the Employment Rights Act 1996, s 1 this right is granted no later than two months after the beginning of employment.

2.37 The right to minimum period of notice From one month's employment, under the Employment Rights Act 1996, s 86.

2.38 Maternity rights These are granted under Employment Rights Act 1996, Pt VIII but have changed in the Employment Relations Act 1999. They give a wide measure of protection for pregnant women and those who have recently given birth. Detrimental treatment of a female employee in that situation will also be sex discrimination.

2.39 The right to a minimum wage This is currently set at £3.60 per hour and different rates apply to younger workers, see the National Minimum Wage Act 1998.

2.40 The right not to be required to work long hours, rest breaks and paid holidays These rights are granted by the Working Time Regulations 1998, SI 1998/1833, which set very basic conditions for workers on health and safety grounds. They involve complicated rules and a number of exemptions but it is still worthwhile considering whether they might apply to any worker seeking advice.

2.41 There are also forthcoming rights contained within the Employment Relations Act 1999 concerning parental leave (which may be useful for parents of an HIV infected child), trade union recognition and changes to individual rights.

2.42 Most of the rights above may not seem at first consideration to be particularly relevant to people who are HIV positive or have AIDS but it must not be forgotten that health status is not all there is to any individual who may, for a range of reasons, have some protection on other grounds.

5 Procedure and remedies for discrimination and breach of individual rights at work

2.43 For all the possibilities outlined in paras **2.33**ff the appropriate first ... will almost always be the Employment Tribunal. In some ... but it would be

2.44 There are some advantages and disadvantages to the Employment Tribunal system. First, the tribunals have substantial experience in the area of discrimination law. Second, the normal costs rule does not apply and costs can only be awarded where the Employment Tribunal decides that a party has 'in bringing or conducting the proceedings acted frivolously, vexatiously, abusively, disruptively or otherwise unreasonably'[1]. In practice this occurs fairly rarely. A disadvantage, however, is that is that there is no legal aid available in Employment Tribunals so that other means of funding cases has to be found, for instance through the trade union, through a law centre or specialist centre such as Terrence Higgins Trust or the Disability Law Service or under a contingency or conditional fee arrangement. Third, the proceedings are relatively straightforward so that, in theory at least, a person can conduct his or her own case. Whilst this might apply in an unfair dismissal case, the more complicated discrimination cases, such as indirect discrimination or disability discrimination are likely to need specialist input.

1 Employment (Constitution etc) Regulations 1993, r 12.

2.45 Most of the rights outlined above have a three-month time limit attached to claims. This can be extended at the discretion of the European Tribunal in those rights arising out of the Employment Rights Act 1996 where it 'was not reasonably practicable' for the claim to be made in time[1]. For discrimination claims the Employment Tribunal's discretion can be exercised if they consider it would be 'just and equitable'[2] for the claim to proceed.

1 Various sections of the Employment Rights Act 1996 depending on the claim eg, s 111 for unfair dismissal
2 See, for example, the Sex Discrimination Act 1975, s 76(5).

2.46 Applications to the Employment Tribunal are generally on Form IT1 but as long as the claim is clear and raises the issues, it does not have to be submitted in that form. It is important to include all potential claims at that point even if they are withdrawn at a later stage because amendments will only be allowed with leave after the deadline has passed.

2.47 In discrimination claims the questionnaire procedure can be used. This should be sent to the employer within 21 days of the application being lodged (or it can be submitted before proceedings). This procedure is very useful for getting information from potential or actual respondents, especially statistical information which might be vital to a case. Standard forms are available from the Equal Opportunities Commission, CRE and DARAS.

2.48 The respondent has 21 days to respond and the case is listed for hearing. This varies but, at the time of writing, the waiting period for a one-day hearing is about six weeks. Almost all discrimination claims are now listed for a directions hearing where the issues are clarified and arrangements made for expert reports, exchange of witness statements and so on. A multi-day case involving discrimination will take somewhat longer to list, currently up to three months. This wait is expected to lengthen as more cases based upon the new rights outlined above are pursued.

2.49 Other issues which affect discrimination cases, for instance that the burden of proof rests on the applicant, should be borne in mind. It is therefore of great importance to prepare well. Consideration should always be given at an early stage to witnesses and whether witness orders might be needed, to documents and discovery and what expert reports or witnesses might be required. This is particularly true of disability discrimination cases, especially where one of the issues might be whether the applicant is disabled within the definition of s 1 of the Disability Discrimination Act 1995 and a medical opinion will almost certainly be expected. It is worth considering that medical practitioners working in the field of HIV and AIDS may be prepared to waive or reduce their fees if the lack of funding is explained.

2.50 In all cases advisers should consider what form of remedy is being sought. It is useful to have an early view of what is likely to be achievable so that settlement negotiations can be constructive. Many clients with HIV and AIDS will be concerned about the publicity (see Chapter 1), the stress and uncertainty of litigation and any lengthy delays, so they may be particularly interested in settling their claim. Consider also any declaratory relief as that may be of value to others in similar situations.

C PROVISION OF GOODS AND SERVICES

2.51 Much of what has been said in the employment field also applies in relation discrimination in providing goods, facilities and services. The Sex Discrimination Act 1975, Pt III, Race Relations Act 1976 and the Disability Discrimination Act 1995 all contain express prohibition in relation to these areas.

2.52 It is perhaps unfortunate that few cases in the area of goods and services have been pursued. Under sex and race discrimination legislation it is important to remember that the main principles still apply. Part III of the Race Relations Act 1976 and Pt III of the Sex Discrimination Act 1975 prohibit discrimination on the grounds of race etc and sex where education and services are provided to the public or to a section of the public. There are, however, a number of exemptions for private households, private clubs and so on. The use of this legislation is inevitably limited for persons with HIV or AIDS.

2.53 We turn, therefore, to the Disability Discrimination Act 1995 and to Pt III (not yet in force). This part of the Act covers a wide section of service providers, whether public or private, including accommodation, legal and health services, leisure facilities and so on. The service has to be one provided to the public. The main exceptions are education and transport and there are some governmental activities (such as the immigration service) which are not covered, see *Amin v Entry Clearance Officer*[1].

1 [1983] 2 All ER 864, CA.

2.54 The main provisions of the 1995 Act which relate to goods and services have similar definition of discrimination to that contained in the employment section: that less favourable treatment is unlawful if it cannot be justified[1] or that there is a failure to make a reasonable adjustment[2].

1 Disability Discrimination Act 1995, ss 19, 20.
2 DDA 1995, ss 20, 21.

2.55 There are some important differences, however, partly due to the multitude of situations to which these sections might apply. The justification ... reference to health and safety and is a subjective test ... complainant to field is not to give the same service but one which is as far as possible equivalent to people without that disability[1].

1 HL Official Report col 266,18 July 1995, Lord Mackay.

2.56 For a person with HIV or AIDS bringing a discrimination claim much will depend on the nature of the disability. As with the employment provisions, a complainant will still have to prove that they are a person with a disability. It will then be a question of the particular form of discriminatory treatment as to how likely they are to succeed. To give an example, it may be that a person with AIDS has a mobility problem so that they have to use a wheelchair. In those circumstances, any failure to make adjustments to the building to accommodate them could be tested and much will depend on the reasonableness or otherwise of that failure.

2.57 Another situation where discrimination may arise is in access to healthcare. For example, where a dentist refuses to treat patients who are HIV positive. This would be contrary to the Disability Discrimination Act 1995 (if the person is also symptomatic) unless it could be justified. As the British Dental Association's own guidelines state that a patient with HIV should be treated, it is unlikely that a refusal to treat HIV positive patients could be justified without further good reason.

D EDUCATION AND TRAINING

2.58 Both the Sex Discrimination Act 1975 and the Race Relations Act 1976 make provision against discrimination in the field of education. This applies in public and private schools, colleges and universities. Generally it is unlawful to discriminate on the grounds of race or sex in admissions, access to facilities, classes or courses or other forms of less favourable treatment. As well as being able to take a claim through the county court, a complaint can also be made to the Secretary of State for Education and there may well be the possibility of a judicial review if the discrimination raises a point of public law. A number of cases about discrimination in education have been dealt with by way of judicial review.

1 Race Relations Act 1976, Pt II and Sex Discrimination Act 1975.

2.59 However, the most useful legislation for a person with HIV or AIDS bringing a discrimination claim will be the Disability Discrimination Act 1995. The Act specifically excludes education from its remit[1] so that there are no analogous provisions to those contained in the other two main anti-discrimination Acts. Training is covered, though this is really limited to Training and Enterprise Councils.

1 Disability Discrimination Act 1995, s 19(5).

2.60 For a child with HIV or AIDS, the provisions contained in the Education Act 1993 in relation to pupils with special educational needs may be of some use. These provide for a statement to be prepared by the local education authority on the child's needs and can be challenged by the parents by way of appeal, if necessary. The Disability Discrimination Act 1995 did insert a new clause into that Act to provide that schools report on the admission of disabled children and steps taken to prevent less favourable treatment and to assist access to disabled pupils[1]. There are guidelines available from DfEE on pupils with HIV which usefully set out good practice in relation to this issue.

1 Disability Discrimination Act 1995, s 29.

E INSURANCE

2.61 One of the commonest forms of discrimination against people who are HIV positive is that they may be refused insurance or that there is an exclusion in a policy of insurance that prevents them from taking advantage of the policy when the need arises. The problems will occur at different times, either when the person needs insurance and finds they are not able to get it, for instance to travel or for mortgage purposes, or when they become ill or after death and the person dealing with the estate discovers there is an exclusion clause in life insurance.

2.62 Both the Sex Discrimination Act 1975 and Race Relations Act 1976 prohibit discrimination in insurance within the goods and services part of those Acts. It is subject, in the case of sex discrimination, to a justification on the basis of actuarial information.

2.63 Again, though, it will be the effect of the Disability Discrimination Act 1995 that will most interest advisers of people with HIV or AIDS. The general principles on insurance are outlined in Ch 8 but there are important new provisions as a result of the Disability Discrimination Act 1995 that need to be explored. The sections above on goods and services include insurance services so that it falls within the general prohibition on less favourable treatment or the duty to make adjustments. Because of the varied nature of insurance services, specific regulations were brought in for transitional arrangements[1]. This meant that policies in place at 2 December 1996 did not have to comply with the Disability Discrimination Act 1995 until their next renewal date. By 2 December 1997 therefore all policies should have complied with the new law. These regulations also state the circumstances in which less favourable treatment is justified[2]:

> '(b) based upon information (for example, actuarial or statistical data or a medical report) which is relevant to the assessment of the risk to be insured and is from a source upon which it is reasonable to rely; and
>
> (c) reasonable having regard to the information relied upon and any other relevant factors'.

1 Disability Discrimination (Services and Premises) Regulations 1996, SI 1996/1836.
2 SI 1996/1836, reg 2(2).

2.64 From this it can be seen that the insurers are likely to provide some other evidence to support their less favourable treatment, which may be the refusal to insure or the existence of an exclusion clause. There have been no cases that have been gone through the system although a number have been settled so it is arguable that an insurer may not be able to justify an exclusion clause. Certainly, anecdotal evidence would indicate that they have not got good [illegible] information upon which to justify the exclusions, given that [illegible] situation both in

2.65 Another situation that may arise is someone who has an insurance related benefit at work. This is likely to be a long-term illness benefit, often called Permanent Health Insurance (PHI) or Permanent Disability Insurance (PDI). This benefit may be linked to pension arrangements and is generally a group policy. Section 18 of the Disability Discrimination Act 1995 covers this situation and makes employers liable for the discrimination. Advisers should be aware that it is useful to proceed against both the employer and the insurer in the employment tribunal although there may well be arguments on who is the correct party. Making the insurer justify the exclusion clause by costly references to actuaries does encourage settlement.

2.66 The Association of British Insurers publish a useful guide which highlights some of the areas of concern and advisers may find this useful even though it is obviously not a definitive statement of the law[1].

1 Available from ABI, 51 Gresham Street, London, EC2V 7HQ.

Court procedure for non-employment cases

2.67 Any claims under the Disability Discrimination Act 1995, Race Relations Act 1976 or Sex Discrimination Act 1975 not under the employment provisions (that is, goods and services, education and insurance) should be commenced in the county court within six months of the date of the discriminatory treatment. Registering a claim with one of the enforcement bodies, namely the Equal Opportunities Commission, CRE or DARAS (soon to be replaced by the Disability Rights Commission) can extend that period by two months.

2.68 The Civil Procedure Rules 1998, which implemented the Woolf reforms from 26 April 1999, must be followed. This means that a great deal of the case must be ready at the issue of proceedings, including medical and other expert reports. It is therefore vital that the gathering of evidence starts immediately on such a case in view of the short time to issue. Legal Aid may be available if the claim is worth more than £5,000 or if a remedy other than a money remedy is sought. In discrimination claims, it is common to ask for a declaration or an injunction and, for the purposes of public policy, this may be something which clients and advisers will wish to consider.

Chapter 3

Social welfare services

Luke Clements
Isabel Manley

Part I Duties and responsibilities of social services providers

A INTRODUCTION

3.01 This chapter describes the statutory responsibilities of social services departments for people with HIV or AIDS. There are no social services statutes which specifically refer to the needs of people affected by HIV or those who have developed AIDS. The relevant law is to be found in those statutes which concern the provision of community care services for disabled people.

3.02 Community care services are generally subdivided into:
(a) residential services: the provision or procurement by social services of a place in a residential care home or a nursing home;
(b) non-accommodation services; these can either be:
    (i) services to a person in his or her home (generally referred to as 'domiciliary' services) such as home help, adaptations, meals on wheels or the provision of a telephone; or
    (ii) services in a community setting, such as at a day centre, or other recreational activities such as outings or holidays.

3.03 Social services departments are primarily responsible for assessing the needs of people with HIV or AIDS, for community- or home-based services and for making arrangements to ensure that these services are actually made available. This obligation brings with it many separate responsibilities: it presupposes, for instance, that social services departments have information systems which advertise the availability of such services and that they work closely with other providers (such as the National Health Service and housing departments). The community care obligations are considered separately at paras **3.05–3.116** under the following subject headings: information and planning; assessment and care plans (and carers' assessments); provision of services (including accommodation, home care etc, children's services and the NHS duties); charging; and complaints.

3.04 The Department of Health has published guidance and issued a number of circulars concerning the social care needs of people with HIV infection and AIDS; these include:
[illegible] voluntary organisations

(b) Children and HIV—guidance for local authorities (1992);
(c) The health and social care of people with HIV infection and AIDS—findings and good practice recommendations from research funded by the Department of Health 1986–1992 (1993);
(d) Women and HIV (1993);
(e) Inspection of local authority services for people affected by HIV or AIDS: overview (1994);
(f) Implementing caring for people: caring for people with HIV and AIDS (1994);
(g) Support grant for social services for people with AIDS 1998/99: LAC (1998).

B SOCIAL SERVICES—DUTY TO INFORM AND PLAN

3.05 Social services departments are under a duty to inform themselves of the number of disabled people in their areas and to prepare an annual community care plan to explain how the authority proposes to meet the community care needs of its population[1]. In addition, authorities are obliged to ensure (by general publicity and personal explanations) that existing service users, as well as those 'who might benefit by help and their families', are informed about what help is available[2].

1 Chronically Sick and Disabled Persons Act 1970, s 1 and the National Health Service and Community Care Act 1990, s 46.
2 Chronically Sick and Disabled Persons Act 1970, s 1(2) and DHSS Circular 12/70, para 5.

1 Registers of disabled persons

3.06 Social services departments are also required to maintain registers of the disabled persons ordinarily resident within their area[1]. Department of Health guidance[2] explains that these registers serve a dual purpose, namely that:
(a) registration can be of benefit to individual service users in certain situations (ie in order to establish a right to certain social security/tax benefits)[3]; and
(b) they fulfil an important community care planning role for ascertaining the demand and potential demand for domiciliary care services.

1 In relation to adult disabled people, the duty is to be found under the National Assistance Act 1948, s 29(4)(g); in relation to disabled children, the duty is found at the Children Act 1989, Sch 2, Pt I, para 2.
2 Appendix 4 to LAC (93)10, paras 2ff.
3 Various benefits for blind persons are dependent upon registration—most notably an extra income tax allowance. Such persons are exempt from the 'all work test' for incapacity benefit and severe disablement allowance together with such other miscellaneous benefits as certain income support premiums and relief from non-dependent deductions for income support, housing benefit and council tax benefit, certain car parking concessions, a small reduction in the TV licence and access to free NHS eye examinations.

3.07 The guidance particularly emphasises the importance of inter-agency collaboration in relation to disabled childrens' registers[1]. Registration is entirely voluntary for both disabled adults[2] and children[3]. Any person assessed as needing community care services must receive them regardless of whether his or her name is on the local authority's register.

1 Paragraph 4.3, vol 6 of the Children Act 1989 Guidance (Children with Disabilities) asserts that 'the creation of a joint register of children with disabilities between health, education and social services would greatly facilitate collaboration in identification and a co-ordinated provision of services'.
2 Appendix 4 to LAC (93)10 at para 3.
3 Paragraph 4.2, vol 6 of the Children Act 1989 Guidance (Children with Disabilities) emphasises that there is no duty on parents to agree to registration and services are not dependent upon registration.

2 Access to files

3.08 Social services authorities are required to provide users with copies of relevant parts of their files, unless the disclosure of information is specifically exempted. The right of access to such files is (at the time of writing) governed by the Access to Personal Files (Social Services) Regulations 1989[1], although these regulations are due to be repealed and replaced by equivalent provisions under the Data Protection Act 1998.

1 SI 1989/206, as amended by the Access to Personal Files (Social Services) (Amendment) Regulations 1991, SI 1991/1587.

3.09 The right of access to a file is activated by a request in writing. The authority may request payment of an administration fee[1] and any additional information which it reasonably requires in order to be satisfied as to the identity of the person making the request and to locate the information sought. Subject to these requirements being satisfied, the authority must comply with the request.

1 A maximum fee of £10.00 can be charged. Authorities should take into account an individual's ability to pay in deciding whether to charge any fee. The 40-day compliance period is not delayed by an authority requesting the fee, but it need not actually supply the information until the fee is paid—see paras 13–16 of App 1 to LAC (89)2.

3.10 If, however, information is required which relates to another individual who can be identified from that information, then the authority cannot release this information without first giving that individual an opportunity to consent to or object to its disclosure. This restriction on disclosure does not apply if the third party supplied the information in connection with his or her employment by the social services authority.

C COMMUNITY CARE ASSESSMENTS

3.11 A social services department cannot provide any community care services to a disabled person until it has assessed that person's need for services[1].

1 Except in cases of emergency: National Health Service and Community Care Act 1990, s 47(5).

3.12 The duty to carry out such community care assessments stems from the National Health Service and Community Care Act 1990, s 47(1). The White Paper[1], which preceded the 1990 Act, explained that the objective of an assessment is to:

could be expected to achieve, taking account of his or her personal and social relationships. Assessment should not focus only on the user's suitability for a particular existing service. The aim should be first to review the possibility of enabling the individual to continue to live at home even if this means arranging a move to different accommodation within the local community, and if that possibility does not exist, to consider whether residential or nursing home care would be appropriate.'

1 *Caring for People* (1989) HMSO.

3.13 Department of Health guidance[1] has emphasised that assessments should:

'not take place in a vacuum; account needs to be taken of the local authority's criteria for determining when services should be provided, the types of services they have decided to make available and the overall range of services they have decided to make available and the overall range of services provided by other agencies, including health authorities. The individual service user and normally, with his or her agreement, any carers should be involved throughout the assessment and care management process.'

1 *Community Care into the Next Decade and Beyond: Policy Guidance* (1990) HMSO, paras 3.15–3.16.

3.14 There are, therefore, three distinct stages in the assessment process:

(a) the actual assessment by the local authority of the person's potential need for community care services;

(b) the local authority decides whether the person's needs are sufficiently substantial to warrant the provision of services. Local authorities carry out this task by comparing the person's assessed 'needs' against a predetermined scale of need (known as the 'eligibility criteria');

(c) if the local authority determine that the person satisfies their eligibility criteria, then it is obliged to provide the services which are considered necessary to meet that person's needs. The final stage of the process then requires that the local authority prepare a 'care plan' which spells out precisely what services it is going to provide (or arrange to be provided).

1 The actual assessment

3.15 Section 47(1) of the National Health Service and Community Care Act 1990 obliges social services authorities to carry out an assessment of an individual's need for community care services where:

(a) the individual's circumstances have come to their knowledge; and

(b) he or she appears to be a member of one of the client groups for whom community care services can be provided, eg he or she appears to be disabled, elderly or ill; and

(c) the individual might benefit from the provision of community care services[1].

1 Whether or not provided by the assessing authority: *R v Berkshire County Council, ex p P* (1998) 1 CCL Rep 141.

3.16 Local authorities must carry out such assessments even if it is unlikely that the disabled person will be entitled to services. *R v Bristol City Council, ex p Alice Penfold*[1] concerned a 52-year-old single mother who suffered from anxiety and depression. She was accepted as being homeless by Bristol City Council who offered her two properties, although she refused both as neither were in the part of the city where her family (and support network) lived. Her solicitors then asked the authority to carry out a community care assessment of her needs, on the basis that she either be offered accommodation under the community care legislation[2] (as opposed to accommodation under the homelessness legislation) or, if she moved elsewhere, that she would need support to replace her family.

1 (1998) 1 CCL Rep 315.
2 Under the National Assistance Act 1948, s 21.

3.17 The authority refused to carry out a community care assessment on the grounds that there was no prospect of meeting any needs that might have emerged in the course of the assessment and that in any event what she really wanted was housing accommodation in her preferred part of the city and 'normal accommodation' was not a service that could be provided under the community care legislation.

3.18 Scott Baker J held:
(a) where there is an apparent need for community care services which a local authority is empowered to provide, then the authority must undertake a community care assessment;
(b) even if it were the case that a service user has no sensible prospect of being awarded services because of constraints upon resources, that does not absolve the local authority from conducting such an assessment;
(c) the discharge by a housing authority of its obligations to homeless persons does not preclude the need for a community care assessment;
(d) a local authority is empowered to provide 'normal' accommodation under the community care legislation[1], provided the provision of the accommodation is a function of need that would otherwise fall to be met by other community care services.

1 National Assistance 1948 Act, s 21, see para **3.46**.

3.19 The duty to assess arises regardless of a specific request for an assessment. In *R v Gloucestershire County Council, ex p RADAR*[1], it was held that the local authority could not discharge its obligation to potential service users (who had in fact previously received services) simply by writing to them asking them to reply if they wanted to be considered for assessment. The court held that 'the obligation to make an assessment for community care services does not depend on a request, but on the "appearance" of need'.

1 [1996] COD 253.

3.20 The purpose of an assessment is to enable the social services department to discover as much about the disabled person's needs, illness, disabilities, preferences etc as is necessary in order to decide whether services should be made available and, if so, the nature of those services.

3.21 Guidance issued by the Department of Health[1] emphasises the importance of treating the assessment of need as a separate exercise from consideration of service response, stating:

'It is easy to slip out of thinking "what does this person need?" into "what responsibility for the delivery or management of services arising from that assessment.'

1 *Care Management and Assessment: Practitioners' Guide* (1991) HMSO.

3.22 In separate guidance[1], the Department of Health explained that the assessment process should take into account particular risk factors for service users, carers and the community generally; abilities and attitudes; health (especially remediable conditions or chronic conditions requiring continuing healthcare); and accommodation and social support needs. The guidance also stresses[2] that assessment arrangements should normally include an initial screening process to determine the appropriate level of assessment. That:

> 'some people may need assistance which does not call for a formal assessment, others may require only a limited or specialist assessment of specific needs, others may have urgent needs which require immediate response. Procedures should be sufficiently comprehensive and flexible to cope with all levels and types of need presented by different client groups.'

1 *Community Care in the Next Decade and Beyond: Policy Guidance* (1990) HMSO para 3.19.
2 *Community Care in the Next Decade and Beyond: Policy Guidance* (1990) HMSO para 3.20.

3.23 The disabled person and, with his or her agreement, any carers should be involved throughout the assessment process and their views and preferences fully taken into account. The guidance states that where a user is unable to participate actively in the assessment, it is even more important that he or she should be helped to understand what is involved and the intended outcome.

3.24 Local authorities must ensure that service users who 'are unable to express their views, for example, those with severe learning disabilities or dementia or those who have been previously disadvantaged, for example, those from minority ethnic groups should, as a matter of priority' have access to an independent advocacy scheme[1].

1 *Care Management and Assessment: Practitioners' Guide* (1991) HMSO, para 3.27.

3.25 The assessment under the National Health Service and Community Care Act 1990, s 47(1)(a) obliges authorities to identify those needs which could potentially be satisfied by the provision of a community care service. Thus, an assessment of a person may reveal that she or he has a need for counselling and financial/benefits advice; also that the episodic nature of his or her HIV or AIDS may mean that, at times, help is required with shopping, housework, laundry and cooking (but not at other times). These needs can be met by the provision of social work or home help services or perhaps by a temporary place in a residential care home. On the other hand, if the assessment suggests that a person may benefit from (for example) medical assistance or a change of tenancy (to a ground floor flat for instance), then these are requirements which are not capable of being satisfied by the provision of community care services and accordingly are not 'needs' for the purposes of s 47(1)(a).

3.26 Department of Health guidance advises that a copy of the assessment of needs should normally be shared with the potential service user, any representative of that user and all other people who have agreed to provide a service.

(i) The duty to co-operate with other agencies

3.27 Where the assessment discloses a possible housing or medical need, s 47(3) obliges the authority to notify the relevant housing or health authority. The social services authority is obliged in such cases to specify what assistance the health or housing authority are requested to provide in order to facilitate the assessment. Although the Act does not oblige either authority to respond or co-operate, separate parallel duties under housing or health legislation may be triggered. For instance, in cases of homelessness, the housing authority will be under a duty to receive applications and to make enquiries under the Housing Act 1996, s 184.

2 Qualifying for services and eligibility criteria

3.28 Once the authority has interviewed the disabled person and any carers or 'significant others' in that person's life, and gathered together all the evidence it considers necessary (medical reports, housing data etc), it is obliged to decide what the individual's community care needs are. Having done this, the authority must make a separate decision (under s 47(1)(b)) as to whether all or some of the assessed needs call for the provision of any community care services. Section 47(1)(b) obliges the authority to 'have regard to' the results of the assessment, rather than obliging it to provide services to meet all the identified needs.

3.29 What an authority is attempting to do at this stage is to match its available resources to the needs of its population. In order to take this decision, the authority has regard to a locally agreed scale of need, known as 'eligibility criteria'. Accordingly, a wealthy authority[1] might have a relatively generous set of criteria, which allows people with low-level needs to have some services whereas a less wealthy authority might adopt more severe criteria which meant that only people in significant need obtained any help. The Department of Health has advised on the procedure for formulating such criteria, in the following terms[2].

1 Or perhaps more accurately, one which had decided to allocate significant resources to its social services department.

2 A letter dated 14 December 1992 written by the Chief Inspector of the Social Services Inspectorate ref: CI(92)34.

3.30 'An authority may take into account the resources available when deciding how to respond to an individual's assessment. However, once the authority has indicated that a service should be provided to meet an individual's needs and the authority is under a legal obligation to provide it or arrange for its provision then the service must be provided. It will not be possible for an authority to use budgeting difficulties as a basis for refusing to provide the service.'[1]

1 A letter dated 14 December 1992 written by the Chief Inspector of the Social Services Inspectorate ref: CI(92)34.

... in this process by defining eligibility criteria:

depending on the extent of the difficulties they encounter in carrying out everyday tasks and relating the level of response to the degree of such difficulties. Any "banding" should not, however, be rigidly applied, as account needs to be taken of individual circumstances. Such eligibility criteria should be phrased in terms of the factors identified in the assessment process.'[1]

1 See note to para **3.30**.

3.32 Eligibility criteria are frequently based upon a risk assessment, ie 'what would the consequences be if services were not provided to the particular person in need?' If the consequence would be a serious risk of physical harm within a short period of time, then the person will be in high-priority category for services (say priority one), whereas if the consequence would be increasing social isolation rather than measurable physical harm the person will be in a lower priority category for services (say priority four).

3.33 The House of Lords in *R v Gloucestershire County Council, ex p Barry*[1] held that such criteria were lawful, albeit subject to four significant caveats:

(a) when a social services department change its criteria, by making them more severe, it cannot withdraw services from an existing user until such time as it has carried out a full reassessment of that individual's community care needs and satisfied itself that that person does not meet the new criteria.

(b) Once a social services department has decided that a particular person should be provided with services, then the services must be provided, regardless of resource constraints.
In *R v Sutton London Borough Council, ex p Tucker*[2], a learning disabled applicant who had sensory impairments (including deafness and myopia) was in hospital awaiting discharge. The social services department accepted that her needs required a place in a specialist care home, but considered that a care home in Birmingham would meet her needs despite the applicant's family and most experts being implacably opposed to an out-of-area placement. The local authority contended, inter alia, that a local placement would be very much more expensive. Having rejected the Birmingham care home as a feasible option, the court ruled that the local placement had to be funded regardless of cost; the authority had decided her needs should be met and it was therefore too late to raise the issue of resources.

(c) Resource availability alone cannot be 'determinative'; Gloucestershire's actions amounted to treating the cut in resources as the sole factor to be taken into account, and that was unlawful.
What the court means by this statement is that the local authority cannot use resource shortages alone as a reason for refusing services. Resources are one of a number of factors which the authority must bear in mind, they cannot be the only consideration.

(d) Resource availability will not be a relevant factor where a disabled person would be at severe physical risk if the services were not provided. In such a case, McCowan LJ held that he could not 'conceive that an authority would be held to have acted reasonably if it used shortages of resources as a reason [for not providing the service]'.

1 [1997] AC 584, 1 CCL Rep 40.
2 (1996) 1 CCL Rep 251.

3 The provision of services and the care plan

3.34 Once a local authority has decided that a person's need for community care services must be met, then it is required to decide what services should be provided and to detail these in writing, in what is known as a 'care plan'. Good practice requires that the authority specify in the care plan what services the individual is entitled to receive, their frequency, who is to provide them, when the arrangements are to be reviewed and so on. A care plan is essentially a statement of the arrangements that are necessary in order that the services be delivered to the qualifying individual.

3.35 A person with HIV or AIDS may be assessed as needing assistance preparing meals and in bathing and requiring social stimulation to help overcome isolation and depression. The local authority might decide that it can meet these needs by providing a home help, meals on wheels and a place at an appropriate day centre. The care plan would specify the days when the various services were provided, the duration, the nature of the service, how transport to the day centre would be arranged etc. The local authority could provide the service itself or buy it in from an independent provider. The care plan might also include details of any charge the disabled person might have to pay towards the cost of providing the service.

3.36 In *R v Islington London Borough Council, ex p Rixon*[1], Sedley J held that a care plan is the means by which the local authority assembles the relevant information and applies it to the statutory ends and hence affords good evidence to any inquirer of the due discharge of its statutory duties.

1 (1997) 1 CCL Rep 117.

(i) Waiting lists

3.37 Once a social services department has decided that the disabled person's needs should be met, then it is required to take immediate steps to provide the necessary services. For this reason it is probably unlawful to respond to such a determination by merely putting the disabled person's name on a waiting list for the service. In *R v Liverpool City Council, ex p Winter*[1], leave was given to challenge an authority's practice of placing people (who it had assessed as requiring a service) on a waiting list. Immediately prior to the substantive hearing, the authority withdrew its defence and agreed to provide the assessed service and pay the applicants' full costs.

1 Unreported but see (1997) 1 CCL Rep 5 and (1998) 1 CCL Rep 118.

3.38 In *Rixon*[1], Sedley J considered that a local authority could not assess someone as needing a service (for instance a day centre placement) and then fail to provide the service, merely because none was available. This reason alone would be insufficient. He asserted:

> '...in my judgment, the respondent local authority has fallen below the requirements of the law...the local authority has, it appears, simply taken the existing unavailability of further facilities as an insuperable obstacle to any further attempt to make provision ...'.

(ii) Choice and care packages

3.39 An assessment may identify needs which are capable of being met by two alternative care packages; for instance a person with HIV or AIDS may be assessed as requiring almost 24-hour care assistance to help with meals, dressing, bathing and to ensure that she suffers no harm. This 'assessed need' could be met either by the provision of 24-hour home care assistance or by him or her moving into a residential care home.

3.40 If an authority can meet the assessed need by two or more different care packages, it is entitled to have regard to the comparative cost of the two options and opt for the cheaper package. Although this principle has been approved by the Court of Appeal in *R v Lancashire County Council, ex p Ingham*[1] local authorities can only make such a choice if both packages objectively meet the disabled person's needs. In *R v Avon County Council, ex p M*[2] the applicant had Down's syndrome. A symptom of this was his entrenched view that he wanted to go to a particular residential home even though an alternative, cheaper home objectively catered for all his other needs. The authority, in deciding what accommodation he needed had regard to a psychologist's report which stated that M's entrenched position was typical of and therefore caused by the Down's syndrome. The authority refused to fund the more expensive home on the ground that it would set a precedent by accepting psychological need as being part of an individual's needs which could force it to pay more than it would usually expect to pay in such cases. Rejecting this argument, Henry J held:

> 'The law is clear. The council have to provide for the applicant's needs. Those needs may properly include psychological needs. Where they do, it is not right to describe the payment in meeting those needs as "forcing the authority to pay more than the usual amount it would be prepared to pay for the individual concerned". The authority would simply be paying what the law required, and not being forced to pay more. So the introduction of the question of precedent in this context is, in my judgment, potentially misleading.'

1 (1997) 1 CCL Rep 29, QBD.
2 [1994] 2 FCR 259, [1994] 2 FLR 1006.

4 Carers' assessments

3.41 Whilst social services departments are unable to provide community care services for carers (unless the carers are themselves also disabled persons), it is essential that in the community care assessment process they take full account of the views, strengths and weaknesses of any carer. The Carers (Recognition and Services) Act 1995 puts this requirement on a statutory footing by obliging the social services authority (if so requested) to carry out a separate assessment of the carer at the same time as it assesses the person for whom the care is provided. The carer can be an adult or a child.

3.42 In order to qualify for an assessment under the Act, a carer must satisfy the following criteria:

(a) a community care assessment (or reassessment) of the person for whom he or she cares must be in the process of being carried out;
(b) the carer must be providing (or intending to provide) a substantial amount of care on a regular basis;
(c) the carer must request a carer's assessment. Department of Health guidance requires social workers to 'inform any carer who appears eligible under this Act of their right to request an assessment'[1].

1 LAC (96)7, para 20.

3.43 The Act entitles qualifying carers to an assessment of their ability to provide and continue to provide care. If as a result of such an assessment it transpires that the carer is no longer able or willing[1] to provide the same level of care, then the authority will have to decide whether to change the service user's care plan by increasing the services provided by another agency or agencies to compensate.

1 Paragraph 9.8 of the practice guidance accompanying the Act states that social workers should not 'assume a willingness by the carer to continue, or continue to provide the same level of support'.

D THE PROVISION OF COMMUNITY CARE SERVICES

3.44 Adults with HIV or AIDS are primarily entitled to services[1] under three statutes:
(a) National Assistance Act 1948: residential or nursing home provision by social services;
(b) Chronically Sick and Disabled Persons Act 1970: domiciliary or community-based care services (for instance, home help, adaptations, day centre placements etc). These services are in practice only available for people who have developed the AIDS symptoms and therefore are to be considered at law as 'substantially and permanently handicapped'[2];
(c) National Health Service Act 1977: domiciliary or community-based care services for people with HIV but who have not yet developed AIDS to the extent that they are considered at law as 'substantially and permanently handicapped'[3].

1 Community care law is complex and involves a number of conflicting legislative provisions: for a detailed analysis of the law see *Community Care and the Law* (1997) Luke Clements Legal Action Group.
2 The definition deriving from the National Assistance Act 1948, s 29.
3 National Assistance Act 1948, s 29. These three statutes are considered separately at paras **3.46–3.71**.

3.45 In addition, the following statutes are also of relevance:
(a) Children Act 1989: children with HIV or AIDS are entitled to services under the Children Act 1989 as well as (in certain situations) the Chronically Sick and Disabled Persons Act 1970;
(b) Community Care (Direct Payments Act) 1996: in general, community care services are either provided directly by social services departments or purchased by them from independent provider organisations. In certain situations local authorities can provide the disabled person with cash in lieu of services (provided that the disabled person then uses that

1 Residential and nursing home accommodation

3.46 Section 21 of the National Assistance Act 1948 obliges social services authorities to provide residential accommodation for persons ordinarily resident in their area who are aged 18 years or over and in need of care and attention which is not otherwise available to them.

(i) Ordinarily resident

3.47 A person's ordinary residence is essentially the place where she or he resides; it is the place which she or he has 'adopted voluntarily and for settled purposes as part of the regular order of his life for the time being, whether of short or long duration'[1]. The Department of Health has issued guidance on 'ordinary residence' as circular LAC (93)7.

1 *Shah v Barnet London Borough Council* [1983] 2 AC 309, [1983] 1 All ER 226.

3.48 The ordinary residence guidance and the National Assistance Act 1948, s 24 emphasise the following basic principles:

(a) where a person is provided with residential accommodation by a social services authority, he or she is deemed to continue to be ordinarily resident in the area in which he or she was ordinarily resident immediately before the residential accommodation was provided;

(b) where a person is in NHS care, he or she is deemed to be ordinarily resident in the area in which he or she was ordinarily resident immediately before admission as a patient to the NHS facility;

(c) where a person was not ordinarily resident in any area prior to admission, then the responsible social services authority will be the one in whose area he or she is at that time;

(d) where a person has no settled or ordinary residence, then he or she is the responsibility of the social services department in whose area he or she is physically present.

(ii) The nature of residential care accommodation

3.49 The National Assistance Act 1948, s 21 enables social services departments to provide residential accommodation in a residential care home or a nursing home or, in exceptional circumstances, in ordinary rented housing accommodation[1]. In general, however, if an authority assesses a person as needing supported lodgings, warden-controlled accommodation or ordinary housing accommodation, then it will refer the need to the relevant housing department and ask for it to assist in the assessment process[2].

1 *R v Bristol City Council, ex p Alice Penfold* (1996) 1 CCL Rep 315.
2 National Health Service and Community Care Act 1990, s 47(3).

Residential care homes

3.50 Independent residential care homes must be registered under the Registered Homes Act 1984. There are special rules for the registration of small homes defined as homes providing for fewer than four people[1]. The social services authority is the registration authority for residential care homes within its area and is required to establish 'arm's length' registration and inspection units to oversee its responsibilities under the Registered Homes Act 1984, Pt I.

1 Registered Homes Act 1984, s 1(4).

3.51 Residential care homes vary enormously and generally specialise in providing accommodation for specific groups, such as the elderly, younger disabled people and people with HIV or AIDS. It is the task of the social services department during the assessment process to identify exactly what services the disabled person requires. If it decides that these services are best delivered in a residential care setting, then the local authority must ensure that these are provided in a suitable home. The local authority will also specify in the care plan any additional services which will need to be specially bought in by the home or other agency to meet all of the user's needs.

Nursing homes

3.52 There are two principal types of nursing home:
(a) ordinary nursing homes: these in general provide, in addition to the basic services one would expect from a residential care home (see para **3.50**) nursing or other medical services;
(b) mental nursing homes: these are homes which provide nursing or other medical treatment (including care, habitation, and rehabilitation under medical supervision) for mentally disordered patients.

Independent nursing and mental nursing homes must be registered. The health authority is the registration and inspection authority for such homes within its area.

3.53 As with residential care homes, nursing homes vary enormously and generally specialise in providing care for specific conditions, such as for people with dementia, drug and alcohol abusers, palliative care and people with HIV or AIDS. It is again the responsibility of the social services department during the assessment process to identify exactly what services the disabled person requires within the nursing home.

Choice of accommodation

3.54 Where a social services authority have assessed a person as requiring residential accommodation in a registered care home or nursing home then it is obliged to make arrangements for accommodating that person at a place of his or her choice in the United Kingdom, provided that[1]:
(a) the preferred accommodation provides a service which meets the disabled person's assessed needs;
(b) the cost of the preferred accommodation is not more than the social services department would usually expect to pay having regard to the assessed needs;
(c) the accommodation is available;
(d) the accommodation complies with the local authority's usual terms and conditions for residential care home contracts.

1 As provided for in the National Assistance 1948 (Choice of Accommodation) Directions 1992, direction 3.

3.55 Where the preferred accommodation is more expensive than the accommodation proposed by the authority, the disabled person can nevertheless insist on being supported by the authority in that accommodation, provided a third party (who is not a spouse[1]) agrees to top up the difference (and that third party can reasonably be expected to pay the sum for the duration of the proposed placement).

1 Special restrictions exist where the third party is a spouse—see direction 4(2) and para 11.13 of LAC (92)27.

3.56 The right to exercise choice over accommodation extends not only to prospective residents, but also to existing residents who wish to move to different or more expensive accommodation.

2 Services for disabled people under the Chronically Sick and Disabled Persons Act 1970, s 2

3.57 These services are in practice only likely to be available for people who have developed the symptoms of AIDS and therefore are to be considered at law as 'substantially and permanently handicapped'. Services under the 1970 Act, s 2, are however, available to disabled adults and disabled children alike.

(i) Substantially and permanently handicapped

3.58 For the purposes of the 1970 Act, a disabled person is a person who is blind, deaf or dumb or who suffers from a mental disorder of any description[1], or a person who is substantially and permanently handicapped by illness, injury or congenital deformity. Guidance issued by the Department of Health[2] advises authorities that they should give 'a wide interpretation to the term "substantial", which the department fully recognises must always take full account of individual circumstances. With regard to the term "permanent", authorities will also wish to interpret this sufficiently flexibly to ensure that they do not fell inhibited from giving help...in cases where they are uncertain of the likely duration of the condition.'

1 Ie a person within the ambit of the Mental Health Act 1983, s 1.
2 Appendix 4 to LAC (93)10 at para 8.

Practical assistance in the home

3.59 Local authorities can provide a wide range of services which constitute practical assistance for the disabled person in his or her home, including house cleaning, ironing, help with shopping as well as services which are primarily concerned with the personal care of the disabled person such as help getting out of and into bed, dressing, help in the bathroom, help with cooking and so on. Many social services departments give a higher priority to these personal care services and will only provide cleaning- or ironing-type services in exceptional circumstances.

Provision of radio, television, library, recreational and educational facilities

3.60 The recreational and educational services under this heading can include a place at a day or other recreational or therapeutic centre as well as drop-in clubs, recreational day trips or outings etc. In relation to educational services to support disabled (adult) students, Department of Health guidance[1] reminds social services authorities that s 2 of the 1970 Act covers funding the personal care requirements of such students to enable them to pursue their studies even if those studies are undertaken outside the local authority's area.

1 Circular LAC(93)12.

Travel and other assistance

3.61 This service provision includes arrangements to enable the disabled person to travel to a day centre or other recreational or educational activity. The Chronically Sick and Disabled Persons Act 1970, s 21 also deals with the criteria for obtaining disabled parking exemptions: the orange badge scheme.

Home adaptations and disabled facilities

3.62 Services under this part of the Act fall into two parts: one relating to adaptations (ie significant works possibly of a structural nature); and the other to the provision of additional facilities (ie works involving the provision of fixtures, fittings and equipment).

(a) *Adaptations* Typically home adaptations concern such matters as stair lifts, ground floor extensions, doorway widening, ramps, wheelchair-accessible showers and so on. In most cases, the local authority will ask the disabled person to apply for a 'disabled facility grant'[1] to help with the cost of such adaptations. Whilst this is appropriate, a failure to qualify for a grant does not of itself absolve the social services department from its continuing responsibility to facilitate the adaptations[2].

(b) *Additional facilities* The Act also requires (where the need has been assessed) social services departments to provide disabled people with additional facilities designed to secure their greater safety, comfort or convenience. This includes fittings such as hand rails, alarm systems, hoists, movable baths, adapted switches and handles. Department of Health guidance has been issued concerning the provision of additional facilities[3].

1 Under the Housing Grants, Construction and Regeneration Act 1996.
2 LAC (90)7, para 15.
3 Circular LAC (90)7 and see also LASSL 20/73.

Holidays

3.63 Where the need has been assessed, social services departments are obliged to 'facilitate' the taking of holidays by disabled people, whether at holiday homes or otherwise, provided under arrangements made by the authority or otherwise[1]. The obligation may extend to the full cost of the holiday including travel and an accompanying carer if necessary[2].

1 *R v Ealing London Borough, ex p Leaman* (1984) Times, 10 February.
2 *R v North Yorkshire County Council, ex p Hargreaves* (1997) 1 CCL Rep 33.

Meals

3.64 The Act covers the provision of meals at day centres, meals-on-wheels and other similar servi

Telephone and ancillary equipment

3.65 The duty under s 2 of the 1970 Act may cover the installation of a telephone line as well as the provision of an appropriate handset, loud telephone bell (or a flashing visual or vibrating signal); amplifiers, inductive couples for personal hearing aids and visual transmission machines such as minicoms, faxes and possibly modems for computer e-mail transmission etc.

Other services available to disabled people

3.66 In addition to the specific services which a social services department is obliged to provide for disabled people where a need has been assessed, it is also under a general obligation to ensure that other services are available. These include the services required under the National Health Service Act 1977, Sch 8 (to be provided for 'ill' people—considered at para **3.67**) and general services for disabled people (for which provision was made under the National Assistance Act 1948, s 29) including:

(a) social work service, advice and support (this includes welfare benefits, debt advice etc);
(b) facilities (at centres or otherwise) for social rehabilitation and adjustment to disability including assistance in overcoming limitations of mobility or communication;
(c) workshop and workshop hostel services;
(d) free or subsidised travel;
(e) assistance in finding accommodation; and
(f) warden services.

3 Services for ill people or to alleviate or prevent illness

3.67 The specific obligations on social services departments under the Chronically Sick and Disabled Persons Act 1970, s 2 are owed to people who are already 'substantially and permanently handicapped'. As noted at para **3.57**, these services are in practice only available for people who have developed AIDS symptoms. In contrast, social services departments have a general obligation to provide a raft of services for people who have an illness whether or not it is has already resulted in them becoming permanently and substantially handicapped or for people who are recovering from an illness or in order to prevent illness. Accordingly these services are of major relevance to people with HIV who have not developed AIDS.

3.68 Illness is defined[1] as including mental disorder within the meaning of the Mental Health Act 1983 and any injury or disability requiring medical or dental treatment or nursing. People who are alcoholic or drug-dependent are also specifically included[2] within the definition.

1 Under the National Health Service Act 1977, s 128(1).
2 Appendix 3, para 3(g) to LAC (93)10.

3.69 The National Health Service Act 1977, Sch 8[1] concerns the provision of the following services by social services departments.

1 In conjunction with directions issued by the Secretary of State on 17 March 1993 as App 3 to LAC (93)10.

(i) Services to alleviate mental disorder

3.70 Social services departments are required to make domiciliary care arrangements for the purpose of preventing mental disorder, as well as for persons who are or who have been suffering from mental disorder. The services being:

(a) centres including training centres and day centres or other facilities including domiciliary facilities, whether in premises managed by the local authority or otherwise, for training or occupation of such persons, including the payment of persons engaged in suitable work at the 'centres or other facilities';

(b) social work and related services to help in the identification, diagnosis, assessment and social treatment of mental disorder and to provide social work support and other domiciliary and care services to people living in their own homes and elsewhere.

(ii) Services to alleviate 'illness'

3.71 Social services departments are empowered to make the following domiciliary care arrangements:

(a) centres or other facilities for training such persons or for keeping them suitably occupied and the equipment and maintenance of such centres) together with any other ancillary or supplemental services for such persons;

(b) meals at these centres, or at other facilities (including domiciliary facilities) and meals-on-wheels for housebound people;

(c) social services including advice and support for the purposes of preventing the impairment of physical or mental health of adults in families where such impairment is likely and for the purposes of preventing the break-up of such families or for assisting in their rehabilitation;

(d) night-sitter services;

(e) recuperative holidays;

(f) facilities for social and recreational activities;

(g) services specifically for persons who are alcoholic or drug-dependent.

(iii) Services under the Mental Health Act 1983, s 117

3.72 Most non-accommodation services that authorities provide for people with a mental health difficulties are delivered under the Chronically Sick and Disabled Persons Act 1970, s 2 (since services under this section are available to persons 'who suffer from a mental disorder of any description'). A small minority of people who receive community care services are however entitled to them under the Mental Health Act 1983, s 117. Such persons must have been detained either under s 3 of the 1983 Act (detention for treatment) or under one of the criminal or imprisonment sections (ss 37, 47, 48). Where such persons cease to be detained, s 117 requires authorities to provide them with 'aftercare services'. These services are potentially unlimited in nature and are services to which the user has specific individual legal rights. From a service user's perspective, the receipt of services under s 117 has the added advantage that social services authorities

4 Services for children with HIV or AIDS

3.73 Social services authorities are under a general duty, by virtue of the Children Act 1989, s 17(1), to safeguard and promote the interests of children 'in need' and in furtherance of this duty are empowered to provide a wide range of services.

3.74 The Department of Health has issued general guidance on good social work practice in relation to children with HIV or AIDS[1] which considers such issues as confidentiality, inter-agency liaison, training, testing and access to services. A particularly difficult issue raised by the guidance concerns the possibility that the circumstances leading to infection may reveal other problems such as drug abuse or sexual abuse.

1 *Children and HIV—Guidance for Local Authorities* (1992).

(i) The Children Act 1989

3.75 Section 17(10) provides that a child shall be taken to be 'in need' if:
'(a) he is unlikely to achieve or maintain, or to have the opportunity of achieving or maintaining, a reasonable standard of health or development without the provision for him of services by a local authority…;
(b) his health or development is likely to be significantly impaired, or further impaired, without the provision for him of such services; or
(c) he is disabled.'

3.76 The definition of a disabled child in the Children Act 1989, s 17(11) closely follows the definition of a disabled adult, ie a child is disabled if he is blind, deaf or dumb or suffers from mental disorder of any kind or is substantially and permanently handicapped by illness, injury or congenital deformity. 'Development' means physical, intellectual, emotional, social or behavioural development and 'health' means physical or mental health.

3.77 A child who is not 'substantially and permanently' handicapped may nevertheless be a child in need by virtue of s 17(10)(a) or (b) of the Children Act 1989 and therefore entitled to assistance.

(ii) The assessment of children in need

3.78 There is no duty to assess under the Children Act 1989 equivalent to that found in the National Health Service and Community Care Act 1990, s 47. Nevertheless, there is a power to assess which is strongly reinforced by guidance. In most cases, children with HIV or AIDS will be entitled to a community care assessment under the National Health Service and Community Care Act 1990, s 47(1) in that they will be potentially entitled to services under the Chronically Sick and Disabled Persons Act 1970, s 2.

3.79 The Children Act 1989[1], however, provides for the assessment of 'children in need' and for such assessments to take place at the same time as assessments under:

(a) the Chronically Sick and Disabled Persons Act 1970;
(b) Pt IV of the Education Act 1996;
(c) the Disabled Persons (Services, Consultation and Representation) Act 1986; or
(d) any other enactment.

1 Children Act 1989, Sch 2, para 3.

3.80 The Children Act 1989 Guidance (vol 2: family support) amplifies what is required in such assessments:

> '2.7 Good practice requires that the assessment of need should be undertaken in an open way and should involve those caring for the child, the child and other significant persons. Families with a child in need, whether the need results from family difficulties or the child's circumstances, have the right to receive sympathetic support and sensitive intervention in their family's life...
>
> 2.8 In making an assessment, the local authority should take account of the particular needs of the child – that is in relation to health, development, disability, education, religious persuasion, racial origin, cultural and linguistic background, the degree (if any) to which these needs are being met by existing services to the family or the child and which agencies' services are best suited to the child's needs.'

(iii) Services for 'children in need'

3.81 Once a child has been accepted as being 'in need' and that need identified by an assessment or otherwise then the Children Act 1989 specifies that a range of support services be made available (these may well be in addition to any community care services available under the Chronically Sick and Disabled Persons Act 1970, s 2). The services are almost unlimited; including, by s 17(6), the giving of 'assistance in kind or, in exceptional circumstances, in cash'.

3.82 Schedule 2, Pt I of the Act deals further with the provision of services for children in need. It gives an illustration of the type of services which may be provided but it is clear that this list is not exhaustive, comprising:
(a) advice, guidance and counselling;
(b) occupational, social cultural, or recreational activities;
(c) home help (which may include laundry facilities);
(d) facilities for, or assistance with, travelling to and from home for the purpose of taking advantage of any other service provided under this Act or of any similar service;
(e) assistance to enable the child concerned and his family to have a holiday.

3.83 The guidance to the Children Act 1989[1] summarises the breadth of powers available to social services authorities in such cases:

> 'this general duty is supported by other specific duties and powers such as the facilitation of "the provision by others, including in particular voluntary organisations of services" (s 17(5) and Sch 2). These provisions

services, guidance and counselling, respite care and a range of other services as a means of supporting children in need (including children with disabilities) within their families. The Act recognises that sometimes a child can only be helped by providing services for other members of his family (s 17(3)) "if it [the service] is provided with a view to safeguarding or promoting the child's welfare". ... The social services department may make such arrangements as they see fit for any person to provide services and support "may include giving assistance in kind, or in exceptional circumstances in cash" (s 17(6)). However, where it is the view that of the social services department that a child's welfare is adequately provided for and no unmet need exists, they need not act.'

1 Paragraph 2.11, vol 2: family support.

3.84 The duties owed to disabled children are underwritten by a requirement[1] that authorities provide services designed to minimise the effect on disabled children within their area of their disabilities and to give such children the opportunity to lead lives which are as normal as possible.

1 Children Act 1989, Sch 2, Pt 1, para 6.

Direct payments in lieu of services

3.85 Social services authorities are, by virtue of the Community Care (Direct Payments) Act 1996, empowered to provide certain service users with direct payments rather than services to enable the service user to use the money to purchase the service he or she requires.

3.86 The Act is primarily an enabling statute, the statutory detail is provided in the Community Care (Direct Payments) Regulations 1997[1]. Policy and Practice Guidance has been issued as LAC (97)11 of which the main rules are:

(a) It is for the local authority to decide whether to offer a particular service user the option of receiving direct payments. If the authority decide on this option, it only becomes effective if the service user consents.

(b) The money paid over by the authority must be spent on purchasing services to meet the need, which that authority has assessed (as a result of a community care assessment).

(c) Direct payments may only be made to persons who can manage (alone or with assistance) such payments.

(d) Direct payments cannot be made to:
- (i) people aged 65 or over, unless the person concerned began receiving them before that age;
- (ii) people with a mental health or drug or alcohol dependency difficulty:
  - (A) patients detained under mental health legislation who are on leave of absence from hospital;
  - (B) conditionally discharged detained patients subject to Home Office restrictions;
  - (C) patients subject to guardianship under the mental health legislation;
  - (D) people receiving aftercare under supervision under s 25A of the 1983 Act or aftercare including supervision or treatment) in consequence of a compulsory court order;

(E) offenders serving a probation or combination order subject to a requirement to undergo treatment for a mental health condition or for drug or alcohol dependency.

(e) Certain categories of people cannot be paid to provide a service under the direct payment scheme, including:
   (i) the payee's spouse or common-law spouse;
   (ii) a person living in the same household as the payee who is the payee's:
      (A) parent or parent-in-law;
      (B) son or daughter;
      (C) son-in-law or daughter-in-law;
      (D) stepson or stepdaughter;
      (E) brother or sister;
      (F) aunt or uncle;
      (G) grandparent;
   (iii) the spouse including a common-law spouse of any person specified in (ii) who lives in the same household as the payee.

(f) The guidance states that even where the close relative is not living in the same household, she or he should still be excluded from the scheme unless the local authority 'is satisfied that that is the only appropriate way of securing the relevant services'.

(g) Direct payments cannot be used for the purchase of permanent residential care and any respite residential care purchased is limited (reg 4) to a cumulative total of four weeks in any 12-month period. However, in calculating the cumulative period, only periods of residential care less than four weeks apart are added together to make a cumulative total.

(h) Direct payments cannot be used to purchase local authority provided services.

(i) The payment made by the authority will be net of any assessed charge (see para **3.100**).

1 SI 1997/734.

Charging

3.87 Local authorities must assess a person's need for community care services before they carry out a financial assessment. They are, however, in general, able to charge for the community care services which they provide. The statutory provisions which relate to residential and non-residential services differ markedly and accordingly these are dealt with separately at para **3.100**. Local authorities are not allowed to charge for any community care services which they provide under the Mental Health Act 1983, s 117 (see para **3.72**).

Children

3.88 The charging rules in relation to the accommodation of children are dealt with by Sch 2 to the Children Act 1989 and the charge assessment procedures for non-accommodation services are dealt with under s 29 of the 1989 Act. These rules are not considered in detail, however they are broadly similar to those which apply to adults, except that for children under 16 years, it is the means of the parent that are assessed. Section 29 also stipulates that no charge can be levied where the parent is in receipt of income support of

Residential care charges

3.89 Local authorities have always been under a duty to charge for residential accommodation (whether at a residential care home or a nursing home). The obligation in relation to adults stems from the National Assistance Act 1948, s 22, although the financial assessment details are spelt out in the regulations[1] and in detailed guidance, the Charging for Residential Accommodation Guidance (generally referred to as CRAG). CRAG is updated annually and can be obtained free of charge from the Department of Health, PO Box 777, London SE1 6XH.

1 National Assistance (Assessment of Resources) Regulations 1992, SI 1992/2977, as amended.

3.90 The charging rules are the same whether the user is placed in a local authority-owned home or an independent one. The assessment procedures have many similarities to those which apply for means-tested benefits; most notably, that there are different procedures for assessing the resident's income and capital. An obvious difference is that under the National Assistance Act 1948, social services departments have no power to assess a couple according to their joint resources. They must look only at the resident's income and the resident's capital. Note however that social services departments have general powers under the liable relative rules[1] to pursue a resident's spouse for a contribution towards the cost of accommodation if they believe it reasonable.

1 Under the National Assistance Act 1948, s 42, spouses are under a duty to maintain each other.

Treatment of income

3.91 The basic principle involved in the assessment of income is that all the resident's income is applied towards the accommodation costs up to the total cost of the accommodation. The resident is only eligible to retain a small sum, known as the 'personal allowance'.

3.92 The personal allowance is intended to enable residents to have money to spend on such minor items as stationary, personal toiletries, treats and small presents for friends and relatives. The allowance is up-rated each year (the figure for April 1999–April 2000 is £14.75 per week).

3.93 Authorities have a discretion to vary the personal expense allowance in certain situations to reduce the severity of the otherwise rigid means testing. CRAG gives various examples of where it may be appropriate for an authority to consider allowing a different amount, where:

(a) a person in residential accommodation has a dependent child, the authority should consider the needs of the child in setting the personal allowance;
(b) a person temporarily in residential accommodation receives income support including an amount for a partner who remains at home;
(c) the resident is the main recipient of an unmarried couples' overall income including, for instance, an occupational pension, the authority can use its discretion to increase the resident's personal expenses allowance in special circumstances to enable the resident to pass some of that income to the partner remaining at home
(d) the resident has a pension or retirement annuity contract, half of which would be ignored had it been an occupational pension, then the authority can use its discretion to enable a similar outcome.

Treatment of capital

3.94 Where the capital of a resident is less than £10,000, it is disregarded for the purpose of the means test. For so long as assessed capital exceeds £16,000 then s/he is not entitled to receive any financial assistance from the local authority in respect of the payment of residential home fees. Capital of between £10,000 and £16,000 is taken into account by attributing a 'tariff income' of £1.00 per week for each £250 or part of £250 from £10,000–£16,000.

3.95 Under the Community Care (Residential Accommodation) Act 1998 and its accompanying guidance[1] the following obligations upon social services departments are made explicit:
(a) local authorities are under a legal duty to carry out community care assessments regardless of whether the person has or does not have capital in excess of £16,000;
(b) if, after an assessment of a person's resources, a local authority determine that they exceed £16,000, this does not exempt the authority from its duty to make arrangements for those people who are themselves unable to make care arrangements;
(c) local authorities should ensure that they have in place procedures to ensure that when the net capital of a resident who is self-funding reduces to £16,000 they undertake an assessment and if necessary step in and take over funding arrangements to ensure that the resident is not forced to use capital below £16,000 other than the notional income from that capital.

1 LAC (98)19.

Treatment of property

3.96 The regulations and CRAG detail what capital assets are taken into account and how they are valued. The capital value of certain assets is disregarded, for instance the surrender value of any insurance policy or annuity.

3.97 The capital value of the resident's house is usually taken into account in full, less 10% for disposal costs. However, there are circumstances in which it is disregarded indefinitely:
(a) the value of a dwelling normally occupied by a resident as his or her home should be ignored if his or her stay in a residential care or nursing home is temporary;
(b) where the resident no longer occupies a dwelling as his or her home, its value should be disregarded where it is occupied in whole or in part by:
  (i) the resident's partner or former partner; or
  (ii) a relative of the resident or member of his or her family who is either:
    (A) aged 60 years or over; or
    (B) is aged under 16 and is a child whom the resident is liable to maintain; or
    (C) is incapacitated.

3.98 Local authorities have an overall discretion to disregard the capital continues to live. The guidance states that in deciding how to exercise the use of this discretion:

> 'Local authorities will have to balance the use of this discretion with the need to ensure that residents with assets are not maintained at public expense. It may be reasonable, for example, to disregard a dwelling's value where it is the sole residence of someone who has given up their home in order to care for the resident, or someone who is an elderly companion of the resident particularly if they have given up their own home.'

The improper deprivation of assets

3.99 Under the Assessment Regulations[1], residents may be treated as possessing actual capital which they have disposed of for the purpose of decreasing the amount of their potential liability for residential care charges. In addition, local authorities have wide powers to set aside gifts made to third parties where one of the objects of the gift was to avoid or reduce liability for residential fees[2].

1 National Assistance (Assessment of Resources) Regulations 1992, SI 1991/2977, s 25(1), as amended.
2 Including powers under the Health and Social Services and Social Security Adjudications Act 1983, s 21 and the Insolvency Act 1986, ss 339 and 423.

Non-accommodation charges

3.100 By virtue of the Health and Social Services and Social Security Adjudications Act 1983, s 17, social services authorities have a discretionary power to charge for most[1] non-accommodation services provided for adults. Section 17(3) provides for the reduction or waiver of charges where the user satisfies the local authority that he or she has insufficient means for it to be reasonably practicable to pay the usual charge for the service. There is no statutory defined procedure for assessing non-accommodation charges, each authority is entitled to develop its own procedures.

1 Ie for all non-accommodation services with the exception of services under the Mental Health Act 1983, s 117.

3.101 Where a user considers the local authority's charge to be too high, the usual procedure will be to pursue the matter through the local authority's complaints procedures. At any panel hearing it may be important to stress that the authority's powers to reduce or waive charges are not limited to a consideration of the service user's financial means. As the authority has an overall discretion as to whether or not to levy charges, it retains a discretion to waive or reduce charges on any ground. Such an overall discretion might be used where, for instance, the service user lacked mental capacity and the services were therefore being put in without consent, or where the service user is at risk of serious and immediate harm if the services are not provided but refuses to have the services if the user is charged for them.

3.102 Department of Health guidance[1] has made it clear that:

> 'once someone has been assessed as needing a service, that service should not be withdrawn even if he or she refuses to pay the charge required.

The authority should continue provision of the service while pursuing the debt, if necessary, through the magistrates' court.'

1 Social Services Inspectorate Advice on Non-Accommodation Charges, January 1994, para 26.

5 Local authority complaints procedures

3.103 Every social services authority is required by law[1] to have a standardised complaints system. The procedures in relation to adult and children's complaints are very similar, with the most significant difference being that at the equivalent (second stage) of children's complaints procedure an independent person must be involved. The complaints process for adults is outlined at para **3.105**.

1 For adults, the complaints procedures stem from the Local Authority Social Services Act 1970, s 7B and the Complaints Procedure Directions 1990; for children, the relevant law is to be found in the Representations Procedure (Children) Regulations 1991, SI 1991/894.

3.104 A complaint may be made by anyone for whom the local authority has power to provide services. Complaints may in addition be made by third parties on behalf of service users, provided the service user agrees to this. The complaints process consists of three distinct stages:
(a) informal or problem-solving stage;
(b) formal or registration stage;
(c) review stage.

(i) Informal or problem-solving stage

3.105 Where a local authority receives representations from any complainant it is required to attempt to resolve the matter informally. At the first stage, a complaint does not have to be registered although many authorities do keep a written record. It is simply an opportunity for the local authority to attempt problem-solving, conciliation and negotiation.

3.106 A significant defect with the informal first stage (as opposed to the next two stages) is the lack of any statutory time-scale for its completion. In practice many authorities specify in their local procedures maximum periods for this phase (not infrequently a period of two weeks).

(ii) The formal stage

3.107 If the complaint cannot be resolved to the satisfaction of the complainant at the first informal stage, then the local authority is required to give the complainant an explanation of the complaints procedure and ask the complainant to submit a written representation if he or she wishes to proceed. This second stage involves the formal registration of the complaint. A complainant is entitled to go straight to this stage, omitting the informal stage if they wish.

3.108 The authority is required to consider the complaint and formulate a comply with the 28-day period the authority must within that period give the complainant an explanation as to why this is so and a date when the response will be given. In any event the response must be forthcoming within three months. The authority is required to notify the complainant in writing of the result of its investigation.

(iii) Review stage

3.109 The complainant may, if dissatisfied within 28 days of receiving the local authority's decision, request that the complaint be referred to a panel for review. Such a request must be made in writing. In such cases the local authority is required to convene a panel hearing, within 28 days of receipt of the complainant's request and at least ten days before the hearing, to provide details of the time and venue of the panel hearing and who will be in attendance. The panel consists of three people, the chairperson is independent and in most cases one wing member is a councillor and the other a senior social services officer.

3.110 Complainants are entitled to make written submissions to the panel before the meeting and to make oral submissions at the meeting. They can be accompanied by another person who is entitled to be present at the whole meeting and to speak on their behalf. The role of the panel is to consider all the relevant evidence, weigh it up, and recommend a particular outcome. It is the panel's job to re-examine the previous decision.

3.111 Within 24 hours of the review hearing, the panel must reach a decision in writing and forward its recommendations (and reasons) to the local authority, the complainant (and his or her representative) and any other person who is considered to have sufficient interest.

3.112 The local authority has 28 days from the date of the panel's recommendations to decide what action should be taken. It must notify in writing all the persons who received copies of the panel's recommendations; the notification must detail, not only the authority's decision, but also its reasons for taking that decision and of any action which it has in consequence taken or which it proposes to take.

6 HIV or AIDS support grant

3.113 Each year the Department of Health provides to social services authorities a specific support grant to assist in the provision of services for people with AIDS. Circular guidance has been issued on the Support Grant Scheme as LAC(98)9. In 1998/99, a total grant of £13.7 million was made available. The scheme operates on a 70:30 basis, authorities providing at least 30% of expenditure from their own resources.

3.114 The general aim of the scheme is to enable social services departments to draw up strategic plans, based on local population needs assessments, for commissioning social care for people with HIV or AIDS and to enable social services departments to finance provision of social care for people with HIV or AIDS including their partners, carers and families.

3.115 The grant can be used to support the costs of HIV or AIDS training related to community care services as well as joint projects established to address the accommodation needs of people with HIV or AIDS as part of a co-ordinated strategy to facilitate community care needs but not for the provision of housing alone.

3.116 The guidance recognises that the prevalence of HIV or AIDS remains concentrated in London and is low elsewhere. It emphasises the important role played by voluntary organisations in developing services for people with HIV or AIDS and the need for local authorities to work in conjunction with their respective health authorities.

Part II Housing and welfare benefits

A INTRODUCTION

3.117 This area is not covered in detail in this book as specialist help may be needed. The Terrence Higgins Trust Advice Centre has teams of advisers who work exclusively in the area and a referral to them might be appropriate. However, advisers should be aware of the main issues that are relevant in order to give their clients a full service.

B ACCESS TO HOUSING

3.118 A client may present as homeless or potentially homeless. This may happen where someone is in shared accommodation which may be overcrowded or otherwise unsuitable because of poor health or problems which have arisen around confidentiality. Advice may need to be sought on whether the person should make a housing register application or present themselves as homeless to the local authority.

3.119 The Housing Act 1996 deals with both housing register applications and the local authority's duties in respect of homelessness. In respect of applications to join the housing register the person may need assistance with presenting the case for the number of points to be allocated to improve their position on the list. Factors to be taken into account include health needs, including the need to be on the ground floor or have access to a lift if there are mobility problems.

3.120 Of course, if the person is homeless, the local authority have a duty to investigate the case, and, if they have reason to believe the person is eligible for assistance, they should place the person in temporary accommodation whilst continuing to investigate. Such investigations will include whether the person may be in priority need, that is, whether there are dependant children or mental or physical health problems. The local authority will also consider whether a person is intentionally homeless and what local connections they have to the area. Clients should be warned that temporary accommodation in accepted as homeless and in priority need (and satisfies the tests on local connection and not intentionally homeless) the local authority must offer temporary accommodation for two years which can continue after that time if there is no change in their circumstances. If a person is not in priority need the local authority need only offer advice and assistance.

3.121 Considering those groups who are affected by HIV and AIDS, in particular, those from abroad, it is important to mention that those 'subject to immigration control' (see chapter 6) are not eligible for local authority housing. The local authority does have duties under the National Assistance Act 1948 and the Children Act 1989, though and some people may be offered housing through this route. There are also some local rules that may apply about length of residence and so on. If a negative decision is received there is a right to a review and then appeal on a point of law to the county court. There is also the possibility of seeking permission for judicial review on the usual grounds.

3.122 If there is no likelihood of the person being found to be homeless, they may want to apply to be placed on the housing register and it may be worth either giving assistance with the form or referring them elsewhere so that their prospect of being housed is as good as possible. If the points assessment is disappointing, a request can be made for re-assessment with additional information.

1 Disrepair, illegal evictions and possession proceedings

3.123 It is sometimes the case that people are less able to cope with poor conditions when they are ill. Help with putting the landlord on notice and getting an independent environmental health officer report may increase the chance of repairs being carried out. Advisers should pay particular care to confidentiality when dealing with private landlords as many people will not want them to know of their health status.

3.124 People faced with the prospect of possession proceedings or an illegal eviction will need urgent advice on how to proceed. Of course, legal aid may be available and there is the possibility of securing injunctions where appropriate or negotiating with the landlord. In some circumstances the person may not want to keep possession as they may prefer to be homeless but care should be taken to avoid any problems of intentional homeless arguments.

2 Transfers and succession

3.125 If the person is in unsuitable accommodation because, for instance, it is not near the hospital they use, they might want to consider a transfer or mutual exchange. This may depend on the individual local authority policy and it is advisable to seek specialist help in making the best case for a transfer.

3.126 The Housing Act 1996 specifies the conditions that have to be met for someone to succeed to a local authority tenancy. It only includes relatives so same-sex couples do not qualify under the Act. However some local authorities have policies which allow them to exercise discretion. This might be an issue that comes up when one of a couple has died, maybe from an AIDS-related illness and their same-sex partner wants to remain in the property.

C WELFARE BENEFITS

3.127 The same rules apply to those affected by HIV and AIDS as to anyone else in relation to access to welfare benefits. That is, that they are complex and involve extreme care and endurance in form filling. There are some benefits that are particularly relevant to people who might be ill and, again, specialist help is available from the Terrence Higgins Trust Advice Centre.

1 Incapacity benefit

3.128 If someone has worked and becomes too ill to carry on working, incapacity benefit is the first benefit to consider. The rules are quite complex but for those who have paid enough contributions and can satisfy the 'all work' test will qualify. Those with symptomatic HIV may be exempt form the all work test if they can get MED4 from their doctor to accompany the application. If refused on the basis of the all work test an appeal can be made within one month.

2 Disability living allowance

3.129 Those who are severely disabled may be entitled to disability living allowance, whether they are working or not. The person has to show that they have difficulties walking outside (the mobility component) and/or have personal care needs (the care component). The mobility component has two rates and the care component three. Which rate they receive will depend on the severity of their symptoms. Usually the person claiming has to show that they have had the condition for three months although there are special rules which may apply to those who have an AIDS diagnosis. The form is complicated and needs particular care when completed so specialist help is useful. If the claim is refused a review can be requested within three months.

3 Income support

3.130 For those unable to work and on a low income, income support may be available. For those with HIV or AIDS, there may also be the entitlement to premiums relating to disability if they supply necessary medical certificates. A refusal (or award at a lower level than expected) can be reviewed within three months.

3.131 There are a number of other benefits which may be relevant including housing and council tax benefit which are administered through the local authority. The social fund provides loans for people for capital items, usually

3.132 There are restrictions on the above benefits for people who are asylum seekers unless the refugee application was made at the port of entry. Also those with a restriction in their passport that there should be 'no recourse to public funds' and people who have been refused on asylum may not be able to claim some benefits. This is complicated and the client should be referred to a welfare rights adviser before they make a claim if they fall into the category of someone with any restriction on their stay in the UK. The benefits authorities do not recognise same-sex relationships and partners in those relationships will not be included in means testing.

Chapter 4

Medical treatment issues: consent and liability

Luke Clements
Terry Donovan

A OVERVIEW

4.01 In marked contrast to the duties and responsibilities of social services providers (see chapter 3), the public law duties of the National Health Service are non-specific and consequently difficult to enforce. The National Health Service Act 1977 remains the primary statute which governs the discharge of health services in the England and Wales.

4.02 Section 1 of the Act places a general duty on the Secretary of State for Heath (in England) and the Secretary of State for Wales to provide a 'comprehensive health service'. It requires them to ensure that the 'comprehensive health service' secures improvements in physical and mental health by developing services aimed at the prevention, diagnosis and treatment of illness.

4.03 Section 3 of the Act subdivides the nebulous 'comprehensive' duty into six general categories of service:

'(a) hospital accommodation;
(b) other accommodation for the purpose of any service provided under this Act;
(c) medical, dental, nursing and ambulance services;
(d) such other facilities for the care of expectant mothers and young children as he considers are appropriate as part of the Health Service;
(e) such facilities for the prevention of illness, the care of persons suffering from illness and the aftercare of persons who have suffered from illness as he considers are appropriate as part of the Health Service;
(f) such other services as are required for the diagnosis and treatment of illness.'

4.04 The 1977 Act has been the subject of considerable amendment. Up until 1989, hospitals were generally funded and managed by district health authorities, who received their funding from regional health authorities. District and regional health authorities were abolished by the Health which received funding from the executive branch of the Department of Health and Welsh Office, now known as the NHS Executive. The National Health Service and Community Care Act 1990 created an 'internal market' by which health authorities funded, but did not provide, services. The hospital and other providers were renamed 'trusts' which then became independent organisations albeit under the NHS umbrella.

4.05 The 1977 Act divided the NHS into two different systems. Part I is primarily concerned with the provision of healthcare in hospitals and 'community health services'; for example, the services provided by district nurses, midwives or health visitors in clinics or individuals' homes and the provision of medical services to pupils in state schools. The responsibility for securing the provision of these services to patients rests with the Secretary of State, although under s 13 of the 1977 Act these have been delegated to health authorities and since 1990 hospital and community health services are provided by NHS trusts.

4.06 The second aspect of the NHS, sometimes described as 'primary care', is dealt with under Pt II of the 1977 Act. This governs the arrangements made by health authorities for the provision of services by general practitioners, dentists, opticians and chemists. The responsibilities of general practitioners and trusts are considered separately at paras **4.09**ff.

1 Guidance

4.07 Whilst the obligations upon the various NHS bodies are spelt out in broad terms by the various statutes, there is a marked lack of detail as to what precisely must be done in any individual case. This lack of statutory detail is expanded upon by detailed guidance issued by the Department of Health in England and the Welsh Office (now the Assembly) in Wales. In general, this is guidance which the relevant person must take into account when making a decision, although it is possible that, in certain situations, it may be binding[1].

1 See *R v North Derbyshire Health Authority, ex p Fisher* (1998) 1 CCL Rep 150 (considered at para **4.21**) and also *R v Islington London Borough Council, ex p Rixon* (1998) 1 CCL Rep 119, (1996) Times, 17 April.

4.08 Copies of Department of Health Guidance can be obtained free of charge from: Department of Health, PO Box 777, London SE1 6XH and Welsh Assembly Guidance from the Health Circular Section, Welsh Office, Crown Buildings, Cathays Park, Cardiff CF1 3NQ. Department of Health guidance issued since 1993 is also accessible on the Internet[1].

1 See www.open.gov.uk; then via department of health/publications/circulars/COIN (circulars on the Internet).

2 General practitioner services

4.09 Under s 29 of the 1977 Act, it is the duty of each health authority to arrange with medical practitioners to provide personal medical services for all persons in the area who wish to take advantage of the arrangements. These services are described as 'general medical services'. As with hospital services, it is not the health authority itself which provides the service; instead, it enters into separate statutory arrangements with independent practitioners for the provision of those services. General practitioners (GPs) are therefore not employees of the health authority; they are independent professionals who undertake to provide general medical services in accordance with regulations which govern that activity[1].

1 National Health Service (General Medical Services) Regulations 1992, SI 1992/635, as amended.

4.10 For the purposes of patients with HIV or AIDS the regulations are of particular relevance in three specific respects.

(i) GPs' obligation to provide general medical services

4.11 Schedule 2, para 12 to the 1992 Regulations require GPs to render to his or her patients all necessary and appropriate medical services of the type usually provided by GPs including:

(a) giving advice, where appropriate, to a patient in connection with the patient's general health and in particular about the significance of diet, exercise, the use of tobacco, the consumption of alcohol and the misuse of drugs or solvents;
(b) offering consultations to patients and, where appropriate, physical examinations for the purpose of identifying, or reducing the risk of disease or injury;
(c) offering to patients, where appropriate, vaccination or immunisation against measles, mumps, rubella, pertussis, poliomyelitis and tetanus;
(d) arranging for the referral of patients, as appropriate, for the provision of any other services under the National Health Service Act 1977; and
(e) giving advice, as appropriate, to enable patients to avail themselves of services by a local social services authority.

4.12 The obligation created by these regulations includes more than merely advising patients as to the availability of the community care services for which the social services department is responsible. It also obliges GPs to actually refer patients to social services departments for the provision of community care services.

(ii) GP's obligation to prescribe drugs and appliances

4.13 The obligation on GPs to render general medical services for their patients brings with it a need to prescribe. This requirement is dealt with in Sch 2, para 43 to the 1992 Regulations which provides:

> 'Subject to paragraph 44, a doctor shall order any drugs or appliances which are needed for the treatment of any patient to whom he is providing treatment under these terms of service by issuing to that patient a prescription form and such a form shall not be used in any other circumstances.'

4.14 The prescription powers of GPs are subject to specific restrictions in to the 1992 Regulations, GPs are prohibited from prescribing certain drugs and other substances (which are listed in Sch 10). These are items which it is thought that patients should obtain at their own expense and are, for the most part, proprietary medicines which are generally brought over the counter at chemists.

1 Ie drugs listed in the Misuse of Drugs Regulations 1985, Sch 2; National Health Service (General Medical Services) Regulations 1992, Sch 2, para 43(3), as amended.

4.15 In addition to the power to prescribe drugs, reg 43 enables GPs to prescribe 'appliances' (ie medical aids, dressings, pads etc) as well as basic equipment to help overcome the effects of disability. In relation to disability equipment, there is frequently an overlap of responsibility with the local social services department's community care duties (see chapter 3). It is therefore common practice for health and social services to arrange joint equipment stores which can be accessed by both social services and the relevant NHS trust.

4.16 The appliances which a GP can prescribe are detailed in two lists known as the 'drug tariff' and the 'appliance list'[1]. The lists enables GPs to provide a range of general items. If more specialist equipment is needed, however, this may be obtained via a hospital consultant (see para **4.20**). Equipment and appliances provided by the GP can include:

(a) stoma and incontinence care equipment;
(b) equipment for people with diabetes;
(c) elastic hosiery, dressings, bandages, trusses etc;
(d) respiratory equipment (including nebulisers, oxygen cylinders etc);
(e) chiropody appliances;
(f) wheelchairs for permanent use, including powered wheelchairs, although in general the disabled person will be referred to the local 'wheelchair service centre' for assessment of the most suitable wheelchair.

1 The drug tariff is a statement published from time to time under reg 18 of the National Health Service (Pharmaceutical Services) Regulations 1992, SI 1992/662. The appliance list contains the details of appliances which have been approved by the Secretary of State for the purposes of s 41 of the 1977 Act.

(iii) GPs' obligation to provide medical certificates

4.17 General practitioners have an important role in relation to the United Kingdom's social security system, both in providing certificates for the purpose of contributory benefits (for instance, sickness notes) and in relation to entitlement to non-contributory benefits such as income support premiums or attendance allowance. Accordingly Sch 2, para 37(1) of the 1992 Regulations provides that GPs are required to issue free of charge to their patients (or their personal representatives) any medical certificate which is reasonably required for certain specified purposes; these being set out in Sch 9 to the 1992 Regulations.

3 Hospital and NHS consultant services

4.18 As noted at para **4.05**, NHS trusts are the major providers of secondary health services in hospitals and similar institutions. Doctors working for such trusts[1] are directly employed by the trusts under an employment contract; a quite different arrangement to the 'independent' provider status of GPs.

1 Ie consultants or junior doctors (which description includes senior registrars, registrars, senior house officers and house officers).

4.19 For the purposes of patients with HIV or AIDS, the role of hospitals and hospital doctors are of particular relevance in the following respects.

(i) Consultant's powers to prescribe drugs and appliances

4.20 An NHS consultant may prescribe any drug, appliance or piece of equipment which he or she considers necessary for a patient's treatment. In general the consultant's employment contract with the NHS trust will restrict this prescribing power, or at least make the provision of expensive items subject to validation by the trust's managers.

4.21 In certain situations it may be unlawful for a health authority to restrict the availability of specialist drugs. In *R v North Derbyshire Health Authority, ex p Fisher*[1] for instance, the court held that the respondent authority had failed, without good reason, to follow government guidance[2] on the prescription of beta-interferon drugs to people with multiple sclerosis and accordingly its actions were unlawful.

1 (1998) 1 CCL Rep 150.
2 Executive letter EL (95)97.

4 Obligation to secure long-term healthcare provision

4.22 The NHS's responsibilities for providing continuing care for patients with chronic illnesses has been the subject of substantial policy guidance. The primary guidance was published in February 1995 as local authority circular LAC (95)5[1]. The circular guidance emphasised at para 1 that:

> 'the arrangement and funding of services to meet continuing physical and mental care needs are an integral part of the responsibilities of the NHS. This includes, but is not limited to, the responsibility to arrange and fund an appropriate level of care from the NHS under specialist clinical supervision in hospital or in a nursing home. It also includes equally important responsibilities around rehabilitation, palliative healthcare, respite healthcare, community health services support and specialist healthcare support in different settings.'

1 Also referred to as HSG (95)8 or in Wales as WHC (95)7.

4.23 The guidance highlighted a number of specific services which must be made available.

(i) Rehabilitation and recovery

or had an inpatient admission for some other acute need. LAC (95)5 and follow-up guidance[1] has stressed that such rehabilitation services should not be limited to patients who have had an acute episode of hospital care, but should also cater for patients who needed longer term rehabilitative care as part of a care package in their own home, a residential care home or nursing home.

1 Executive letter EL (96)8.

(ii) Palliative healthcare

4.25 Palliative care should be distinguished from the care of 'terminally ill' people who are defined by the Department of Health as people with an active and progressive disease for which curative treatment is not possible or not appropriate and whose death can reasonably be expected within 12 months.

4.26 Guidance expressly[1] requires health authorities to provide:
(a) palliative healthcare, on an inpatient basis, fully funded by the NHS in hospital, hospice or in a limited number of cases in nursing homes capable of providing this level of care;
(b) specialist palliative healthcare to old people already in nursing homes;
(c) palliative healthcare support to people in their own homes or in residential care.

1 EL (93)14, EL (94)14 and EL (95)22.

4.27 The guidance, however, advises that where:

> 'it is decided on the basis of assessment that a person's needs make a placement in a residential care or nursing home appropriate, the local authority will generally be responsible for arranging such a placement (although precise responsibilities will have been agreed between local authorities and health authorities). Although not in need of specialist in-patient palliative care the time of their initial assessment and placement, some people placed in this way may eventually become terminally ill or enter the terminal phase of a long-term condition. Some of these patients may come in time to require specialist palliative care. Health authorities will be responsible for providing such specialist care. Depending on the individual's needs, specialist palliative care could be provided by means of a placement for temporary or permanent specialist in-patient care elsewhere (for which new placement the health authority would bear the cost) or by additional specialist healthcare to the person in the home where they live (in which case the health authority would fund only the additional care).'

(iii) Continuing in-patient care

4.28 The guidance LAC (95)5 requires health authorities to arrange and fund an adequate level of inpatient care, on a short- or long-term basis, for people:
(a) where the complexity or intensity of their medical, nursing care or other clinical care or the need for frequent not easily predictable interventions requires the regular (in the majority of cases this might be weekly or more frequent) supervision of a consultant, specialist nurse or other NHS member of the multi-disciplinary team;

(b) who require routinely the use of specialist healthcare equipment[1] or treatments which require the supervision of specialist NHS staff;
(c) have rapidly degenerating or unstable condition which means that they will require specialist medical or nursing home supervision.

1 *R v North and East Devon Health Authority, ex p Coughlan* (1999) 143 Sol Jo LB 21, CA.

4.29 In addition, patients who have finished acute treatment or in-patient palliative care in a hospital or hospice, but whose prognosis is that they are likely to die in the very near future should be able to choose to remain in NHS-funded accommodation or, where practicable and after an appropriate and sensitive assessment of their needs, to return home with appropriate support.

(iv) Respite healthcare

4.30 The same guidance states that the NHS 'has important responsibilities' for arranging and funding respite care and that all health authorities must arrange and fund an adequate level of care, particularly in respect of people who:
(a) have complex or intense healthcare needs and will require specialist medical or nursing supervision or assessment during a period of respite care;
(b) during a period of respite care require or could benefit from active rehabilitation;
(c) are receiving a package of palliative care in their own homes but where they or their carer need a period of respite care.

4.31 The guidance emphasises that in making arrangements for respite care, health authorities should pay careful attention to the wishes of patients and their carers. In more recent guidance[1] it was stressed that there would be other situations in which the NHS should be the service responsible for respite care, for example: 'where carers have been providing a level of healthcare which is not reasonably available in a residential setting'.

1 EL (96)8.

(v) NHS specialist or intensive services for people in nursing or residential care homes

4.32 The NHS is responsible for the healthcare needs of all people, regardless of whether they are in a hospital, residential care home or living in the community. The only exception to this general rule relates to the provision of general nursing to people living in a nursing home; in such cases, the responsibility for the general nursing and basic equipment (such as incontinence supplies) lies with the home all other medical care (including specialist nursing etc) remains the responsibility of the NHS.

4.33 The guidance states that nursing care such as incontinence advice, stoma care or diabetic advice are services that should be provided by the NHS to nursing home residents (ie free of charge). Likewise, community health services such as physi provided by the NHS, as well as specialist medical or nursing equipment (for instance specialist feeding equipment) not available on prescription and normally only available through hospitals.

(vi) Community health and primary care services for people at home

4.34 The NHS has a crucial role in the provision of continuing care for people at home via such services as district nursing and nursing auxiliaries as well as the provision of specialist medical or nursing equipment not available on prescription (such as wheelchairs, special beds, commodes, incontinence pads). These may be supplied by the NHS to people living at home as part of its community health services. Again, this is an area where there are considerable overlapping responsibilities between health and social services.

B THE NHS'S COERCIVE POWERS IN RELATION TO PATIENTS WITH HIV OR AIDS

4.35 Article 5(1)(e) of the European Convention on Human Rights permits detention by a state of (amongst others) 'persons for the prevention of the spreading of infectious diseases'. Accordingly UK domestic legislation contains a number of such measures.

1 Power to order a compulsory medical examination

4.36 The Public Health (Control of Disease) Act 1984, s 35[1] provides that a magistrate may, if satisfied by a written certificate issued by a medical practitioner, order that:
(a) a person is suffering from a notifiable disease (including AIDS); or
(b) the person, though not suffering from such a disease, is carrying an organism that is capable of causing it (ie HIV); and
(c) in his or her own interest, or in the interest of his or her family, or in the public interest, it is expedient that she or he should be medically examined; and
(d) she or he is not under the treatment of a registered medical practitioner (or the medical practitioner who is treating him or her consents to such an order).

1 As modified by the Public Health (Infectious Diseases) Regulations 1988, SI 1988/1546.

4.37 Where an order has been made under s 35, a warrant may additionally be issued, permitting the officer to obtain entry into any premises (by force if necessary) to enforce the order.

2 Power to order removal to a hospital

4.38 The Public Health (Control of Disease) Act 1984, s 37[1] provides that a magistrate may order a person to be removed to a hospital, if:
(a) the relevant health authority consent; and

(b) the magistrate is satisfied that the person is suffering from a notifiable disease (which includes AIDS); and
   (i) that his or her circumstances are such that proper precautions to prevent the spread of infection cannot be taken, or that such precautions are not being taken; and
   (ii) that serious risk of infection is thereby caused to other persons; and
   (iii) that accommodation is available in a suitable hospital.

1 As modified by the Public Health (Infectious Diseases) Regulations 1988, SI 1988/1546.

3 Power to detain

4.39 The Public Health (Control of Disease) Act 1984, s 38 enables a magistrate to order that a patient be detained in hospital, if satisfied that the patient:
(a) is suffering from a notifiable disease (which includes AIDS); and
(b) would not, on leaving the hospital, be provided with lodging or accommodation in which proper precautions could be taken to prevent the spread of the disease.

The application is made by the local authority and may be made ex parte. Kennedy and Grubb[1] suggest that the above powers under s 37 and s 38 only apply to patients with AIDS and not to persons with HIV infection alone.

1 Kennedy and Grubb *Medical Law* (1994, 2nd edn) Butterworths.

4 Confidentiality of and access to medical information

(i) Access to personal information

4.40 The previous legislation concerning access to health records[1] has now been repealed and replaced by the Data Protection Act 1998. Section 7 of this Act provides individuals with a right of access to any information held on them by the relevant authority, provided the request is made in writing and upon payment of any fee required (subject to a maximum fee of £10).

1 Data Protection Act 1984 and the Access to Health Records Act 1990.

4.41 Section 30 of the 1998 Act provides for regulations to be made which may restrict the duty of disclosure of information which has been collected by health, education or social services. These regulations have not yet been published but it is likely that they will reflect the previous rules which enabled information to be withheld if the authority considered that its disclosure was 'likely to cause serious harm to the physical or mental health of the patient or someone else'.

4.42 The Access to Medical Reports Act 1988 gives (with limited exceptions) individuals the right to see any medical report which has been prepared on them for an insurance company or an employer.

(ii) Confidentiality

4.43 Section 2 of the Data Protection Act 1998 provides for special safeguards it defines as including, inter alia, information as to a person's 'physical or mental health or condition' or 'his sexual life'. It is unlawful to process sensitive personal data unless one of the conditions stated in Sch 3 to the Act is satisfied. The schedule lists ten restrictive grounds, which include (no 8) 'the processing is necessary for medical purposes'. For this ground to be satisfied the processing of the data must be undertaken by a health professional or a person who owes an equivalent duty of confidentiality to a health professional. 'Medical purposes' is defined[1] as including preventative medicine, medicinal diagnosis, medical research, the provision of care and treatment and the management of healthcare services.

1 Data Protection Act 1998, Sch 3, para 8(2).

4.44 Additional statutory obligations of confidentiality exist for persons who have been examined or treated for any sexually transmitted disease. The National Health Service (Venereal Diseases) Regulations 1974, reg 2 provide that health authorities must take all necessary steps to ensure that the identity of any persons examined or treated for any sexually transmitted disease is kept confidential. This obligation to maintain confidentiality permits the disclosure of information to a GP or other health professional involved in the 'treatment of persons suffering from such disease or for the prevention of the spread thereof'[1].

1 National Health Service (Venereal Diseases) Regulations 1974, reg 2(a). The absolute importance of confidentiality required by the Regulations in relation to persons with HIV or AIDS was emphasised in *X v Y* [1988] 2 All ER 648.

(iii) HIV testing

4.45 HIV testing involves the taking of blood from a patient and accordingly is unlawful unless the patient gives informed consent or there is an exceptional overriding situation which legitimises the action.

4.46 The Department of Health has issued guidelines for pretest discussion on HIV testing (1996) which state that testing for HIV infection should only be undertaken with informed consent, individuals having received information about how HIV is transmitted, the significance of both positive and negative results and a discussion of the particular needs and interests relevant to the individual.

4.47 The guidelines state that informed consent has three components, namely that the individual:
(a) must be competent to consent;
(b) should understand the purposes, risks, harms and benefits of being tested and those of not being tested; and
(c) must consent voluntarily.

4.48 The guidelines detail the issues that should be discussed with individuals contemplating HIV testing; these are described as five stages:
(a) discussion about the nature of HIV infection, transmission and risk reduction;
(b) risk activities and the need for a test;
(c) discussion of the advantages and disadvantages of testing and the implications of the positive and negative result for the individual;

(d) the test procedure and providing the result; and
(e) obtaining informed consent.

4.49 In relation to persons who are unwell, but unaware that their symptoms may be due to HIV the guidelines advise that although all five stages must be followed it may be:

> 'inappropriate to enter into lengthy discussion on risk reduction or the pros and cons of a test when the individual is very unwell, although only in exceptional circumstances should a test ever be performed without informed consent'.

4.50 British Medical Council guidelines[1] to doctors state that:

> 'Only in the most exceptional circumstances, where a test is imperative to secure the safety of persons other than the patient and where it is not possible for the prior consent of the patient to be obtained, can testing without explicit consent be justified.'

1 June 1993.

Ante-natal care

4.51 The guidelines state that HIV testing during pregnancy is most appropriately dealt with in the context of obtaining consent to the wider range of general ante-natal tests, although 'specific consent to an HIV test must be obtained'. They reiterate the government's policy of offering ante-natal HIV testing to all women in high prevalence areas and emphasise the specific advantages of knowledge of serostatus for pregnant women.

Mental capacity and informed consent

4.52 All adults are presumed to be capable of handling their own affairs unless the contrary is shown. Where an adult is incapable or considered 'vulnerable', then a variety of legal provisions can apply. The present state of the law is highly confused and in drastic need of reform. Substantial proposals for reform have been made by the Law Commission, in its report *Mental Incapacity*[1].

1 1995 Law Commission Report No 231.

4.53 The Mental Health Act 1983 is not primarily concerned with the needs of vulnerable adults. The central provision of the 1983 Act concerns the admission to hospital of any person suffering from a specified mental disorder 'of a nature or degree which makes it appropriate for him to receive medical treatment in a hospital' (s 3(2)(a)). The Act is also concerned with the provision of treatment; s 63 (subject to ss 57 and 58) provides that 'the consent of a patient shall not be required for any medical treatment given to him for the mental disorder from which he is suffering'.

4.54 Patients detained in hospital may or may not have 'decision-making capacity'. The Act is not however concerned with this question, but rather whether it is 'necessary for the health or safety of the patient or for the

4.55 In a series of cases, the court has therefore distinguished between the policy of the 1983 Act and the law of capacity. For instance, in:

(a) *B v Croydon District Health Authority*[1]: the court held that, although a patient had capacity to refuse treatment, it was nonetheless lawfully given under s 63 of the 1983 Act because it was 'for' her mental disorder;

(b) *Re C (adult: refusal of treatment)*[2]: the court refused a declaration as to the legality of treatment (the removal of a gangrenous leg) because the treatment did not relate to the patient's 'treatment'. Although the court was in no doubt that the patient was mentally ill within the meaning of the Mental Health Act 1983, s 1 it held that he had sufficient capacity to understand the risk to him if his leg was not amputated;

(c) *Re C (a minor)(detention for medical treatment)*[3]: the court allowed the use of wardship powers under the Children Act 1989, s 100 (rather than use of powers under the 1983 Act) to detain, for treatment, a 16-year-old with anorexia nervosa.

1 [1995] Fam 133, [1995] 1 All ER 683.
2 [1993] 1 FLR 940.
3 [1997] 3 FCR 49, [1997] 2 FLR 180.

Capacity

4.56 The law is concerned with the ability of a person to perform a specific legal act, such as making a will; marrying; giving property away; or being able to manage his or her affairs. Whether a person does have mental capacity or not is a legal, not a medical, question. Capacity will vary depending on the nature of the act that is to be undertaken. Frequently, the courts will place a great deal of weight on the evidence of a doctor, but, ultimately, it is a legal decision. A person may have mental capacity at law to conduct a simple transaction (for instance, handling his or her social security moneys), but not sufficient capacity for a complex matter, such as conducting medical negligence litigation.

4.57 It is presumed that a person is capable until the contrary is proved and then it is presumed that the person is mentally incapable until the contrary is proved. The standard of proof is 'the balance of probabilities'.

4.58 There are various tests of capacity, depending on the nature of the action to be undertaken. For instance[1], to make a will, a person must understand:

(a) the nature of the act and its effects;
(b) the extent (as distinct from the value) of the property of which or she is disposing; and
(c) appreciate the claims to which he or she ought to give effect.

1 An excellent text on this subject is *Assessment of Mental Capacity: guidance for doctors and lawyers* (1995) BMA.

4.59 To marry, a person must:

(a) appreciate that he or she is taking part in a marriage ceremony;
(b) be able to follow the words;
(c) understand the nature of the contract he or she is entering into;
(d) understand the rights and responsibilities that marriage involves; and
(e) be free from the influence of any 'morbid delusions'.

4.60 To create an enduring power of attorney, a person must appreciate that:
(a) the attorney will be able to assume complete authority over his or her affairs;
(b) the attorney will be able to do anything with the person's property which he or she could have done;
(c) the attorney will continue if the person becomes mentally incapable and;
(d) if he or she becomes mentally incapable, the power is irrevocable without confirmation by the court.

4.61 If a decision has to be made on behalf of a person who lacks mental capacity and that decision relates to the person's 'property' or 'affairs' then there are a number of legal mechanisms available to assist, ie enduring powers of attorney and the Court of Protection, considered at para **4.63**. Unfortunately, these words have been given a restrictive interpretation and in effect are limited to issues concerning 'business matters, legal transactions and other dealings of a similar kind'[1].

1 *Re F (mental patient: sterilisation)* [1990] 2 AC 1.

4.62 Where the matter does not concern 'property or affairs', (for instance a decision has to be made where the person lives, or whether contact should be allowed with a third party) then in relation to persons over 18 years of age, the law is significantly deficient. Frequently all that can be done (legally) is to invoke the inherent jurisdiction of the High Court (considered at para **4.78**).

The Court of Protection

4.63 The Court of Protection is an Office of the Supreme Court and is now governed by Pt VII of the Mental Health Act 1983. The court has wide powers to 'do or secure the doing of all such things as appear necessary or expedient' concerning persons who lack mental capacity. The court can only take action however, in relation to a person's property and affairs and only after it has been satisfied (after considering medical evidence) of the necessary mental incapacity. The court can, in particular, take action:
(a) for the maintenance or other benefit of the patient;
(b) for the maintenance or other benefit of the patient's family;
(c) for making provision for other persons or purposes for whom or which the patient might be expected to provide if he were not mentally disordered; or
(d) otherwise, for administering the patient's affairs (s 95).

4.64 Generally the court will do this by appointing a 'receiver' although in certain situations, this is not necessary, for instance when the patient's only assets consist of:
(a) social security benefits;
(b) a pension or similar payment from a government department or local authority;
(c) entitlement under a discretionary trust;
(d) property which does not exceed £5,000 in value (in such cases a 'short order' can be made avoiding the necessity of a receiver).

4.65 Where a receivership order has been made, the incapacitated person is generally referred to as a 'patient' of the Court of Protection. A separate administrative agency exist the Public Trust Office, whose address is the same as for the court: Stewart House, 24 Kingsway, London WC2B 6JX, tel 0171 269 7300.

5 Powers of attorney

(i) General powers

4.66 An individual has always had the power to appoint somebody else to act as his or her agent with regard to his or her financial affairs. The power may be in general terms or limited to specific acts. The power is presently contained in the Powers of Attorney Act 1971. A power of attorney may be general in terms (allowing the attorney to do anything that the 'donor' could do) or it may be limited to a specific act (for instance, signing a contract for the sale of land).

4.67 The problem with ordinary powers of attorney is that the donor must be mentally capable when she or he grants the power and the authority of the attorney ceases immediately the donor ceases to have mental capacity. Powers of attorney can only be used to determine questions concerning a person's 'property and financial affairs'.

(ii) Enduring powers

4.68 The Enduring Powers of Attorney Act 1985 enables attorneys to be appointed whose powers would continue even after the donor had become mentally incapable of managing his or her affairs.

4.69 The procedure for creating such powers is straightforward. A pre-printed form is completed and signed by the donor and each attorney (their signatures are witnessed)[1]. The power can come into force immediately or only after the attorney has lost his or her capacity.

1 See Appendix III.

4.70 The attorney is under a duty to apply to the Public Trust Office as soon as he or she has reason to believe that the donor is (or is becoming) mentally incapable. Before applying, the attorney must give notice of his or her intention to apply for registration of the enduring power to the donor, the donor's relatives and any 'co-attorney'. At least three relatives must receive the notice (and the Act states the priority of relative). People served with these notices have the power to object to registration. Failing an objection, the registration takes effect within about five weeks.

4.71 As noted at paras **4.62**ff, powers of attorney do not, however, enable the attorney to make long-term arrangements about healthcare matters or where the person should live or with whom she or he should have contact etc.

(iii) Social security appointees

4.72 The Social Security (Claims and Payments) Regulations 1987, reg 33 allows for an appointee to be appointed where the claimant is 'unable for the time being to act'. Guidance suggests that a person is unable to act if they 'do not have the mental ability to understand and control their own affairs, for example because of senility or mentally illness'. Appointees do not apply to people who are hospital in-patients[1].

1 Social Security (Hospital In-patients) Regulations 1975, SI 1975/555, reg 16(2).

4.73 The Benefits Agency is the authority responsible for the appointment, supervision and revocation of appointeeships. The appointee is personally responsible for ensuring that the social security monies are applied in the patients' interests.

4.74 In relation to home proprietors acting as appointees, Age Concern states that:

> 'Although the home proprietor may be prepared to manage an individual's financial affairs, large groups of homes may have a specific finance department, it should be remembered that no available guidance recommends this. It should therefore be considered only as a last resort and all the parties involved must ensure that the appropriate safeguards are observed.'[1]

1 *Resident's Money* (1996).

4.75 Where the home proprietor is a local authority, it often acts as the appointee or receiver for those living in its home.

(iv) Guardianship

4.76 Section 7 of the Mental Health Act 1983 provides for the making of a guardianship order in relation to mentally disordered people where 'it is necessary in the interests of the welfare of the patient or for the protection of other persons that such an order be made'. Guardianship orders can therefore be made in relation to persons who do not lack mental capacity.

4.77 Under s 8 of the 1983 Act the guardian (normally the social services department or, rarely, a family member) has three limited powers:
(a) to require the patient to reside at a place specified;
(b) to require the patient to attend at places for medical treatment, occupation, education or training; and
(c) to require access to the patient to be given.

(v) The court's inherent jurisdiction

4.78 The High Court has power (both inherent and statutory) to make a declaration as to whether an Act is lawful or not.

4.79 The Law Commission, when reviewing this power, commented as follows[1]:

> 'A declaration by the High Court does not answer the question "who decides?". Nor does it answer the question "what will be best?" It has been said that "th

camera photographing the relevant legal terrain. It registers what exists and declares what it finds".'

1 *Mental Incapacity* (1995) No 231.

4.80 In spite of the fact that the declaration cannot change anything, the court has expressed the view that certain serious procedures should always be referred to it for a declaration in advance (ie sterilisation or withdrawal of artificial feeding). It has also expressed a willingness to respond to new and difficult dilemmas, such as those that may arise when a patient, who has lost capacity, appears to have refused consent to a particular procedure being performed.

4.81 The declaration procedure has now been used in several reported cases about the cessation of artificial sustenance for a patient in persistent vegetative state[1]. It has been used to clarify the effect of purported refusals of treatment[2]. It has also been invoked where the parents of a disabled woman, who was alleged to lack capacity to decide for herself, were disputing whether she was being prevented from having contact with her mother. Although the case never came to a full hearing, Eastham J accepted that there was jurisdiction in the High Court to make a declaration about such a matter[3]. In *Re S*[4], declarations were sought as to whether a stroke victim should remain within the jurisdiction to receive treatment and care at his home in England.

1 *Airedale National Health Service Trust v Bland* [1993] AC 789.
2 *Re C (adult: refusal of treatment)* [1994] 1 WLR 290.
3 *Re C (mental patient: contact)* [1993] 1 FLR 940.
4 [1995] 3 All ER 290.

C CLINICAL NEGLIGENCE AND HIV

Substantive law

(i) Negligence

4.82 Cases involving sub-standard medical treatment of patients who are HIV positive, will be first and foremost claims in clinical negligence (more traditionally known as medical negligence). The test of clinical negligence was set out in the leading case of *Bolam v Friern Hospital Management Committee*[1]. In this case McNair J said:

> 'The test as to whether there has been negligence or not is not the test of the man on the top of a Clapham omnibus, because he has not got the special skill. The test is the standard of the ordinary skilled man exercising and professing to have that special skill. A man need not possess the highest expert skill; it is well-established law that it is sufficient if he exercises the ordinary skill of an ordinary competent man exercising that particular art.
>
> A doctor is not guilty of negligence if he has acted in accordance with the practice accepted as proper by a responsible body of medical men skilled in that particular art…a doctor is not negligent, if he is acting in

accordance with such a practice, merely because there is a body of opinion that takes a contrary view.'[1]

1 [1957] 1 WLR 582.

4.83 This was a judgment at first instance but it was given approval by the House of Lords in *Maynard v West Midlands Regional Health Authority*[1].

1 [1984] 1 WLR 634.

4.84 In practice, the test is summarised as whether the standard of care fell below that of the reasonably competent practitioner in the field at the time. This reflects the fact that medical science is constantly changing and this is particularly true of HIV medicine. Advances over the last 10 to 15 years have been considerable and so an acceptable standard of care or state of knowledge for a doctor in, say, 1985 is unlikely to be acceptable in 1999. Thus, in a case set in 1985 it is important to remember to apply the test as per a reasonable standard for 1984.

4.85 The second part of the *Bolam* formula is often called the 'reputable minority defence' and it is one that claimant medical negligence lawyers have consistently tried to challenge. For example, in a claim against a GP, the claimant's advisers will instruct an independent GP expert to comment upon whether the treating doctor provided an acceptable standard of care. Suppose that the alleged negligence took place in 1997 and that the plaintiff's expert says that there is a claim because the standard of care fell below that which should have been expected from a reasonably competent GP treating a patient with HIV in 1997. However, the defence lawyers will then instruct their own experts who may say that the plaintiff's expert has set out a counsel of perfection and that, in fact, there is still a reputable minority of GPs who would have treated the patient in exactly the same way as the doctor against whom the claim is being brought.

4.86 What is a reputable minority? This is perhaps best illustrated when looking at claimants in cases that do not proceed. Typically, the independent expert will be saying that, in his or her practice, the treatment would not have been acceptable, but that it has to be conceded that for a significant number of practitioners, it would be regarded as acceptable. In those circumstances the case cannot usually proceed because it is anticipated that there will be a strong *Bolam* defence.

4.87 Also, it is worth remembering that, when McNair J set out the test, it was a direction to a jury, which means that the question of whether the treatment itself was acceptable is still a question of fact which, in the modern context, must be decided by the judge. However, this is a slippery point to grasp and generally, the judiciary is reluctant to intervene in issues of clinical judgment.

4.88 That said, it should perhaps be emphasised that, in most clinical negligence cases, the *Bolam* test is adopted in a fairly straightforward manner. Its limitations might be discussed and indeed, they often come as a great disappointment to the client, but, for the average practitioner, it is extremely rare for the semantics of the test to become an issue in a case. This is not to suggest that claimant lawyers are complacent about the test—indeed it is the discussion see *Bolitho v City and Hackney Health Authority*[1] in which, inter alia, the plaintiff's lawyers put forward submissions for revised *Bolam* tests which would stress that the views of medical experts must only be accommodated by the court if those views themselves withstood logical analysis. Therefore, the question of whether the defendant has provided an adequate standard of care is ultimately always a question for the court to decide upon, having heard the facts of the particular case and considered the independent medical evidence.

1 [1998] Lloyd's Rep Med 26.

4.89 There has been much learned debate on the issues raised in *Bolitho*, much of it conflicting, but, in essence, the law remains unchanged. Nevertheless, the lawyer should still question whether that reputable minority is acting in a reasonable and responsible way. To put it another way, is it possible that on a commonsense analysis, the reputable minority is also acting negligently?

(ii) Causation

4.90 Establishing negligence is only half—and usually the easiest half—of the battle. The basic proposition on causation is that the negligent act or omission must have, on the balance of probabilities, caused or materially contributed to the injury complained of. If the negligence made no difference to the final outcome, then there is no case to answer. This is often extremely difficult for clients to accept—'but I could have died!'. Alternatively and this is perhaps more likely in an HIV case, the patient did die, but of causes unrelated to the negligence. Once again, there will be no case, no matter how clear the negligence.

4.91 Difficulties arise where the injury may or may not have been caused by the negligence. Take, for example, an ex-intravenous drug user who is HIV positive. He has had chronic ill-health resulting from both his drug abuse and HIV and is generally weak, although his condition has been stable for some time due to changes in lifestyle and good healthcare. He moves to a new area and develops a chest infection. The GP is called. He fails to recognise the early signs of pneumonia and that the patient is particularly vulnerable. Within a few days, the patient dies. Negligence is established because the GP clearly does not conduct a proper examination or inquire about the patient's history, but the question arises as to whether this made any difference to the eventual outcome. The patient was already in a weakened state and it is likely that even with proper treatment he may have died from acute pneumonia. The question for the case causation expert is whether, but for the negligence, the patient would have lived. Unfortunately the answer is seldom a clear 'yes' or 'no' and lawyers then have to push the expert into estimating percentage chances of recovery. If the expert can say that it is more likely than not that the patient would have survived or not been injured, then the case on causation will be established. *Hotson v East Berkshire Health Authority*[1] is one of the leading cases on causation in the medical context.

1 [1987] AC 750.

4.92 The defendant in a clinical negligence case will usually be one of the following:

(a) the NHS trust or health authority which is responsible for the hospital in which the treatment took place. Hospital staff are not personally responsible, as the trust or health authority is vicariously for their acts and omissions;
(b) in the case of a private hospital, the company or charitable trust which owns it (although the treating doctor may also be personally liable, as an 'independent contractor');
(c) the GP in person, as indemnified by his or defence association—usually the Medical Defence Union, or Medical Protection Society;
(d) in the case of private medical treatment given by a hospital consultant, the consultant will be the proper defendant and, once again, he or she will be indemnified by a defence association;
(e) in a product liability claim, the manufacturer, or, in some circumstances, the supplier of the product.

(iii) Which type of expert?

4.93 Most cases will require two experts, one to advise on negligence and one to advise on causation. With negligence, the rule is like for like. Thus if the case involves failings by a GP, you need an independent expert GP to advise on the standard of care. If it is a hospital claim, your independent expert should be in the same discipline as the consultant who was in charge of the patient's care.

4.94 For causation, the choice of expert will depend upon the injury sustained. For example, in the pneumonia case discussed above, where a GP failed to diagnose pneumonia, a chest physician would have to advise on causation. If a person becomes depressed or has a psychological or psychiatric reaction to the alleged negligence, then experts from those disciplines will have to advise on condition and prognosis.

4.95 The independent expert should always be of consultant status. The only exception to this are GPs, who do not usually become consultants and so you should instruct a senior partner in a general practice who has experience of medico-legal work.

4.96 Experts can make or break a case and it is thus important to choose them carefully. Ideally the experts should have experience of medico-legal work—although this is less necessary for causation experts. He or she should be very experienced, but still in current practice (retired experts have a very limited shelf-life) and should not approach the task with any preconceptions, or policy views on clinical negligence. If a solicitor is in any doubt about which expert to instruct, he or she should speak with a specialist practitioner, or consult AVMA (Action for Victims of Medical Actions, tel 0181 686 8333) or APIL (Association of Personal Injury Lawyers, tel 0115 958 0585) both of which hold databases of experts.

4.97 The expert advising on negligence will not ordinarily require any specialist knowledge of HIV medicine. This is because usually he or she will be commenting upon care given by a fellow non-specialist—for example the local GP. However, on causation it is important to have an expert with specialist knowledge of HIV. This is because he or she will need to have a detailed understanding of the special factors that apply to patients with HIV. The best place to find such experts will be at one of the centres of excellence for HIV treatment. In London, the Koblar Centre at Chelsea and Westminster Hospital has medical experts in many disciplines who specialise in HIV cases: dermatologists, psychiatrists and physicians. The letter of approach to the expert should give brief details of the case, name the doctor or hospital against which the claim is contemplated and explain how the case will be funded. Generally the medical notes should be obtained before contacting the expert, but should not actually be sent until he or she has agreed to report.

(iv) Product liability or claims against drug companies

4.98 The law of product liability is found primarily in the Consumer Protection Act 1987. The basic proposition is that the primary liability for defective products rests with the manufacturer of the product. A doctor becomes a 'supplier' of the product when prescribing medicine to a patient. A supplier has a responsibility to identify the manufacturer to a claimant when any damage is caused by a defect in the product. If that cannot be done, then the liability rests with the supplier. If the supplier makes changes to the product or its packaging, or prescribes it for a purpose not envisaged by the manufacturer, the supplier may in turn be classed as a manufacturer and face liability for damage caused by defects.

4.99 In the context of an HIV case, a product liability claim is most likely to arise from medication or in relation to the kits used for testing for HIV.

4.100 The Act imposes strict liability. Thus, if a medicine is defective and the patient suffers a personal injury, then the manufacturer, or the supplier if he cannot identify the manufacturer, will be liable. The claimant does not have to prove negligence and, therefore, the *Bolam* test does not apply and the reputable minority defence is not available. However, the claimant will still have to establish a causal link between the injury and the allegedly defective product.

4.101 The Act includes approximately 16 possible defences. It has been suggested that the Act has not fulfilled its promise, but this may be because personal injury lawyers have stuck to the traditional channels for compensation claims through negligence: breach of statutory duty and breach of contract. In other jurisdictions, particularly in the USA, this area of the law is more developed. Therefore, if a claimant in this country is damaged by a product that was manufactured by a US company, it may be worth considering if a product liability claim can be commenced.

4.102 In the HIV context, potential product liability claims are most likely to arise in the following two scenarios:

(a) where medication or equipment causes injury which was not expected and which might be defined as a hitherto unknown risk. For example, an adverse reaction to a drug which was not discovered during the research and development stage of the drug;

(b) a claim where manufacturing defect has occurred and the product has not reached the consumer in its intended form.

4.103 The Act provides a defence to the first scenario to the effect that where scientific knowledge at the time of supply was such that a manufacturer could not be expected to have known about the potential risk, there would be no liability. Thus, for the claimant's advisers, the question will be whether the research and development stage of the product was thorough and whether the manufacturer should, in fact, have known about the potential risk.

4.104 The law for the scenario in para **4.102**(b) is contained in the Consumer Protection Act 1987 and indeed, most product liability claims concern consumer products. An example would be a hairdryer which, due to a manufacturing or design fault, operates at too high a temperature and burns the hair.

4.105 In the context of HIV claims, an example might be medication which is not given in its intended form. For example, the treating doctor, rather than prescribing a whole batch of expensive medication to one patient, decides to break up the packaging and supply smaller batches to a number of patients. In doing that, the GP may have become a 'manufacturer' for the purposes of the Act because he has changed the product. If a patient then suffers an illness because of this, a product liability claim might arise.

4.106 Another possible example of a product liability claim would be where an HIV testing kit is defective. There are various kits available, some of which are more reliable than others. Therefore, if, due to a manufacturing defect, a testing kit were to show a positive result that is false, a potential claim might follow.

4.107 Many patients who are HIV positive are keen to become involved in study trials for the development of new products. In such trials, manufacturers and doctors have to operate under strict protocols and ethical guidelines. This is a large subject which cannot be discussed here, but if a potential claim arises, it is important to check that the protocols and guidelines were followed and that no unnecessary risks are taken.

4.108 There has not yet been a successful product liability claim in a medical context in this country. By definition, product injury usually affects large groups of people and there have been a number of unsuccessful group actions. Generally a claim involving a medical product is likely to overlap with a clinical negligence claim and despite the strict liability imposed by the Consumer Protection Act 1987, a negligence claim is a more established path in the UK courts.

(v) Procedure and legal costs

4.109 These are two very large subjects, which cannot be dealt with in this text, but the following points are notable. In April 1999, Lord Woolf's reforms were implemented with the introduction of the Civil Procedure Rules 1998. In broad terms, the aim of the reforms is to reduce legal costs and delay by introducing proactive judicial case management. Legal procedures are to be simplified and lawyers encouraged to get on with cases rather than allowing them to become bogged down obtuse legal argument. At the time of writing, it is too early to gauge the effect of the reforms, not least because many of the rules are still in the process of being clarified by practice directions and indeed practice itself.

4.110 It is difficult to question the aims and ideals of the reforms, as litigation has undoubtedly been expensive and slow. However, there are sometimes very good reasons why clinical negligence cases are slow and expensive. First, they are dependent upon medical experts who are themselves busy clinicians with many other commitments. Therefore, lawyers often have to wait many months for the right expert to either examine a client, or to prepare a report and there may be two or three equally busy experts advising on the same case. Trying to reconcile the schedules of the experts with the very strict time limits that the courts will impose is likely to result in serious difficulties for claimants who are already disadvantaged by illness or injury.

4.111 Legal aid remains for clinical negligence cases, at least for the time being. However, its scope has been reduced and the new rules, in tandem with the Woolf reforms, rely heavily on the concept of proportionality between costs and the likely level of damages. This is not unreasonable, as £50,000 to £100,000 can easily be spent litigating a case that might be worth only £10,000. Once again, though, in clinical negligence cases, particularly those involving HIV, this may lead to injustice. This is partly to do with the way in which damages are calculated (see para **4.117**). For example, in a case involving the death of an adult person, who is not married and who has no dependants, the level of damages is likely to be below the level at which legal aid would be granted. Thus, even if there is strong reason to believe that the death may have been caused by clinical negligence, legal aid will not be available to investigate the claim.

4.112 The reduction of legal aid was accompanied by a relaxation of the rules on how legal claims might be funded. Thus, conditional fee agreements, often wrongly described as 'no win–no fee' have been allowed and in theory, a claimant can ask a lawyer to conduct a case without charging. Liability for the defendant's costs remains, but a number of insurance products have been introduced to protect the claimant from having to pay them in the event of the case being lost. In the clinical negligence field, conditional fee agreements and insurance policies are very much in their infancy and there has not yet been a large uptake. The insurance policies are expensive—often thousands of pounds—and most of them require solicitors to carry out an expensive pre-contract investigation of the claim. This usually means all of the work involved in obtaining independent experts' reports which will generally cost between £2,000 and £5,000.

4.113 Funding a case privately is generally prohibitively expensive, although some clients will have legal expenses insurance, which will allay some of the costs.

(vi) Quantum

4.114 Compensation can be divided into two types of damage. The first is known as general damages—which covers the person's pain, suffering and loss of amenity. The second is special damage and future loss which covers all of the expenses that the person has been put to, or will be put to because of the injury. Thus, it will include things like loss of earnings, medical expenses, care expenses, cost of therapy, the cost of adapting accommodation and any other expenses that might reasonably be connected to the injury.

4.115 General damages tend to be very low. At the top of the scale are the most serious brain injury cases, for example, where a person is left in a persistent vegetative state. In those claims, general damages will be in the region of £150,000. It is the special damage and future loss which might bring the value of the claim up to £2–3 million.

4.116 There are not yet any reported cases to give direct guidance on the level of damages for a person who is negligently infected with HIV. Claims have arisen in a number of countries where people were infected with HIV through contaminated blood products. In the UK, this gave rise to the haemophiliac litigation, which went to the Court of Appeal, albeit on a discovery point. See *Re HIV haemophiliac litigation*[1]. The action was against the government for breach of statutory duty under the National Health Service Act 1977. The allegations focused on:

(a) the government's failure to produce sufficient UK blood products and continuing to rely upon imported blood products from the USA;
(b) failure to use heat-treated blood products (which destroys HIV);
(c) failure to screen out infected blood donors in the UK;
(d) failing to use tests to detect infected blood;
(e) failing to revoke licences that allowed the use of commercially produced blood from the USA.

1 [1990] NLJR 1349 at 962.

4.117 The case went to the Court of Appeal, not on its issues, but because of the government's refusal to disclose documents concerning the blood transfusion service. The substantive cases were agreed in a settlement in 1990 with the plaintiffs and so the liability issues were never tested by the courts. Subsequently, in 1992, the government settled the remaining claims of plaintiffs who had been infected through blood transfusions. That said, the class of persons who may have been infected is still not closed and under the scheme the Secretary of State still has a discretion to admit late applications. Infected persons have to make their application within 12 months of becoming HIV positive, or before 31 December 1999, whichever is sooner. Applicants must have been infected with HIV through blood transfusion, tissue transfer or treatment with blood products. Haemophiliacs are excluded, as they were covered by the previous scheme. The treatment has to have taken place in the United Kingdom and extends to private hospitals, provided that the blood or tissue was supplied by the NHS. It is not only limited to patients—it also covers heterosexual partners and the spouses or children of the person who has been infected. It is notable that homosexual partners are excluded. The tariff is as follows:

Infected blood or tissue recipients

Type	*Amount*
Infant	£41,500 each
Single adult	£43,500 each
Married adults without dependent children	£52,000 each
Infected person with dependent children	£80,500 each
Infected intimate of the above:	
Adults/spouse/partner	£23,500
Child who is married	£23,500
Other child	£21,500

4.118 The above figures were calculated with reference to general damages for similar illnesses and thus may give some guidance.

4.119 The scheme also makes provisions which concern undertakings which preclude proceedings against certain specified government departments and health authorities (interestingly it does not preclude medical negligence actions). Provisions are also made concerning legal costs, although it is only in the case of minors that court appearances will be necessary.

4.120 Reported awards in other cases involving infectious diseases give some guidance as to the approach to be taken. *Molinari v Ministry of Defence*[1] concerned a 26-year-old man who developed leukaemia as a result of exposure to radioactive material when he was working on nuclear submarines as a 16-year-old naval apprentice. He became ill and had to undergo medical treatment which was ultimately successful, but damaging in itself. He was awarded £40,000 for general damages, which took into account the chance of remission and his anxieties about further relapse. Also, the judge allowed a claim for provisional damages so that Mr Molinari might return to court within five years for a further compensation should he suffer a relapse.

1 [1994] PIQR Q33.

4.121 This is not directly analogous to an HIV case, but it does involve a person contracting a devastating illness through the negligence of another party and thus includes discussion of the psychological and physical implications for the victims. Leukaemia is also an illness in which a premature death is a possibility.

4.122 Another source of comparison are the awards for asbestosis. See, for example *Mulgrew v Upper Clyde Ship Builders Ltd*[1]. This involved a 66-year-old ship worker who had been exposed to asbestos throughout his working life. He developed the first symptoms of mesothelioma in 1994 and the condition was diagnosed in 1995. His prognosis was poor with a life expectancy of only a year, whereas had it not been for the condition he would have been likely to survive until the age of 75. Instead, he would be increasingly dependent on strong painkillers and the last three months of his life would be 'distressing and degrading'. He was suffering depression about leaving his wife and grandchildren and, having seen his own brother die of the condition, the nature of his own death. He was awarded general damages of £45,000.

1 (1996) 96(3) QR6.

4.123 A person infected with HIV need not have such a poor prognosis, as life expectancy has improved and much will depend upon whether he or she has developed full-blown AIDS at the time of trial. If that is the case, then updating the above awards to account for inflation, an appropriate figure for general damages is likely to be in the region of £45,000–£50,000.

4.124 In contrast, if a person has simply been exposed to the possibility of contracting AIDS (for example, a needle stick injury to a healthcare worker), the damages would be much lower. For example *Howell v Bolton Hospital National Health Service Trust*[1] concerned a hospital worker who suffered a needle stick injury from a syringe in an ophthalmology department. She suffered no physical injury, but developed a psychological reaction in that she became concerned that she might have contracted AIDS or hepatitis. She developed a depressive disorder and remained apprehensive until seven months after the accident when she was seen by a consultant haematologist who reassured her that she was not likely to have contracted any infections. She was awarded damages of £2,000. For any lawyer instructed in such a claim, it will obviously be very important to look closely at the circumstances of the injury (for example, if it was a needle that had been used on an HIV positive patient the risk would obviously be much greater). Also, the patient's condition and prognosis would have to be established very clearly before any settlement is reached. Repeat HIV tests over an appropriate period is the only way of being sure.

1 (1996) 96(1) QR 7.

4.125 In cases of clinical negligence involving people who are already HIV positive, the issue will usually be to what extent life expectancy and/or quality of life has been damaged by the alleged negligence. When considering this, it is worth remembering the substantive law on causation. The claimant has to establish that on the balance of probabilities (ie more likely than not) his or her condition has been made worse than it otherwise would have been. When the starting point is a person whose life expectancy and general health has already been compromised by being HIV positive, the general damages will have to look at the difference between how ill the claimant was before the negligence and how ill they have become in consequence of it.

4.126 Inevitably, this is a very difficult exercise which involves lawyers attempting to persuade medical experts to talk in percentages to compare conditions which can be difficult to measure in the first place. However, things are improving. Anti-virals, better awareness and informed research have all led to improvements in quality of life and life expectancy for those who are HIV positive. In the late 1980s, most lawyers would probably have advised that any claim involving clinical negligence with a patient who was already HIV positive would probably fail on causation, as the assumption would have been that it is more likely than not that the person will have become ill and died quite quickly in any event.

4.127 That is much less likely to be the advice now. Clinical negligence lawyers are used to bringing cases that involve cancer patients who have received sub-standard treatment and have their already compromised health compromised even further. An HIV case is essentially no different. Moreover, perhaps paradoxically, as the state of medical negligence improves prognosis, the chance of winning a clinical negligence claim and the level of damages in that claim will increase.

4.128 Claims involving misdiagnosis of the condition are more likely to arise from false positives being given on test results. The issues of negligence and causation will focus on the circumstances in which the testing was carried out: did the doctor follow the correct procedures; were the test kits defective; was the laboratory at fault in its analysis or reporting procedures; was the patient given adequate counselling before and after the test; and did the doctor have proper reporting and administrative systems? In short, every step of the procedure has to be looked at carefully.

4.129 In quantum terms, the claim will focus on the effect that the incorrect misdiagnosis has on the patient and whether this is made worse by the manner in which the news is given. Almost inevitably, the news will be received traumatically and some patients may have a reaction which amounts to a clinically recognised condition (for example, a depressive illness or post-traumatic stress disorder). This will give rise to a claim in general damages, together with a claim for special damage and future loss for factors such as loss of earnings. Once again, analogies can be drawn with cancer claims, in which people have been incorrectly informed that they are suffering from cancer and, as a result, give up jobs and make other life changes which have serious financial implications.

4.130 These cases are to be distinguished from those where accurate information causes distress. The issue was considered by the Court of Appeal in 1996 in the case of *AB v Tameside and Glossop Health Authority*[1]. The health authority found that one of its health workers was HIV positive and decided to inform certain patients of the very remote risk of their having been infected. It was decided that it was not practical to inform each patient face to face, so that immediate counselling and reassurance might be given. Instead, letters were sent to the patients' GPs explaining the situation and asking them if they knew of any reason why a standard form of letter should not be sent directly to the patients.

1 (1996) 35 BMLR 79, CA.

4.131 The health authority subsequently sent standard letters to a number of patients informing them of the situation, the remote risk and offering counselling and/or blood-testing. A number of the patients suffered an adverse reaction and sued the health authority for nervous shock. The thrust of the plaintiff's claim was that it was reasonably foreseeable that a recipient of a standard letter might suffer shock and psychiatric illness as a result.

4.132 The trial judge decided that the health authority did not exercise due care and that they should have realised that the best method of informing a patient, no matter how remote the risk, was face to face, through the patient's GP or another experienced health worker. To give the news by letter carried a foreseeable risk that some vulnerable patients might suffer psychiatric injury above the ordinary shock and distress which was natural in most individuals.

4.133 The decision was reversed by the Court of Appeal on the basis that the relevant standard of care was to take reasonable care in all the circumstances and that the judge had not considered 'all of the circumstances'.

4.134 There are two important provisions on quantum which effectively discriminate against homosexual couples. When the European Convention on Human Rights is fully adopted into domestic legislation, this position may change, but at present the Fatal Accidents Act 1976 effectively limits the two heads of compensation to heterosexual couples. First, under s 1, the classes of person who may claim as a dependent allow a non-married partner to bring a claim for dependency but only if he or she was living with the deceased 'as the husband or wife of the deceased'. This phrase is not further defined in the Act, but the Marriage Act 1949 and arguably the ordinary usage of the words 'husband' and 'wife' denote a heterosexual relationship. Given that the dependency claim can often be the largest element of the damages, this is a significant disadvantage.

4.135 Second, under s 1A of the Act, the statutory bereavement award of £7,500 is also limited to the wife or husband of the deceased (although in this section it is not even extended to a heterosexual partner who was living with the deceased as a husband or wife).

Testing for HIV

4.136 The General Medical Council has published guidelines on the ethical issues arising from HIV testing, which may be found in its booklet *Serious Communicable Diseases*[1]. It is an excellent guide to the ethical and practical difficulties facing healthcare workers in their treatment of patients and in terms of protecting their own safety. For example, on consent to testing it states:

> 'The information you provide when seeking consent should be appropriate to the circumstances and to the nature of the condition or conditions being tested for. Some conditions, such as HIV, have serious social and financial, as well as medical, implications. In such cases you must make sure that the patient is given appropriate information about the implications of the test and appropriate time to consider and discuss them.'

1 October 1997, GMC.

4.137 On injuries to healthcare workers, it states:

> 'If you or another healthcare worker has suffered a needle stick injury or other occupational exposure to blood or body fluids and you consider it necessary to test the patient for a serious communicable disease, the patient's consent should be obtained before the test is undertaken… You should not arrange testing against the patient's wishes or without consent other than in exceptional circumstances, for example where you have good reason to think that the patient may have a condition such as HIV for which prophylactic treatment is available. In such cases you may test an existing blood sample, taken for other purposes, but you should consult an experienced colleague first.'

4.138 However it then warns that the decision might still be challenged in the courts and may result in either criminal charges, or a complaint to the General Medical Council. This perhaps reflects the uncertainty of the exact legal position. Ethical issues are unlikely to arise in clinical negligence cases, which, almost by definition tend to be concerned with clinical errors. However, of course, to the patient the distinction is not particularly important.

4.139 Confidentiality is a very important issue for patients who are HIV positive; for example, a patient might not want his or her family GP to know about the diagnosis. The guidelines state that the patient's wishes must be respected, except where the doctor feels that a failure to disclose the information would put a healthcare worker or other patient at serious risk of death or serious harm, for example, when dealing with violent patients. In those circumstances, the confidentiality can be broken, but the patient must be informed beforehand. Also, the doctor must be prepared to justify his or her decision if it is challenged. Somewhat at odds with this is the advice on giving information to close contacts:

> 'You may disclose information about a patient, whether living or dead, in order to protect a person from risk of death or serious harm. For example, you may disclose information to a known sexual contact of a patient with HIV where you have reason to think that the patient had not informed that person and cannot be persuaded to do so. In such circumstances you should tell the patient before you make the disclosure and you must be prepared to justify a decision to disclose information.'

4.140 This is somewhat surprising, as it is arguable that were it widely known it might discourage patients from being tested for HIV and seeking appropriate medical care. Thus, the patients' sexual partners would still be at risk and the patient would be at even greater risk. The point has not been tested by the courts in the UK, but in the USA it was considered. In a well-publicised action, Mark Christian, the former partner of the actor Rock Hudson, sued Hudson's estate, his secretary and his physicians. Apparently, Mr Hudson had continued to have sex with Mr Christian several months after learning that he was HIV positive, but without disclosing the information to Mr Christian. The allegation was that Mr Hudson, his physicians and secretary had conspired to conceal the knowledge of the condition and that Mr Christian had thereby been put at risk. The claim against the estate and the secretary was successful, but the claim against the physicians was discontinued. The case is obviously not a precedent under English law and unless the circumstances are exceptional, it is difficult to imagine an English court finding that a physician has a duty of care to the sexual partner of the physician's patient.

4.141 If a doctor believes that he or she has been infected with HIV he or she must promptly seek advice from a suitably qualified colleague (for example, a consultant in occupational health). The doctor should not rely on his or her own assessment of the risk that it posed to patients, but must seek advice on how his or her professional practice should be modified and whether current employers and prospective employers should be informed. There may also be a need for appropriate medical supervision.

4.142 Infected healthcare workers provide ready material for sensational stories in the popular press and heighten public anxiety. There have been cases of patients who have been infected with hepatitis by a doctor but it is probably correct to say that in this country there are no reported cases of a patient having been infected with HIV. Indeed, it would seem that generally it is the healthcare workers who are at greater risk, rather than the patients.

Chapter 5

Families and children

Alison Burt
Julia Thackray

A INTRODUCTION

5.01 This chapter will look at family law issues of particular relevance to clients with HIV and AIDS, focusing on how clients can provide for the future of their children and how the courts will deal with disputes relating to the upbringing of children with HIV or AIDS or in families affected by HIV.

5.02 It is likely that, given the current patterns of HIV infection, many solicitors will begin to see more family clients affected by HIV. In the USA, it is estimated by the orphan project of New York that by 2000 there will be in excess of 30,000 orphans in New York city alone resulting from HIV-related deaths[1]. While the numbers of HIV positive children in this country are still relatively small[2], recent medical studies anticipate an increase in heterosexual transmission and the number of children born to HIV positive mothers[2]. It is much more difficult to quantify the number of children affected rather than infected by HIV and AIDS; a recent study by Barnardo's estimated that at least 3,000 children in the UK are affected by HIV and that most of them are under the age of ten[3].

1 Senak, M *HIV and the Law–A Guide to Our Rights and Challenges* (1996) Insight Books, Plenum Press NY.
2 There are 380 vertically infected children (ie born to HIV positive mothers) as at October 1996: see Sharland, Gibb, Williams, Walters and Novelli *Paediatric HIV Infection: Archives of Disease in Childhood* (1997) pp 76, 293–297.
3 Imrie J, Coombes Y *No time to waste: The scale and dimensions of the problem of children affected by HIV or AIDS in the United Kingdom* Essex: Barnardos, 1995.

5.03 The advances in the treatment of AIDS have changed the lives of families affected by HIV and AIDS. Both children and adults with HIV are enjoying longer symptom-free periods. Those with an AIDS-related diagnosis may also stay healthy for longer than had been expected in the past. New medication has enabled doctors to reduce the risk of vertical transmission to the babies of HIV positive women and to improve the care of HIV positive infants. These developments have led to changes in good practice, particularly in relation to HIV testing, because the potential benefits of diagnosis and treatment are so much greater. Wider treatment options have given parents living with HIV and AIDS more time to plan arrangements for the care of their children.

5.04 In spite of these developments, families affected by HIV and AIDS face tremendous difficulties. In order to plan for their children, parents will need to consider disclosing their HIV status to their children, to potential carers and to professionals such as teachers or social workers. Some families will also be coping with poverty, poor housing and immigration problems. Lawyers advising families in these circumstances need to be alert to the range of practical and emotional difficulties which they face.

5.05 Good practice may involve challenging misconceptions about our clients. Advisers may need, for example, to ensure that the issue of sexuality is treated fairly in contact disputes, that clients with drug problems are not defined by their addiction or that a client with mental health problems is not discounted because of those problems. In the same way, advisers need to ensure that the fact that the client or a child is HIV positive is given only its proper place in proceedings so that it is not given any undue significance.

5.06 This chapter will first look at the legal framework of the Children Act 1989, then looking at how the provisions of the Act may be used by parents with HIV and AIDS in planning for the future of their children in the event of the parents' death or incapacity through illness. The next section will consider how the courts adjudicate in disputes over arrangements for children before looking at the duties and powers of authorities to provide practical assistance for children of clients with HIV or AIDS. Finally, the issue of consent to medical treatment for children and young people will be considered.

B PARENTING, CUSTODY AND GUARDIANSHIP OF CHILDREN AFTER INCAPACITY OR DEATH OF A PARENT

5.07 This section will look at ways in which parents living with HIV and AIDS can make plans for their children in the event of their illness or death. The ways in which carers can formalise their status if they find themselves looking after children whose parents are ill or have died will also be considered.

5.08 The episodic nature of HIV or AIDS means that many people will experience periods of acute illness and periods of relatively good health. Some parents, therefore, may require assistance with the care of their children, during periods of illness, or as respite care, but may not need a full-time carer for the children. Other parents may have this sort of assistance available to them, but may wish to provide certainty for the children in the event of their death.

5.09 It is easy to understand why parents find it difficult to contemplate the possibility that at some point they may become unable to care for their children because of illness. For HIV positive parents who are asymptomatic, or who are responding well to the new combination therapies, it may seem easier to postpone these decisions. For those who are already ill, the loss of their children, even to the think about. Planning also brings with it difficulties of disclosure; parents may not have told their children or the proposed carer about their status. Seeking advice will also necessitate disclosure of details of the parent's health.

5.10 Although advisers may find it difficult to broach the subject of planning when there appears to be no urgent need to do so, there are many advantages for parents who consider these questions at an early stage. In the event of sudden illness, parents who have made arrangements for their children will not have to cope with the additional burden of trying to make long-term decisions in an emergency. Arrangements which are discussed in detail with proposed carers (and, if appropriate, with the children themselves) are much less likely to break down in the long-term or to lead to disputes between proposed carers. Parents will have the security of knowing that their wishes will be respected and children may be helped by the knowledge that the arrangements for their care have been approved by their parents.

5.11 Assistance for parents who are faced with the prospect of planning for their children's future may also be available from voluntary agencies. The Positive Options scheme, for example, is a Barnardo's initiative, providing invaluable support for parents by helping them identify potential carers and arranging a package of both immediate and long-term support for their children[1].

1 Fratter, J 'Positive Options Planning Scheme', Chapter 7 of *HIV Infection and Children in Need* (1993) BAAF.

1 The Children Act 1989—framework and principles

5.12 Most of the options available for parents wishing to plan for the future of their children are set out in the Children Act 1989. The framework of the Act will be looked at before considering in some detail the variety of orders and agreements available for parents and carers to use. The Act sets out a number of important principles relevant to the type of applications considered in this chapter.

(i) Welfare of the child is paramount

5.13 When a court determines any question with respect to the upbringing of a child or the administration of a child's property, the child's welfare will be the court's paramount consideration[1]. This principle applies to most Children Act applications. For example, even where a parent is seriously ill or dying, the court will always make the needs of the child the priority.

1 Children Act 1989, s 1(1).

(ii) Delay is prejudicial to the welfare of the child

5.14 In court proceedings determining questions relating to children, delay is a factor that will generally be considered prejudicial to the welfare of the child[1].

1 Children Act 1989, s 1(2).

(iii) Principle of no order

5.15 When the court is considering whether to make an order under the Children Act, it must consider whether to make an order would be better than not making an order at all[1]. The 'no order' principle is one that the court must have regard to in every case.

1 Children Act 1989, s 1(5).

2 Parental responsibility

5.16 Parental responsibility now forms one of the cornerstones in planning for the future of children. It is defined in s 3(1) of the Act as:

> 'All the rights, duties, powers, responsibilities and authority which by law a parent of a child has in relation to the child and his property.'

5.17 No further definition is given, but the guidance refers to bringing the child up, caring for the child and making decisions about the child[1] as elements of parental responsibility. The guidance further indicates[2] that the exercise of parental responsibility is to be left largely to the discretion of the adults involved, although within the definition of the minimum standards of care imposed by the criminal and civil law. The court will intervene in the parents' exercise of their responsibility only when to do so is in the best interests of the child. Case law also recognises that as children get older and gain understanding, parental responsibility diminishes and the child takes more responsibility for her own decisions.

1 *The Children Act 1989, Guidance and Regulations* Vol 1, Court Orders, para 2.2.
2 *An Introduction to the Children Act 1989* (1989) HMSO p 9 para 2.2.

(i) The importance of parental responsibility in planning for children

5.18 Parental responsibility allows a person who is caring for a child to determine questions relating to all aspects of the child's upbringing. Issues such as religion, medical treatment and education are aspects of parental responsibility that have been considered by the courts[1] and in relation to which court orders have been made.

1 Hershman, D and McFarlane, A *Children Law and Practice* Family Law (1998) Jordan Publishing Ltd at **C[259]** lists many of the issues dealt with in the case law.

5.19 In practice, many people look after children for whom they do not have parental responsibility and may do so for some time without problems. A carer who is a close relative of the child, particularly an unmarried father, may experience few practical problems because his authority is likely to be accepted by schools and hospitals even if he does not have parental responsibility. A carer who is not related to the child, however, may find that her relationship to the child is not recognised by the relevant authorities until she obtains parental responsibility. For example, if a dispute arises among family members, a carer without parental responsibility will find herself overruled by others who do have parental requires major medical treatment, a carer without parental responsibility may be unable to make crucial decisions.

5.20 Carers may acquire parental responsibility in a number of ways which are considered at paras **5.21–5.29**.

(ii) Who has parental responsibility?

5.21 All mothers automatically have parental responsibility for their children, as do married fathers[1]. Unmarried fathers may acquire parental responsibility by written agreement with the mother or by order of the court granting parental responsibility; in addition, they may obtain parental responsibility by adopting the child, being granted a residence order or subsequently marrying the child's mother.

1 Children Act 1989, s 2(1) as extended by the Family Law Reform Act 1987. References to a person's parents being married at the time of the birth include parents who marry during pregnancy. Subsequent marriages legitimate a child and grant parental responsibility to the father.

5.22 People other than the biological father may only acquire parental responsibility by the grant of a residence order in their favour or by adopting the child. A person appointed as guardian also acquires parental responsibility when the appointment takes effect.

5.23 It is possible for more than one person to have parental responsibility at any one time. The addition of another person with parental responsibility does not extinguish the parental responsibility of the first. Where more than one person has parental responsibility problems can arise if they disagree, but the grant of parental responsibility to a person with whom the children do not live does not give that person the right to interfere with matters of the children's day-to-day care[1]. If a care order has been granted in respect of a child, the local authority will have parental responsibility for the child for the duration of the care order. The child's parents will retain parental responsibility, but disputes between local authorities and parents can give rise to complex legal issues, as the court has only limited jurisdiction to intervene after the making of a final care order[2].

1 *Re P (a minor) (parental responsibility order)* [1994] 1 FLR 578.
2 See Hershman and MacFarlane *Children: Law and Practice* at **D[314]–[370]**.

5.24 Parental responsibility may not be surrendered or transferred, but a person with parental responsibility may arrange for some or all of that responsibility to be met by another person[1]. Normally a carer to whom parental responsibility has been delegated will only be able to make relatively minor decisions unless there is a written agreement defining the parameters of his or her decision-making ability.

1 Children Act 1989, s 2(8).

(iii) Parental responsibility agreements

5.25 Unmarried fathers only may obtain parental responsibility by agreement with the mother. The Children Act 1989 provides that agreements made in accordance with the court rules[1] will confer parental responsibility on the father. The agreement must be recorded on form C(PRA), and must be witnessed by a court official and lodged at the Principal Registry of the Family Division. Where a mother is ill and has agreed that the unmarried father should care for the children after her death, she should be advised to enter into a parental responsibility agreement with the father, or appoint him guardian before she becomes too ill to do so.

1 Parental Responsibility Agreement Regulations 1991, SI 1991/1478 and the Parental Responsibility Agreement (Amendment) Regulations 1994, SI 1994/3137.

(iv) Parental responsibility orders

5.26 If a father wishes to obtain parental responsibility and the mother has died or does not consent, he will have to apply to the court for a parental responsibility order. Only an unmarried father may apply for this kind of order. Where a mother is ill because of HIV or AIDS, a father may wish to apply for parental responsibility so that he will be in a better position to care for the children in the event of her illness or death. Even if he will not be the children's primary carer, he may still apply for parental responsibility so that he can be involved in current and future decisions relating to the children.

5.27 On an application for parental responsibility, the court must consider the welfare principle and the no order principle, but the court does not need to have specific regard to the welfare checklist[1]. The Court of Appeal has held that the essence of a parental responsibility order is simply to confirm the legal status of the father[2]. In the recent case of *Re C and V (minors) (parental responsibility and contact)*[3], Ward LJ indicated that by granting a parental responsibility order, the law could confer on the father the 'stamp of approval' which would often be in the interests of the child; formal recognition of the father could help to create a positive image of the absent parent and develop the child's self-esteem.

1 Children Act 1989, s 1(3).
2 *Re S (parental responsibility)* [1998] 2 FLR 921.
3 [1998] 1 FLR 392, [1998] 1 FCR 52, CA.

5.28 The courts have considered what factors should be taken into account upon an application for parental responsibility. The Court of Appeal, on an application for an order for parental rights under the Family Law Reform Act 1987, s 4[1], held that the decisive factors were the degree of commitment shown by the father to the children, the degree of attachment between the children and the father and the reasons for the father's application. Subsequent cases under the Children Act 1989 have confirmed that this list is not exhaustive, but fathers who meet these criteria can generally expect to be granted parental responsibility[2]. In cases where the mother is ill with HIV or AIDS, the court may consider it to be particularly important that the father should have parental responsibility so that he can make decisions if the mother is no longer able to do so.

1 *Re H (illegitimate children: father: parental rights)(No 2)* [1991] Fam 151, [1991] 1 FLR 205.
2 See *Re P (parental responsibility)* [1998] 2 FLR 96 for circumstances in which the court may refuse parental responsibility.

5.29 In addition to obtaining parental responsibility by agreement or parental responsibility order, a father may also obtain

3 Section 8 orders

5.30 The Children Act 1989, s 8 provides for four types of order, which form the main framework of private law applications to the court.
(a) Residence orders allow the court to determine with whom a child will live.
(b) Contact orders provide for the residential parent to make the child available for contact with the absent parent, other relative or significant person.
(c) Specific issue orders are flexible orders allowing the court to adjudicate on any particular question that arises in relation to an aspect of parental responsibility, such as issues of religion, education, medical treatment and change of the child's surname.
(d) Prohibited steps orders direct that any step that may be taken by a parent in the exercise of parental responsibility shall not be taken without the consent of the court. Prohibited steps orders may be used, for example, to prevent the removal of a child from the jurisdiction or from the care of the residential parent, to prevent a change in the child's surname or education, or to prevent the child from having contact with a specific person.

(i) Welfare checklist

5.31 The court will apply the basic principles set out at paras **5.13–5.15**. Where plans for children involve the making of a s 8 order, and where that application is opposed, the court must also consider the following factors:
(a) the ascertainable wishes and feelings of the child concerned (considered in the light of her age and understanding);
(b) her physical, emotional and educational needs;
(c) the likely effect on her of any change in circumstances;
(d) her age, sex, background and any characteristics of hers which the court considers relevant;
(e) any harm which she has suffered or is at risk of suffering;
(f) how capable each of her parents, and any other person to whom the court considers the question to be relevant, is of meeting her needs;
(g) the range of powers available to the court under this Act in the proceedings in question[1].

1 Children Act 1989, s 1(3).

5.32 Whilst regard to the welfare checklist is mandatory in the applications listed at para **5.30**, the court may have regard to the checklist in considering the welfare of the child in other applications.

4 Residence orders

(i) Meaning and importance

5.33 A residence order is an order 'settling the arrangements to be made as to the person with whom a child will live'[1]. Usually, a residence order is granted to resolve a dispute about where a child should live; there is no requirement for all carers to have a residence order simply to reflect the status quo.

1 Children Act 1989, s 8.

5.34 In addition to resolving disputes between carers, however, there are two other important effects of a residence order. The grant of a residence order to a child's carer automatically confers parental responsibility for the duration of the order and may often be the only way for the carer to obtain parental responsibility. A parent who has obtained a residence order may appoint a guardian whose appointment will take effect immediately on her death, with priority over the surviving parent[1]. Residence orders, therefore, have three main purposes: settling disputes about where a child should live, granting parental responsibility, and strengthening the appointment of a guardian.

1 Children Act 1989, s 5(7).

5.35 The courts have held that it is entirely appropriate for a residence order to be granted, even where there is no dispute about where a child will live, in order to grant the carer parental responsibility. In the case of *B v B (a minor) (residence order)*[1], a grandmother had looked after the child for many years and applied for a residence order, with the consent of the mother. Initially, the application was refused on the basis that there was no need for an order as there was no dispute. On appeal, a residence order was granted and the court held that it was appropriate to grant a residence order for the sole purpose of conferring parental responsibility. This decision sets a useful precedent for parents with HIV and AIDS whose children who are already being looked after by a friend or relative.

1 [1992] 2 FLR 327, [1993] 1 FCR 211.

(ii) Shared residence

5.36 A residence order may be granted to one or more people who may live together or apart. A shared residence order will work only if there is a certain level of co-operation between the child's carers; shared residence orders are often made by consent. In a 1996 case[1], the foster carers of a child wished to adopt her. They were not married and, therefore, under the legislation only one could apply to adopt the child. The foster father applied to adopt and an application for shared residence for both foster carers was made. Cazalet J held that it was not inconsistent to grant both an adoption and a joint residence order. It was in the interests of the child to have security and a permanent base and this could be achieved by both carers having parental responsibility.

1 *Re AB (adoption: joint residence)* [1996] 1 FLR 27.

5.37 Shared residence orders, where the carers live apart, are not generally favoured by the courts. Children whose parents have separated are usually considered to need the stability of one home, with one parent having residence and the other having contact. There are cases, however, where this model does not apply; children live within a wide range of family set-ups and clients may wish to make a variety of arrangements for their children. Where there is some positive benefit to the child, in what courts have described as unusual circumstances, shared residence orders may…

cared for by those who live apart, the court can attach directions to the residence order providing for the periods of time that the child will spend in each household. An order made in favour of the child's biological parents who live apart at the time that the order is made will cease if the parents subsequently live together for six months[2].

1 *A v A (minors) (shared residence order)* [1994] 1 FLR 669.
2 Children Act 1989, s 11(5).

5.38 Shared residence orders are often appropriate where the mother shares the care of her child with a partner who is not the biological father of the child and who cannot therefore obtain parental responsibility by agreement. The courts have made orders in favour of both the male and female partners of mothers who share responsibility for child rearing. In the case of *Re C (a minor) (residence order: lesbian co-parents)*[1], a shared residence order was granted to the mother and her female partner. On the evidence in that case, it was in the best interests of the child that such an order be made.

1 [1994] Fam Law 468.

5.39 A shared residence order may also be appropriate where a parent has periods of illness and another person cares for the child during those periods. Once that carer obtains a residence order, the carer will be able to share parental responsibility with the parent and the carer will retain the residence order and parental responsibility if the parent dies.

(iii) Who may apply for a residence order?

5.40 Some applicants are entitled to apply as of right for any s 8 order[1]. Parents, guardians and those with residence orders may apply for any s 8 order without leave[2]. Certain other applicants may apply only for residence or contact orders without the leave of the court. Within this category are step-parents, any person with whom the child has lived for a period of at least three years or any person who has consent of those with parental responsibility[3].

1 Children Act 1989, s 10(4).
2 CA 1989, s 10(4).
3 CA 1989, s 10(4)(c).

5.41 In all other cases, a person will require leave of the court before making any application under s 8 of the Children Act 1989. The grant of leave does not raise a presumption that the substantive application will succeed[1].

1 *Re A (section 8 order: grandparent's application)* [1995] 2 FLR 153.

5.42 In deciding the question of leave, the court will consider the following factors:
(a) the nature of the proposed application;
(b) the applicant's connection with the child;
(c) any risk that there might be of the application disrupting the child's life to an extent that he would be harmed by it;
and if the child is being looked after by the local authority:
(d) the authority's plans for the future; and
(e) the wishes and feelings of the child's parents[1].

1 Children Act 1989, s 10(9).

(iv) Effect and duration of a residence order

5.43 If the person to whom the residence order is granted is not a parent or guardian, the parental responsibility granted will last only for the duration of the residence order. For example, where a mother and her partner (not the father of the child), obtain a joint residence order, which is later varied and granted solely to the mother, the stepfather's parental responsibility for the child will end when the shared residence order is discharged. The scope of the parental responsibility granted to someone who is not a parent or guardian is also limited. The holder may not give or refuse consent for the child to be freed for adoption, or adopted, nor may the holder appoint a guardian.

5.44 If a father is granted a residence order and would not otherwise have parental responsibility, the court must also make a parental responsibility order under s 4 of the Children Act 1989[1]. In this case, even if the residence order comes to an end, the parental responsibility order will not automatically end.

1 Children Act 1989, s 12(1).

5.45 While a residence order is in force, the child's surname must not be changed and the child must not be removed from the UK without the written consent of every person with parental responsibility or the leave of the court. The only exception to this provision is that the holder of the residence order may take the child out of the jurisdiction for up to one month[1].

1 Children Act 1989, s 13(1).

5.46 A residence order will end when the child reaches 16 years of age, unless there are exceptional circumstances which require the order to continue. A residence order will also end on the making of a fresh residence order, the discharge of the order by the court, the making of a care order or if the parents live together for more than six months.

5.47 Where an application for a residence order is contested the court will consider the welfare of the child by applying the 'welfare checklist'.

5 Guardianship

5.48 By appointing a guardian, a parent can choose someone to take over his or her role as parent if he or she should die. Guardianship is an important tool in providing for future care for children and is one that is easily employed. The Children Act 1989, s 5(3) provides that a parent with parental responsibility may appoint another individual, or more than one person, to be the child's guardian(s) in the event of the parent's death.

5.49 Guardianship confers parental responsibility on the guardian either on the death of the person who has made the appointment, or on the death of the last surviving parent with parental responsibility. Where there is more than one person with parental responsibility it is particularly important to advise clients carefully about when the appointment will take effect. The parental responsibility granted by guardianship lasts until the child is 18 unless the guardianship is terminated. By contrast, parental responsibility granted by way of residence order lasts only for as long as the residence order itself and generally not beyond the child's sixteenth birthday.

5.50 The simple formalities required for the appointment of a guardian enable parents with HIV or AIDS to choose a permanent carer without the need for anyone to apply for a court order. Because the appointment takes effect immediately on the death of the parent, the child will not be left in limbo while applications for parental responsibility or residence are processed by the court.

5.51 It may be that parents do not have a potential guardian in mind. Here, voluntary agencies or social services may be able to assist parents who are HIV positive in finding suitable carers who can become involved with the family at an early stage with a view to caring for the children in the event of the parents' deaths. Foster carers and those giving respite care while parents are ill may ultimately become suitable long-term carers.

5.52 There may be difficulties in relation to the appointment of guardians when cultural expectations play a part. In a number of cultures it may be expected that the father will make appropriate arrangements for the children; it may be difficult for the mother to assert her wishes. Clients may find mediation helpful in reaching arrangements by consent. In some areas, social services will provide this kind of assistance; many voluntary organisations also offer mediation.

5.53 If it is proposed that a family member should come from abroad to look after children on the death of the parents, it is essential to obtain specialist immigration advice for the carer to obtain entry clearance and to be permitted to remain in the country to care for the children. It may be that an application for a residence order will be necessary to confirm that the appointed guardian is the person with whom the children should live.

(i) Nature and method of appointment

5.54 The appointment of a guardian must be made in writing, dated and signed by the person making the appointment[1]. The appointment may be made as part of a will, but need not be. Parents should ensure that the prospective guardian understands the nature of the appointment and agrees to undertake that responsibility. It may also be appropriate for parents to discuss their plans with the children. This may raise difficult questions for parents who have chosen not to disclose their HIV status to their children, or to the prospective guardian. Parents should also be advised to keep a copy of the document containing the appointment in a safe place and to give copies to the guardian and to a trusted person or professional.

1 Children Act 1989, s 5(5). Alternative provisions are made for the signing of appointments of guardians at the direction of the appointor.

5.55 It is important to advise parents that if they appoint their spouse as guardian, the appointment will be revoked on divorce unless the terms of the appointment specify otherwise. More than one guardian may be appointed, but if a parent has already appointed a guardian and subsequently wishes to appoint a second guardian to act jointly with the first, then this should be made clear so that the first appointment is not revoked.

Appointment of guardian by sole parent with parental responsibility

5.56 Where the person appointing a guardian is the only parent with parental responsibility, the appointment will take effect on death of that parent. The most common example of this situation is when an unmarried mother wishes to appoint a guardian for her child. The father will not have parental responsibility (unless he has obtained it by court order or by agreement) and the mother's appointment will take effect on her death.

Appointment of guardian by one of two parents with parental responsibility

5.57 Where a guardian is appointed by one of two parents with parental responsibility, the guardianship will not take effect on the death of the appointor if the other parent is alive at that time. The guardianship will take effect only when both parents with parental responsibility have died[1]. If the mother appoints a guardian and the father subsequently acquires parental responsibility, the appointment will take effect on the death of the father. The exception is if the mother has a residence order in her favour immediately before her death then her appointment will take effect on her death as if there were no parent with parental responsibility still living[2].

1 Children Act 1989, s 5(7).
2 CA 1989, s 5(7)(b).

5.58 Where one parent with parental responsibility would prefer that her chosen guardian, rather than the other parent with parental responsibility, should look after the children on her death, she must obtain a residence order. After her death, the guardian will share parental responsibility with the remaining parent.

5.59 If both parents have parental responsibility, it is possible for them to make a joint appointment, to take effect on the death of the last surviving parent. It is also possible for each to appoint a different guardian. In this situation, upon the death of the second parent, both appointments take effect[1] and the separately appointed guardians would become joint guardians. In any of these situations, if a conflict arises between the two guardians, either could apply to the court to resolve the dispute.

1 Children Act 1989, s 5(8).

5.60 If a guardian whose appointment has not yet taken effect has concerns about the children, she is in the same situation as any other potential carer. She has no rights as a guardian until the death of the second parent; in the meantime, all she can do is to make an application for a s 8 order, for which she may need leave[1].

1 Children Act 1989, s 10(4).

Appointment of guardian by a guardian

5.61 Once an appointment has taken effect, the appointed guardian will have parental responsibility for the child and can herself appoint a guardian[1].

Appointment of guardian by the court

5.62 The court may appoint a guardian for a child who does not have any parent with parental responsibility, or where the child is the subject of a residence order and the person to whom residence had been granted has died[1]. Such an order may be made upon application or where the court already has before it family proceedings in relation to the child.

1 Children Act 1989, s 5(1).

(ii) Termination of guardianship

5.63 Guardianship can come to an end in four ways. The appointor may revoke the appointment by destroying the document appointing the guardian or by creating a later appointment. Where the appointor has appointed her spouse as guardian for the child, the appointment will automatically be revoked upon divorce, unless there is a contrary intention contained in the appointment instrument[1]. An appointment of a guardian may also come to an end if the guardian disclaims the appointment in writing[2]. In addition, the court may order that an appointment be brought to an end on the application of anyone with parental responsibility, the child (with leave of the court) or the court itself, if the court considers it appropriate[3].

1 Children Act 1989, s 6(1)–(4).
2 CA 1989, s 6(5).
3 CA 1989, s 6(7).

(iii) Challenging an appointment

5.64 A father who has not obtained parental responsibility for his child during the mother's lifetime would need to take court action if he wished to challenge the mother's appointment of guardian. If the father applied to the court for a residence order, a parental responsibility order, or an order that he should be appointed as guardian and was granted one of those orders, then he would share parental responsibility with the guardian appointed by the mother. Within those proceedings he could also request that the court terminate the guardianship, or he could support any application made by another person to replace the appointed guardian.

6 Adoption

5.65 Some parents with HIV or AIDS may express a specific preference for their children to be adopted; they may not be aware of the existence of other options, such as residence orders, or they may feel that only adoption will give their child a sense of secure attachment to the new parents. As with a residence order, an adoption order means that the adopters acquire parental responsibility. Unlike a residence order, it also has the effect of extinguishing the parental responsibility of the birth parents and anyone else who had parental responsibility at the time when the adoption order was granted[1]. It is an irrevocable order which is intended to ensure that the child becomes a permanent member of a new family.

1 Adoption Act 1976, s 12(1) and (3).

5.66 In most cases, a residence or guardianship order is likely to be a more appropriate and effective tool both for HIV positive parents who are making plans for their children and for carers who are seeking to formalise arrangements after the death or incapacity of a parent. Although it is increasingly accepted that some degree of contact with birth families should continue after an adoption order has been made, it is still the case that adoption implies a degree of severance with the child's birth family. This may be inappropriate where one or both parents have died, but the child has strong relationships with other relatives.

5.67 The other disadvantage of adoption is the lengthy, cumbersome and potentially expensive nature of the procedure involved. Before the application is made, the child must live with the adopters for 13 weeks (if the adopters are related to the child or the child has been placed by an adoption agency or by social services) or one year in all other cases[1]. If the parents are still alive, the court must be satisfied either that each parent or guardian of the child agrees unconditionally to the making of an adoption order or that her consent should be dispensed with[2]. Schedule 2 to the Adoption Rules 1984 requires that the court must be supplied with a detailed report setting out factual matters and the views of the reporting body[3], usually social services. The procedure is considerably more complicated than in Children Act 1989 applications and the parties are much more likely to require representation.

1 Adoption Act 1976, s 13(1), (2).
2 AA 1976, s 16(2).
3 Where the child has been placed for adoption by an approved adoption agency, that agency must prepare the report. In all other cases, the local authority will do so.

5.68 An adoption order cannot be made in favour of more than one person unless the adopters are married to each other[1]. The court will only make an adoption order in favour of one partner to an unmarried relationship if satisfied that the relationship is stable and enduring. It may be possible for the court to grant a joint residence order to both partners once the adoption order has been made[2].

1 Adoption Act 1976, s 14(1).
2 *Re AB (adoption: joint residence)* [1996] 1 FLR 27.

5.69 Where either the parents or new carers feel that an adoption order is the best solution, it is often worth enlisting support from the local authority as far in advance as possible. The social worker's views (as set out in the Sch 2 report) will have considerable influence over the court's decision and it may also be possible to obtain a contribution towards the adopter's legal costs from local authority funds.

5.70 Adoption will generally be appropriate only where the child is still very young and where it is agreed that she should make a new start with a new family. There may be exceptional cases, for example where the child of a parent who is seriously ill with AIDS has lived with another carer for over a year, and both the parent and the carer seek the permanence of an adoption order in favour of the carer. The emotional impact of an adoption order for a parent, who must cope both with her illness and the prospect of relinquishing parental responsibility, should not be underestimated. Where a parent is in favour of adoption but wants the proceedings to take place after her death, she should set out her wishes in writing so that they can be

7 Financial provision

5.71 In addition to arrangements for the physical care of the children, parents may want to consider financial provision. Financial provision after death is dealt with in Chapter 9. This chapter will briefly outline some of the legislation dealing with financial provision for children.

5.72 Most child maintenance is now dealt with through the Child Support Agency (CSA), rather than through the courts. The CSA identifies the parent with care and the absent parent for the child in question and assesses the liability of the absent parent to contribute to the maintenance of the child.

5.73 The Matrimonial Causes Act 1973 allows the court, within divorce proceedings, to make a wide range of orders between husband and wife, including financial support for children. This may be in the form of a lump sum payment, transfer of property (including the transfer of a tenancy), or maintenance where this is not covered by the CSA. The courts' jurisdiction to make child maintenance orders is now limited to certain cases including those where one of the parties is not habitually resident in the UK[1]; where a child over 16 years of age is not in full-time education and/or is receiving 'advanced education'[2]; where the order is required for expenses attributable to the child's disability[3]; and where there is scope for a 'topping up' of a CSA assessment[4]. All these orders rely on the parent against whom a claim is made having sufficient income or capital to make such a claim worthwhile.

1 Child Support Act 1991, s 44(1).
2 CSA 1991, s 55(1) definition of 'child' and 'full-time' and 'advanced education' and s 8(8) for the court's jurisdiction.
3 CSA 1991, s 8(8).
4 CSA 1991, s 8(6).

5.74 There are a number of factors to be weighed in the balance when the court is considering a financial application within divorce. The welfare of any child of the family is the 'first consideration'[1] and on applications for orders for the benefit of the child there is a specific checklist of factors[2] to be taken into account, including the child's financial resources and needs and any physical or mental disability. A child who is HIV positive or has AIDS may need medical or other care requiring a higher financial contribution from the absent parent.

1 Matrimonial Causes Act 1973, s 25(1).
2 MCA 1973, s 25(3).

5.75 The Children Act 1989[1] provides that applications may be made to the court by a parent, guardian, person with residence order or the child themselves for financial provision for the child from the other parent[2]. Again, orders for periodical payments, lump-sum and property transfer may be made, but the benefit of capital orders will not usually last after the child reaches 21 years of age or finishes full-time education. The criteria to be considered by the court are listed in Sch 1 to the Children Act 1989[3]. It should be noted that the 'no order' principle does not apply and the child's welfare is not of 'paramount' importance on a financial application.

1 Children Act 1989, s 15 refers to Sch 1 which sets out the financial provision available for children.
2 CA 1989, Sch 1, para 3(1).
3 CA 1989, Sch 1, para 4(1).

5.76 Some local authorities provide regular payments in the form of 'residence allowances' to non-parent carers. These payments are discretionary and are usually made only when the carers would otherwise experience hardship. Where no residence allowance is available, social services may still be willing to help with the cost of essential equipment for the child.

5.77 Parents who are terminally ill and who wish to make provision for their children will need to consider doing so under the terms of a will or by establishing a trust. Financial provision after death is dealt with in Chapter 9.

8 Case studies

5.78 A single mother would like her mother to look after the children if she becomes too ill to look after them full time and to take full responsibility for them after her death. The children's father is not involved in their care. He and the mother were never married and he does not have parental responsibility.

If the mother appoints her mother as guardian, the appointment will take effect on her death.

The grandmother and the mother could also apply for a shared residence order so as to give the grandmother parental responsibility. It could be argued that the grandmother having parental responsibility would provide security and stability for the children. It may still be possible to persuade the court to make a residence order if the grandmother and the mother live separately.

5.79 The mother and father of three children were married, but are separated. Both are seriously ill and they agreed that in the event of the death or incapacity of either, the maternal aunt would look after the children. Both appointed her as guardian. The mother died and the children went to live with the aunt.

As the father was living at the time of the mother's death, her guardianship appointment did not take effect. The aunt could apply for leave to seek a residence order. If the father consents to her application then it is likely to be granted at an early stage.

5.80 The mother lives with her husband. She takes most of the responsibility for the care of the children, but the children spend a lot of time with their father. Both mother and father are ill. The relationship is under pressure; both are ill from time to time. The husband is frequently aggressive and sometimes violent to the wife. The mother is anxious to provide for the children if she is no longer able to do so. She fears that the husband's health is more vulnerable than her own and that even if he is physically well he is unable to cope with the pressure of looking after the children full time. The mother would like her sister to look after the children after her death; the husband would like his sister to take over the children's care after his death, if their mother has already died. It is difficult for the couple to talk about the future.

> The mother's appointment of her sister as guardian will not take effect until after the death of her husband. She is concerned about what happens if she dies first. She enlists the help of social workers already involved with the family to assist in reaching an agreement and putting it in writing. It is agreed that as long as he is well enough the husband will look after the children. At the point where he can no longer do so, the maternal aunt is to take over the care of the children and the husband will agree to a residence order in her favour. The mother writes a statement supporting such an application, setting out her reasons for wanting the children to be with her sister rather than the husband's family. It is hoped that this would be useful evidence if the husband decided later not to comply with the agreement.

C HIV AND AIDS AS A FACTOR IN CHILDREN ACT DISPUTES

5.81 This section will consider the application of the Children Act 1989 to children's cases where HIV or AIDS is an issue. The issues considered here relate mainly to disputes about contact and residence, or other s 8 applications.

1 The welfare checklist

5.82 In resolving most Children Act 1989 disputes, the court will focus on the general principles set out above and in particular on the welfare checklist at s 1(3) of the Act. The factors set out in the list are not in any particular order, and their relative importance will vary from case to case. The purpose of the list is to ensure that the court considers every important issue. HIV or AIDS should not be treated as a separate issue; instead the court should consider how it affects each of the issues set out in the welfare checklist.

(i) Wishes and feelings of the child

5.83 The importance which the court attaches to children's views will depend on the age and maturity of the child, as well as the nature of the order sought. Generally, the views of children over the age of 11 or 12 will be given great weight[1]. Usually, the court welfare officer will be responsible for ascertaining the wishes of the child.

1 See *M v M (minor: custody appeal)* [1987] 1 WLR 404; *Re P (a minor) (education)* [1992] 1 FLR 316; *Re S (minors) (access: religious upbringing)* [1992] 2 FLR 313.

(ii) The child's needs

5.84 Where residence is in dispute, the court will require details of the proposed arrangements for the child (such as accommodation, financial support and childcare for working parents) in order to assess whether the child's needs will be met. It is often helpful to set out the day-to-day routine which the child will follow and to explain any reasons why her emotional needs will be better met in one home than another.

(iii) The effect of any change

5.85 It is generally accepted that change has a negative effect on children, particularly when they are very young. As a result, courts will be reluctant to disturb the status quo unless the long-term benefits for the child are likely to outweigh the disadvantages of disruption[1].

1 *D v M (minor: custody appeal)* [1982] 3 All ER 897; *Re G (a minor) (custody)* [1992] 2 FCR 279.

(iv) The child's characteristics

5.86 These may include special factors such as racial or cultural needs, the fact that the child has AIDS or HIV, or the need of a very young baby to be cared for by her mother.

(v) Harm which the child has suffered or is at risk of suffering

5.87 This may include ill-treatment or impairment of the child's health or development.

(vi) Capacity of parents and others

5.88 The court will look at the extent to which the adults involved in the case will be able to meet the needs of the child. The needs of the adults themselves will be relevant only in so far as they affect those of the child.

2 Evidence and procedure

5.89 In most cases, issuing an application to the court should be seen as a last resort. Where a dispute has arisen, practitioners should encourage their clients to try other methods of resolution, such as mediation. In some cases, providing accurate information about the nature and transmission of HIV or AIDS may break down misconceptions which form part of the basis of the dispute.

5.90 When an application has been issued, the court will list a directions appointment at which a further attempt will be made to resolve the dispute. If this proves impossible, directions for the filing of evidence will be given. Some courts will expect to be told at this stage what witnesses are to be called.

5.91 If a doctor or other expert will need to examine the child with a view to preparing a report for the court, the court must give permission for the child to be examined[1]. Leave will also be required before any expert will be allowed to see the statements and other reports filed at court[2]. The court will generally wish to know the name and qualifications of the expert before giving leave and the directions should define the issues which the expert is to address. In cases where the child or one of the parties is ill because of AIDS, medical evidence may be necessary. For example, a person seeking residence will need to show that she will [illegible] treatment is already being given, the treating clinician will often be the best person to approach. However, where the medical evidence is likely to be controversial, it may be useful to instruct an outside expert (usually a consultant) who specialises in the treatment of HIV and AIDS and has experience in preparing court reports and giving evidence.

1 Family Proceedings Rules 1991, SI 1991/1247, r 4.18(1).
2 FPR 1991, r 4.23.

5.92 The court will usually be assisted by an independent welfare report. The recommendations set out in the welfare report will be central to the decision of the court. Case law indicates that judges or magistrates who wish to depart from the recommendations in the welfare report should ensure that they explain their reasons for doing so[1]. The person preparing the report will interview the parties and see them with the children, often at home as well as in the court welfare office. In s 8 and other private law cases, the court welfare officer will be asked to prepare a welfare report; social services may be asked to do so where they have had extensive involvement with the family. In cases involving the local authority, a guardian ad litem will be appointed at the beginning of the proceedings to represent the interests of the child. The guardian's report will set out their own views and those of the child if the child is old enough to express them[2].

1 See *W v W (a minor: custody appeal)* [1988] 2 FLR 505; *Re B (minors) (access)* [1991] Fam Law 287; *Re CB (access: attendance of court welfare officer)* [1995] 1 FLR 622, but see also *Re V (residence review)* [1995] 2 FLR 1010.
2 For a full explanation of the role of the guardian, see Hershman and McFarlane **D[421]–[609]**.

5.93 On the basis that delay is prejudicial to the child, the court will exercise strict control over the timetable for the preparation of the case and the listing of the final hearing. The child will not be required to attend the final hearing as her views will be set out in the welfare report. The person who prepared the report will usually give oral evidence. Parties will be required to give evidence and to be cross-examined by the other party's representative. They may be asked detailed questions about their health. Where a parent is too ill to attend court, it may be possible for the court to accept written evidence if the formalities in the Civil Evidence Act 1995 are followed so as to make the written evidence admissible[1].

1 Civil Evidence Act 1995, ss 1–6.

3 Where the child is HIV positive or has AIDS

5.94 Because it must consider the child's physical needs and special characteristics, the court will need accurate medical information about how HIV will affect the child's life. Medical research indicates that two thirds of children born with HIV are likely to survive beyond the age of two; some may remain asymptomatic during childhood[1]. HIV positive children often experience developmental delay and may also suffer from a wide variety of infections. They will require high standards of medical care, hygiene and nutrition if they become ill. Adolescents with HIV will require sensitive and supportive counselling on the implications of their status for their future health and relationships. Courts will need both specific information about the current medical needs and prognosis of the child who is the subject of the proceedings and more general information about how the child will continue to be affected by HIV status as he or she grows up.

1 European Collaborative Study 'Children Born to Women with HIV-1 Infection: Natural History and Risk of Transmission' (1991) Lancet 337: 253-260.

5.95 Where the question of residence is in dispute, or where a parent is contesting a local authority application for the child to be removed from her care, the court will want to be assured that the person who cares for the child will be able to meet the child's needs. It will be vital for parents to show that they have good relationships with the professionals responsible for the child's medical care and that they are able to monitor the child's health. They will also have to show that they can provide the emotional support that the child will need.

5.96 The case of *Re W (a minor)*[1] considered the relevance of a child's HIV status to a residence application. The five-year-old child, whose mother had died of AIDS-related illness, was a ward of court. The child was to be looked after outside the family and there was a dispute between two sets of potential carers as to where the child should live. The judge directed that the question of the child's HIV status should be considered before a decision was taken in relation to residence. The Official Solicitor applied for an order giving authority for a blood sample to be taken from the child so that an HIV test could be carried out.

1 [1995] 2 FCR 184.

5.97 The medical evidence before the court indicated that it was important to ascertain the child's status because it would determine the treatment of any illnesses which the child might contract. Childhood illnesses, although not serious for other children, might have a serious effect on a child who is HIV positive and such illnesses need to be treated quickly. The doctor felt that the test should only be carried out if there was a significant risk that the child was HIV positive. He considered that in this case there was such a risk because the child's mother had died of an AIDS-related illness. The local authority opposed the application on the grounds that it was not in the child's best interests. They argued that knowledge of the child's status would only benefit the child if it confirmed that the child was HIV negative. If the test results were positive, the stress of that knowledge and the resulting stigma might harm the child. The local authority also suggested that the question of whether the child was HIV positive was not relevant to the question of residence. The court held that there was a significant risk that the child was HIV positive and that the child's status should be ascertained. The judgment indicated that the child's status was an important factor to be taken into account when determining the question of the child's residence.

5.98 Because judges are likely to be so concerned about the implications of the child's HIV status, there may be a risk that other equally important issues will be overshadowed. A child who is HIV positive but otherwise healthy may have more urgent needs than those which are related to health. The use of the checklist should ensure that all of the relevant issues are considered by the court.

4 Where a parent has HIV or AIDS

5.99 The extent to which the court will need to consider the fact that a parent is HIV positive will depend on the nature of the application before the court. For example, where an HIV positive parent seeks a residence order, the court will have to consider the implications of her status in much greater detail than if she seeks only a few hours' contact every fortnight. In each case, the court's consideration must focus on the extent to which the child's welfare is affected, or is likely to be affected, by the fact that the parent is HIV positive or has AIDS.

(i) Disclosure

5.100 A parent who is HIV positive may not wish to disclose her status to the court or the other party. If she discloses the information to her solicitor, that disclosure will be confidential and also protected by legal professional privilege. The client should be advised however that the solicitor's duties to the court mean that the solicitor cannot mislead the other party or the court in any way. For example, the solicitor could not write a letter denying that the client is HIV positive if he or she knows that this is not the case.

5.101 It is less clear whether the solicitor is under a positive duty to disclose her client's status in the absence of any questions on the subject. In a 1993 Practice Direction, the President of the Family Division stated that parties and their representatives are under a duty to disclose to the court all matters relating to children[1]. A number of obiter High Court judgments support this view[2], but the House of Lords has not upheld the argument that such a duty exists[3].

1 *Practice Direction (Family Proceedings: Case Management)* [1995] 1 WLR 332, sub nom *Practice Direction: Case Management* [1995] 1 FLR 456 .

2 *Essex County Council v R* [1993] 2 FLR 826; *Re DH (a minor) (child abuse)* [1994] 1 FLR 679; *Oxfordshire County Council v P* [1995] 1 FLR 552.

3 See the majority decision in *Re L (a minor) (police investigation: privilege)* [1996] 2 All ER 78, H L .

5.102 There does not seem to be any clear authority which requires all HIV positive parents to disclose their status to the court. A parent who is HIV positive but otherwise healthy and who seeks only contact may justifiably argue that her status will not affect the child, or become evident to the child, in the foreseeable future. She should however be advised that her case may be prejudiced if that information comes to the attention of the court by other means and if the judge feels that she should have disclosed her status. A parent who seeks a residence order runs a much greater risk if she chooses not to reveal her status. The court is much more likely to hold that the child will be affected if her primary carer becomes ill, even if the treatment options now available mean that the parent may remain healthy for many years. A parent who is already ill will generally have to provide some details of her illness and her prognosis and she will find it very difficult to conceal the nature of her illness from the court.

5.103 Where a parent has decided to disclose her HIV status to the other party but feels unable to do so directly, it may be possible for the court welfare officer to assist, perhaps as part of the conciliation process. Parents may, however, be worried that the other party will reveal details to neighbours or relatives and that they will lose control of the information. It is difficult for advisers to offer concrete reassurance on this point. Documents filed with the court, other than court orders, are confidential and must not be shown to anyone other than parties to the proceedings, their advisers and court welfare officers[1]; any threatened breach of this rule can usually be dealt with in the Children Act 1989 proceedings. It is less clear whether a party can prevent the disclosure of her HIV status if it does not involve the disclosure of court papers. A letter to the other party's representatives reminding them of the confidential nature of the information may be adequate. If there are strong reasons to fear that another party will disclose that information, the possibility of seeking an injunction order within the High Court's inherent jurisdiction should be considered.

1 Family Proceedings Rules 1991, SI 1991/1247, r 4.23.

(ii) UK case law

5.104 There are surprising few reported cases in England and Wales where the HIV status of the parent or party other than the child has been an issue. It is difficult to know whether this is because there have been so few cases dealing with this issues, or because HIV positive parents who are unhappy with the courts' approach do not feel that they are in a sufficiently strong position to engage in extended or appellate litigation.

5.105 Anecdotal evidence indicates that there is still a great deal of misinformation about HIV and AIDS amongst those involved in family cases. For example, one HIV positive father was encouraged to give an undertaking not to kiss his children or to allow them to have any contact with his male partner. In cases such as this, it is clear that homophobia and prejudices about HIV have led to decisions which are both inconsistent with expert evidence and wholly inappropriate.

5.106 Although courts are becoming more liberal when considering parents' sexuality, gay parents will invariably find that their personal lives are scrutinised. In a 1992 case, Booth J held that the mother's lesbianism was an important factor in the balancing act that was involved in considering with which parent the child should live[1]. Since then, the courts have been willing in numerous cases to grant shared residence orders to lesbian co-parents and the issue seems to be less controversial. There have been fewer Children Act cases relating to gay men. In 1996 the Scottish Court of Session granted an adoption order to two gay men. The resulting judgment indicates that the courts are now less likely than in the past to allow issues of sexuality to prevail over the best interests of the child[2]. In practice however, gay and lesbian parents still face considerable prejudice.

1 *C v C (custody of a child) (No 2)* [1992] 1 FCR 206.
2 *AMT (known as AC) (petitioners for authority to adopt SR)* [1997] Fam Law 225.

(iii) American case law

5.107 The courts in many American states have dealt with disputes about custody and access where one of the parties is HIV positive or has AIDS. In the absence of case law from this jurisdiction, it is interesting to consider the approach adopted by American courts

5.108 Most American states decide custody disputes by considering the best interests of the child in the light of the particular facts of the case and follow the Uniform Marriage and Divorce Act 1979 which provides that non-custodial parents are entitled to access unless it would seriously jeopardise the child's 'physical, mental, moral or emotional health'[1].

1 Uniform Marriage and Divorce Act 1979, s 407(a), 9A ULA 207 (1979).

5.109 In cases where courts have considered the visitation rights of HIV infected parents, their findings have varied widely. In considering an application for access by a father who had AIDS, a New York court accepted expert medical evidence that there was no risk that the virus would be transmitted to the child. The court referred to the strength of the relationship between the child and her father, to the father's 'reasonable and responsible' reaction to his disease and to his exemplary conduct as a parent. He was granted substantial unsupervised contact in spite of the mother's allegations that he would not be able to look after the child[1]. By contrast, a New Jersey court held that a father with AIDS should have only supervised contact with his child because of his illness[2].

1 *Jane W v John W* 137 Misc 2d 24, 519 NYS 2d 603 (1987).
2 *Jordan v Jordan FV* 12-1357-84 Middlesex County, NJ Supp.

5.110 In 1986, a court in Indiana rejected the custody application of a father who was HIV positive but asymptomatic, in spite of very substantial evidence that the mother was quite incapable of caring for her daughter. The trial judge ignored medical evidence about the risk of transmission and gave the simple fact of the father's HIV status as the sole reason for denying him access as well as custody. The decision was overturned by the Indiana Court of Appeals, who criticised the prejudice which the judge had exhibited towards the father. The Court of Appeals did not give any guidelines as to how courts should balance the HIV status of parents with other factors relating to the child's welfare[1].

1 *Stewart v Stewart* No S485–1128 (Sup Ct Marion City, Ind, 9 Oct 1986) 521 NE 2d 956 (Ind Ct App 1988).

5.111 In another case in New York, a court considering an application for custody by maternal grandparents refused to grant an order requiring a father to take an HIV test. The grandparents did not argue that there was any risk of transmission, but instead suggested that the father was likely to be HIV positive and that, as a result, his life expectancy would be shorter and also that he would be more likely to commit suicide. Psychiatric evidence indicated that even if the father did have a shorter life expectancy this fact would not justify removing the children from his care, and that he had no suicidal tendencies. The court found that there was no sufficiently compelling reason to order an HIV test[1].

1 *Doe v Roe* 526 NYS 2d 718 (Sup Ct 1988).

5.112 In the majority of the American cases it is clear that the courts have tried both to consider the issue of the parent's status within the context of the child's welfare and to avoid resorting to stereotypical assumptions about the implications of HIV. In some cases they have gone further and refused to condone societal prejudices against HIV positive parents. In a case before the appellate court in Ohio a mother argued that the father must be HIV positive because of his homosexuality and that contact should be refused both because of the risk of transmission and because the children would be stigmatised by their peers. The court dismissed the mother's fears and held that it would not be serving the best interests of the child if it allowed itself to be influenced by society's prejudices against homosexuals and HIV positive people[1]. This judgment is consistent with other cases in which the American courts have specifically disregarded the question of 'community bias'. A similar stand has yet to be taken by the English courts.

1 *Conkel v Conkel* 31 Ohio App 3d 169, 173, 509 NE 2d 983, 987 (1987).

(iv) Factors which the court should consider

5.113 The first concern of many judges will be the risk of transmission of the virus to the child. There is ample medical evidence that casual contact between parents and children cannot transmit the infection. Medical research indicates that there is no risk involved in kissing, hugging, or sharing of eating utensils or bathrooms[1]. It will be important to ensure that the court welfare officer and the judge have access to accurate and up-to-date information about the nature and transmission of HIV and AIDS. Providing copies of the medical evidence should be enough to dispel any anxiety in this respect. The second chapter of *HIV Infection and Children in Need*[1] contains a useful summary of medical research about transmission. Organisations such as Body Positive or the Terrence Higgins Trust can also provide information about this issue.

1 See Newell, M and Peckham, C 'Transmission of HIV Infection' in *HIV Infection and Children in Need* (1993) BAAF, Ch 2 for a review of the medical evidence.

5.114 Where one of the parents is ill or likely to become ill, the court will need to consider the impact of that illness on the child. A parent who is ill and who seeks residence will need to show that her illness will not prevent her from meeting the child's physical needs. The court will also want to know about the emotional support available to the child so that she can ask questions and come to terms with the parent's illness. It may be useful to obtain evidence of the support available to the proposed residential parent, both now and in the future, from relatives, friends and social services. If the ill parent has always been the child's primary carer, she can also argue that the disruption to the child of moving to another home outweighs the effect of her illness.

5.115 If the parent who is ill seeks contact rather than residence, the other party may argue that the child will be distressed by seeing the effects of that illness. Child psychologists agree however that children are more likely to be damaged by attempts to shield them from the illness of a parent than by allowing them to confront that fact. A child whose parents are separated may already have experienced a conflict of loyalties and feelings of guilt and anger. If contact with a parent is prevented without explanation, or if the child is aware that a parent is ill but is given no further information, further emotional damage will occur. Where a parent is dying, contact will help children to prepare to say goodbye and to participate in the grieving process[1]. If the principle of contact is disputed, it may be necessary to obtain psychiatric or psychological evidence about the child's needs in relation to contact.

1 See Swindell, J 'Helping Children and Families Cope with Bereavement' in *HIV Infection and Children in Need* (1993) BAAF, Ch

5.116 The court may also be concerned that living with or having contact with a parent who is HIV positive may expose the child to society's prejudices against HIV and AIDS. Similar arguments have been used in cases involving gay and lesbian parents. In a case of this kind, the HIV positive parent can argue that she is the best person to discuss her status with the child and to give the child support in coping with any discrimination which she may encounter.

5.117 There are strong grounds for arguing that a court should not be allowed to attach disproportionate emphasis to the fact that a parent is HIV positive or has AIDS. It may be useful to suggest that a court should consider how the welfare of the child would be best served without considering the parent's status and only then go on to assess how the child is likely to be affected by the fact of that status.

D LOCAL AUTHORITY SUPPORT FOR CHILDREN AND FAMILIES

5.118 Many social services departments now provide specialist services for families affected by HIV or AIDS. Sometimes the provision of these services is intended to provide 'back-up' support so that families can continue to look after children at home. Parents may also be able to obtain help in planning for the care of their children at a point when they can no longer do so themselves. In some cases, where planned arrangements break down or where there is no one available to look after the children, the local authority will assume responsibility for care of the children.

5.119 Some parents will be worried by the prospect of approaching social services for support. Clients who are drug-users, ex-drug users, women who have chosen to have children knowing they are HIV positive or those whose immigration status is uncertain will often have experienced discriminatory treatment or judgmental attitudes. They are likely to feel anxious about involving the authorities in their most intimate concerns. They may also fear that information about their status will be disclosed to other agencies without their knowledge. They will often have little idea of the standards of service and level of support that they can expect; they may find that they are not being treated in the way that they would like but feel unable to assert their wishes.

5.120 It is here that advisers can help by telling clients about the types of services that they should receive from their local authority and what expectations they should have. Advisers can also help families complain if they do not receive the support to which they are entitled.

1 Local authority duties—the law

5.121 Part III of the Children Act 1989 sets out the duties owed by local authorities to children and families in its area. Some duties (such as the provision of family centres) are owed to all children. Other duties are owed only to children who are considered to be 'in need'. This section will focus on the duties owed to children 'in need', which are more likely to be relevant to families affected by HIV and AIDS.

5.122 Section 17 of the Children Act 1989 imposes a duty on every local authority to 'safeguard and promote the welfare of children…in need…by providing a range and level of services appropriate to those children's needs'. Section 17(10)(a)–(c) states that a child is in need if:

'(a) he is unlikely to achieve or maintain, or to have the opportunity of achieving or maintaining, a reasonable standard of health or development without the provision for him of services by a local authority under this Part;
(b) his health or development is likely to be significantly impaired, or further impaired, without the provision for him of such services; or
(c) he is disabled.'

5.123 Health includes physical or mental health; development may include physical, intellectual, social, emotional or behavioural development[1]. The guidance under the Children Act 1989 does not say who should decide whether a child meets these criteria. The definition of 'need' is deliberately wide[2]. It seems clear that a child who has AIDS, is HIV positive, or is cared for by someone who is ill with AIDS meets the criteria. The Act confirms that any services provided to a child in need may include services for the child's family if they are provided 'with a view to safeguarding or promoting the child's welfare'[3].

1 Children Act 1989, s 17(11).
2 *The Children Act 1989 Guidance* Vol 2, para 2.4.
3 CA 1989, s 17(3).

2 Types of service

5.124 The powers and duties of local authorities in relation to children in need are set out in s 17 and Pt I of Sch 2 to the Act. They include the following.

(a) **Advice, guidance and counselling**[1] Most social services departments offer counselling for children and families affected by HIV and AIDS. This may include supporting parents who wish to disclose their status to their children and helping families to make long-term plans.
(b) **Day care**[2] Day care refers to any care or supervised activity offered during the daytime such as nurseries, play groups, after-school clubs and child-minding. The guidance specifies the standards which must be met by the services provided[3]. Most authorities have policies which specify that all staff working with children should be given training about HIV and AIDS.
(c) **Financial help**[4] The local authority has the power to offer financial assistance as part of its services for children in need but it is under no duty to do so. Courts are very reluctant to interfere with local authority decisions about financial help; attempts to obtain an order requiring a to provide money for families of children in need have generally met with failure.
(d) **Home help**[5] This can include laundry facilities.
(e) **Travel assistance and holidays**[6] Travel assistance means that the local authority can provide transport to enable children or families

can also provide assistance so that the child and her family can have a holiday.

1 Children Act 1989, Sch 2, paras 8(a), (b).
2 CA 1989, ss 18, 19, 71–78 and Sch 9.
3 *The Children Act 1989 Guidance* Vol 2, Ch 6.
4 CA 1989, s 17(6).
5 CA 1989, Sch 2, para 8(c).
6 CA 1989, Sch 2, paras 8(d), (e).

5.125 This list of services does not in any way limit what the local authority can offer. The Act imposes a duty on the local authority to publish information about the services which it provides and to inform those who might benefit from them[1].

1 Children Act 1989, Sch 2, paras 1(2)(a), (b).

3 The assessment process

5.126 In order to decide what services it should provide in order to meet its duties, the local authority may carry out an assessment of the needs of the child and her family. Volume 2 of *The Children Act 1989 Guidance* sets out the way in which the local authority should approach the assessment process[1]. Usually, a social worker will visit the family at home and discuss the help that they require.

1 Further details can be found in the HMSO publication *Protecting Children—A Guide for Social Workers Undertaking a Comprehensive Assessment* (1988).

5.127 The Guidance states that:

> 'Good practice requires that the assessment of need should be undertaken in an open way and should involve those caring for the child, the child and other significant persons. Families with a child in need, whether the need results from family difficulties or the child's circumstances, have the right to receive sympathetic support and sensitive intervention in their family's life.'

5.128 Families affected by HIV and AIDS can expect to be assessed by a social worker, usually from a specialist team, who has a good grasp of the issues which are likely to affect them.

4 The provision of accommodation

5.129 This section deals with the voluntary accommodation by local authorities of children and young people who cannot be cared for at home. It does not relate to care proceedings in which the local authority seeks to remove the child from her home without the consent of those who have parental responsibility. The local authority has the power to provide accommodation when a parent asks it to do so. It only has a duty to provide accommodation, however, when a child in need appears to require accommodation because no one has parental responsibility for her, because she is lost or abandoned, or because the person caring for her is prevented from doing so, for whatever reason and for however long[1].

1 Children Act 1989, ss 20(1)(a)–(c).

5.130 The whole thrust of the Act and its Guidance is that local authorities should provide support that enables children to live at home with their parents wherever possible. A less drastic option than long-term accommodation is to ask for the provision of respite care, either to give carers a regular and planned break every few weeks or months, or during periods when the carer is too unwell to look after the child. The episodic nature of HIV or AIDS requires social services to act quickly and to be flexible in the provision of accommodation.

5.131 Social workers should work in partnership with parents when considering the provision of accommodation. The Guidance states:

> 'The Act assumes a high degree of co-operation between parents and local authorities in negotiating and agreeing what form of accommodation can be offered and the use to be made of it.'[1]

1 *The Children Act 1989 Guidance* Vol 2, para 2.25.

5.132 Parents (or other carers who have parental responsibility) can ask social services to provide accommodation for a child under s 20 of the Children Act 1989. The local authority cannot do so if anyone who has parental responsibility and who is willing and able to look after the child, objects to the provision of accommodation.

5.133 Any person who has parental responsibility can remove the child at any time[1]. If social services are worried about the child being removed from the accommodation, they must start care proceedings; accommodating a child under this provision does not confer parental responsibility on the local authority. In practice, difficulties can arise where parents seek to remove a child who has been accommodated for longer periods. If there has not been a clear agreement about the circumstances in which the child will return to the parents, the local authority may not support the parents' plans and may even start care proceedings. For that reason it is essential wherever possible for parents to draw up a detailed agreement with social services about the purpose and duration for which the child will be accommodated.

1 Children Act 1989, s 20(7) but see s 20(10) which allows a local authority to provide accommodation where a parent with a residence order (or equivalent) has given consent even if another person with parental responsibility objects and s 20(11) which allows a local authority to accommodate a young person over 16 years of age in spite of parents' objections if the young person consents. The same exceptions apply where a person with parental responsibility seeks to remove a child from local authority accommodation.

(i) Planning accommodation

5.134 Parents who are fully involved in the planning process will be in a better position to ensure that the accommodation provided is suitable for their children. Advisers can usefully refer to the provisions of the Children Act 1989, s 20 and Vols 2 and 3 of *The Children Act 1989 Guidance and Regulations* which, read together, impose numerous requirements on local authorities who accommodate children.

5.135 The terms of the regulations require the local authority to make immediate welfare of the child, before the placement begins or as soon as is practicable afterwards[1]. The Act imposes a duty (so far as is reasonably practical and consistent with the welfare of the child) on the local authority to ascertain the child's wishes[2]. The wishes of the child's parents and anyone else with parental responsibility must also be considered. Due consideration must be given to the child's religious, racial, cultural and linguistic background[3]. The authority is under a specific duty to provide accommodation near to the child's home and to accommodate siblings together[4].

1 Arrangements for the Placement of Children (General) Regulations 1991, SI 1991/890, reg 3(1).
2 Children Act 1989, s 20(6)(a).
3 CA 1989, s 22(5)(c).
4 CA 1989, s 23(7)(a), (b). Both duties apply only so far as is practicable and consistent with the welfare of the child or children.

5.136 Of course, some of these considerations may conflict with each other. When a child has grown accustomed to an emergency placement and a more appropriate long-term placement then becomes available it may be difficult to decide whether the child should move to an unfamiliar environment. Clients will have their own preferences as to potential carers, which will vary from family to family. The child may already have developed a relationship with a respite carer; if possible, parents will want to ensure continuity of care by asking for the child to be placed with that carer. Parents who are experiencing periods of illness will want to ensure that the child is placed sufficiently near to the family home for them to be able to visit regularly. In some families, the main priority will be to ensure that the child is placed in a family of similar cultural or religious background. The carers should be educated in HIV-related issues and that they must be committed to maintaining the family's confidentiality and supporting parents' decisions as to disclosure of their HIV status.

5.137 Sometimes a child will have to be accommodated in an emergency, perhaps where a parent becomes suddenly ill. The Guidance recognises that it may not be possible to draw up a long-term plan in those circumstances but requires local authorities to prepare a firm plan as soon as possible[1]. The social worker should also meet with the child and the parents to discuss the planned placement[2], as well as writing to summarise the plans, their likely duration, arrangements for contact, the role of the parents on a day-to-day basis and who is responsible for implementing the plan[3].

1 *The Children Act 1989 Guidance* Vol 3, para 2.18.
2 *The Children Act 1989 Guidance* Vol 3, para 2.70.
3 *The Children Act 1989 Guidance* Vol 3, para 2.72.

(ii) Local authority responsibilities while child is accommodated

5.138 The Act and Guidance impose further duties on the responsible authority after the child has been accommodated. Of particular importance to parents is the duty to promote contact between the child, the parents, anyone else with parental responsibility and friends or relatives connected with the child[1]. The authority can provide financial assistance to the child, relatives or friends to ensure that these visits take place[2].

1 Children Act 1989, Sch 2, para 15.
2 CA 1989, Sch 2, para 16.

5.139 Parents can also ensure that the suitability of the placement is reviewed regularly. The Review of Children's Cases Regulations 1991[1] together with Ch 3 of Vol 4 of the Guidance sets out in detail the procedures which must be followed.

1 SI 1991/895.

5.140 The local authority must maintain the child financially during accommodation. However, parents should be warned that the local authority is also under a duty to consider whether parents should provide a financial contribution. Parents in receipt of income support or family credit cannot be required to do so[1]. The local authority can only require a contribution if it considers it reasonable to do so, and the amount sought must be one which it is reasonably practicable for the parents to pay[2].

1 Children Act 1989, Sch 2, para 21(4).
2 CA 1989, Sch 2, paras 21(2) and 22(5).

5.141 The authority must ensure that the child's educational needs are met during the period of accommodation. The local education authority must be notified of the placement[1]. Because the local authority will not have acquired parental responsibility for the child, it will not be able to authorise medical treatment or tests (including an HIV test); only the parents or another person with parental responsibility can do so. If there is a dispute between the parents and the local authority, the authority would have to apply to the court to decide whether the child should be tested.

1 Arrangements for Placement of Children (General) Regulations 1991, SI 1991/890, reg 5.

5 Confidentiality

5.142 The volume and comprehensive nature of information which will inevitably be compiled by social services is likely to include details of the HIV status of the child or parents. Individuals can request access to their files[1] in order to find out what information is held by the local authority. Parents may be concerned that information may be released to other professionals, such as the child's teachers, or to the child. Feelings of impotence resulting from the need to ask for help from social services will be exacerbated if families feel that they may lose control over the dissemination of such intimate information.

1 Pursuant to the Access to Personal Files Act 1987 and the Access to Personal Files (Social Services) Regulations 1989, SI 1989/206.

5.143 The Department of Health Guidance relating to children and HIV emphasises the need for confidentiality. Many local authorities have developed their own policies to prevent unnecessary disclosure and some ensure that information about a child's HIV status is kept separately from the main set of case records. A good social worker will explain very clearly the agency's policy on confidentiality. The family can ask for assurance that disclosure will be given only if it is essential in order to receive the service in question, and then only if the individual whose status is being disclosed gives her informed consent. The National Foster Care Association advises that information should be disclosed only on a strict 'need-to-know' basis and that, for example, where the child is healthy there is no need to disclose her HIV status to a school or nursery.

5.144 There will, however, be occasions where there is a conflict between the authority's duty of confidentiality and its other duties. For example, when a child is placed with local authority foster carers, the authority must provide the foster carers with a statement giving all necessary information about the child, including health[1]. It is difficult to see how a social worker could comply with this requirement without disclosing the status of an HIV positive child to foster carers. If the child's parents are not willing to consent, the local authority may place itself in breach of its duties under the regulations by failing to disclose the child's status to the foster carers. Another dilemma for social workers may arise if a young person who is HIV positive is having a sexual relationship with another young person in the care of the authority; should priority be given to the duty of confidentiality owed to the first person, or the potential risk of transmission to the second person?

1 Foster Placement (Children) Regulations 1991, SI 1991/910, reg 5(6) and Sch 3, para (1).

5.145 Where conflicts of this kind arise, good practice indicates that social workers should always try first to obtain consent to disclosure of the relevant information. If disclosure is considered to be unavoidable, the authority should give full reasons for its decision to disclose. Some local authorities have drawn up specific guidelines on this topic. For example, the policy of the London Borough of Camden is that disclosure without consent should be made only 'where the health and well-being of a third party are of paramount importance'.

6 Regional practices

5.146 Specialist social workers can provide very useful support for families and are more likely to be sensitive to the family's concerns about confidentiality. It is often worth contacting the policy section in the relevant social services department to find out what local provisions are available. The Local Government Management Board is in the process of drawing up guidelines on good social work practice in this area. Those guidelines will apply to all authorities and it may be useful for advisers to refer to them when families have not received an adequate standard of service.

5.147 The type of services provided by each authority will of course vary according to the scale and pattern of infection in that area. In Scotland, for example, 51% of HIV positive reports are associated with the use of intravenous drugs[1]. As a result, families affected by HIV or AIDS are often coping at the same time with serious drug dependency problems, turbulent family backgrounds, mistrust of or conflict with social services and lack of support from extended family. Lothian social services offers a range of services including support for children and families at home (counselling, advocacy, home care etc), supported accommodation to keep families together, hospice care for the whole family and day care, respite and foster care for children. The service emphasises the need to keep children at home with their parents wherever possible, the importance of confidentiality, and the need to make sensitive decisions about difficult issues such as the HIV testing of children. The authority recognises that both the episodic nature of AIDS and the often chaotic lives of some families require a great deal of flexibility in the services offered. Experienced foster carers have been recruited to specialise in looking after HIV positive children and are given regular training about HIV and AIDS; all Lothian foster carers are required to accept that any child placed with them may be infected.

1 O'Hara, G 'Caring for children and families infected and affected by HIV/AIDS: A Social Work Perspective' Ch 7 *HIV Infection and Children in Need* (1993) BAAF.

5.148 The London Borough of Newham has particularly high numbers of families affected by HIV and AIDS; each year between 15 and 20 babies are born to women who are HIV positive. A conservative estimate suggests that at least 125 families in the borough are affected by HIV. The majority are of African origin. In addition to offering services such as family assessments, co-ordinated respite and childcare, advocacy and assistance with transport, the specialist team are often able to ensure the allocation of black social workers with a good understanding of the cultural needs of families who are planning for the future of their children. The authority has focused on consultation with service users, particularly HIV positive women and as a result has developed initiatives to provide short local holidays for children and their families and to consider supported housing provision.

5.149 The London Borough of Camden anticipated that it would need to provide for a very large number of children infected with HIV who would be born to drug-using parents. By the early 1990s the numbers of infected children were considerably lower than those predicted and financial and policy initiatives were redirected to other areas. A comprehensive review of the borough's provision and policies for families and children affected by HIV or AIDS is now underway. Social workers in the borough find that they are approached for assistance when informal guardianship arrangements break down, or when children who were previously asymptomatic develop AIDS-related symptoms in adolescence.

7 Challenging local authority decisions

5.150 Parents who are dissatisfied with a decision made by a local authority can consider various ways of challenging the authority. They may be able to assert their views by withdrawing themselves or the child from the service provided; if the local authority has not obtained parental responsibility, it will not be able to prevent parents from removing their children. Parents may prefer to try to resolve the disagreement by negotiation, or may seek to contest the decision in a more concrete fashion.

5.151 If the dispute is not too far advanced, it may be useful to ask for a meeting with the relevant social worker or team leader. Sometimes the presence of solicitor or other representative helps to ensure that parents feel confident in expressing their views and that their concerns are respected.

(i) Local authority complaints procedure

5.152 The Representations Procedure (Children) Regulations 1991[1] set out the procedure to be followed by local authorities in dealing with complaints relating to children and families. The local authority must supply a copy of its complaints procedure[2] and appoint an independent person to investigate the complaint[3]. Within 28 days of receivin draw up a response to the complaint and notify the complainant of that response[4]. If the response is not satisfactory, the complainant may ask for it to be considered by a review panel[5]. A successful complaint is likely to result at most in an apology or an offer to correct information held in social services' files or given to other agencies. Sometimes however a complaint will ensure that the desired services are provided.

1 SI 1991/894.
2 SI 1991/894, reg 4(1).
3 SI 1991/894, reg 5.
4 SI 1991/894, reg 8(1).
5 SI 1991/894, reg 8(2).

(ii) Complaint to the local government ombudsman

5.153 The ombudsman is an independent person appointed by Parliament to investigate complaints of local authority maladministration. Before approaching the ombudsman, the complainant is required to have given the local authority and opportunity to respond to the complaint, usually via the authority's own complaints procedure. The ombudsman can generally deal only with the process of decision-making, rather than the merits of the decision itself[1]. The ombudsman can award financial compensation as well as recommending changes in local authority practice and policy.

1 The procedure for complaining to the ombudsman is set out in a free booklet (obtainable from the Commission for Local Administration in England, 21 Queen Anne's Gate, London SW1H 9BY) and in Pt III of the Local Government Act 1974.

(iii) Judicial review

5.154 This is a process by which the High Court reviews the validity and legality of administrative decisions. The court can consider only the decision-making process, not the merits of the decision, unless it is so unreasonable that no reasonable authority could have reached that decision[1].

1 *Associated Provincial Picture Houses Ltd v Wednesbury Corpn* [1947] 2 All ER 680.

5.155 It is difficult to persuade a court to criticise the exercise of an authority's discretion, particularly in relation to the provision of services. While it is possible to argue, for example, that an authority which blames its refusal to provide a specific service on budgetary constraints has attached too much weight to that consideration and too little weight to the needs of the family, case law indicates that courts are reluctant to interfere with the balancing exercise conducted by the authority. In a 1994 case, Auld J held that a local authority could decide how much weight to attach to financial considerations when setting the range and level of day-care facilities it would provide for children in need in its area[1].

1 *R v London Borough of Barnet, ex p B* [1994] 1 FLR 592.

(iv) European Convention on Human Rights

5.156 A complaint to the European Court of Human Rights can be made only when domestic remedies have been exhausted. The majority of Convention cases relating to children allege a violation of art 8, the right to 'family life'. Article 8 can be used to prevent unjustified interference by the state, but it cannot be used to require the state 'positively to re-establish conditions of family life already impaired by the persons concerned'[1]. It remains to be seen whether following incorporation of the Convention into UK law whether families will be in a better position to argue that restrictions imposed on local authority services are capable of constituting a breach of this provision.

1 *X v Austria* (Application 8245/78), Decision of 6 May 24 DR 98 (1981).

(v) Other means of challenge

5.157 Parents can contact their own member of Parliament or councillor to try to enlist support against a decision made by social services. In some cases, a threat to release news of the decision to the media may achieve the desired outcome.

E CHILDREN AND YOUNG PEOPLE—CONSENT TO TREATMENT

5.158 Doctors treating children and young people must ensure that they have obtained valid consent before carrying out treatment. Parents have the right to consent to treatment on behalf of their children until the age of 18. Young people between the ages of 16 and 18 have the right to consent to their own surgical, medical or dental treatment[1]. Disputes may arise between parents and children about treatment issues. This will be looked at in more detail at paras **5.162–5.166**.

1 Family Law Reform Act 1969, s 8.

5.159 Young people under the age of 16 may give valid consent to their own treatment if they have sufficient understanding and intelligence. In the case of *Gillick v West Norfolk and Wisbech Area Health Authority*[1], the House of Lords held that it was not a question of a child's physical age, but the child's capacity to understand advice, consider it and make a decision that determined the right to consent to treatment. This level of understanding is now referred to as *Gillick* competence. In a case considering the capacity of an adult psychiatric patient[2], the court held that the test for competence was whether the patient could understand the 'nature, purpose and effects of the proposed treatments'. There were three stages to a patient's decision-making process to be considered: comprehending and retaining information relating to the treatment; believing the information; and weighing it up to reach a decision. *The Children Act 1989 Guidance* indicates that responsible authorities should ensure that young people are aware of their rights to consent or refuse treatment. Many health authorities have produced their own good practice guidelines about the assessment of young people's capacity and obtaining consent.

1 [1986] AC 112, [1985] 3 All ER 402, HL.
2 *Re C (refusal of medical treatment)* [1994] 1 FLR 31.

5.160 For those who are too young, or do not meet these criteria, the consent of a person with parental responsibility or of the court must be obtained. In limited circumstances, the consent of an adult without parental responsibility will be valid. The Children Act 1989 provides that whilst a person may not surrender or transfer parental responsibility, some or all of th may be delegated to another person[1]. A carer to whom parental responsibility has been delegated may be able to consent to treatment, but such consent is likely only to be accepted by medical practitioners in the case of relatively minor treatment, unless a written agreement is available. Similarly, the provision in the Children Act 1989 for a carer without parental responsibility to 'do what is reasonable in all the circumstances of the case for the purpose of safeguarding or promoting the child's welfare'[2] may also allow a carer to consent to very minor treatment[3].

1 Children Act 1989, s 2(9).
2 Children Act 1989, s 3(5).
3 Plomer, A' Parental Consent and Children's Medical Treatment' (1996) Fam Law 740.

5.161 In emergencies, doctors may treat a child without consent where the best interests of the child demand the treatment: 'a doctor may safely carry out treatment in an emergency if the doctor believes the treatment to be vital to the survival or health of an infant or the impossibility of alerting the parent before the treatment is carried out.'[1] Generally, however, the consent of a person with parental responsibility will be required.

1 *Gillick v West Norfolk and Wisbech Area Health Authority and the DHSS* [1986] AC 112, per Lord Templeman at 200.

1 Disputes between parents and children

5.162 Difficulties may arise where a young person who is competent in the *Gillick* sense disagrees with her parents about treatment. Where that dispute cannot be resolved, parents or the treating authority, may ask the court to adjudicate. In the case of *Re C (refusal of medical treatment)*[1] the High Court held that it could make a finding as to whether an individual was capable of consenting to or refusing medical treatment and could rule by way of an injunction, or declaration on the basis of that finding.

1 [1994] 1 All ER 819, [1994] 1 WLR 290.

5.163 In the Court of Appeal case of *Re W*[1] it was held that where a child of any age who was *Gillick* competent (in the context of the particular treatment in question) consented to treatment, this could not be overridden by the parents. The courts, however, could override the minor's consent to treatment and those with parental responsibility would need to apply to the court to ask for treatment to be withheld[1]. In *Re B (wardship: abortion)*[2], the local authority applied for the termination of the pregnancy of a 12-year-old girl. The girl wanted the abortion, but her mother opposed it. The High Court held that although the mother's wishes were important, the child's best interests were of overriding importance. In a 1995 case[3] a mother attempted to ensure that her children would never be given blood transfusions. She insisted that the children carry cards making it clear to doctors that she did not consent to the use of blood products on religious grounds. The father, however, did not object to these forms of treatment. The court held that the mother could not override any consent that might be given by the father or the court.

1 *Re W (a minor) (medical treatment: court's jurisdiction)* [1993] Fam 64, sub nom *Re W (a minor) (consent to medical treatment)* [1993] 1 FLR 1, per Lord Donaldson.
2 [1991] 2 FLR 426, [1991] Fam Law 379.
3 *Re S (minors)* (8 February 1995, unreported).

5.164 Where the young person herself is refusing treatment, courts are generally more willing to override such a refusal, particularly where her health will be at risk if treatment is not given. In *Re R (a minor) (wardship: medical treatment)*[1] the Court of Appeal held that whilst the child may be able to consent to treatment he or she may not be able to prevent treatment, if the court or parents consent. In this case a mentally disturbed 15-year-old was suffering from suicidal thoughts and hallucinations. She refused to take anti-psychotic medication. The local authority applied for her to be made a ward of court and for leave to administer medication without her consent. The judge at first instance applied *Gillick*. He held that she had capacity to consent to treatment and that it was not for the court to overturn the decision in *Re R*[1]. The Official Solicitor asked for guidance on the question of whether the child was competent in the *Gillick* sense and, if so, whether the parents or the court had power to override the decision of a competent minor.

1 [1992] 1 FLR 190.

5.165 The court held that the fact that a child was deemed to be *Gillick* competent did not terminate the parents' right to consent to treatment. The court, however, had the power to override the decisions of both parents and competent minors where to do so would be in the best interests of the minor.

5.166 This position was confirmed in the important case of *Re W (a minor) (medical treatment: court's jurisdiction)*[1]. The Court of Appeal confirmed that the refusal of even a competent minor was not decisive, but that it was an important consideration for doctors, parents and the court in deciding whether to recommend treatment or to give consent on behalf of the child. In this case, the court considered that the wishes of a 16-year-old girl were of reduced significance because the anorexia from which she suffered affected her ability to make an informed choice. Medical evidence indicated that the anorexia itself created; 'a compulsion to refuse treatment or only to accept treatment which is likely to be ineffective'[2]. Balcombe J commented that if the court's powers were 'to be meaningful there must come a point at which the court, while not disregarding the child's wishes can override them in the child's best interests, objectively considered.'

1 [1993] Fam 64, [1992] 4 All ER 627, CA.
2 [1993] Fam 64.

2 Disputes between parents and medical practitioners

5.167 Adults generally have the right to decide whether to accept treatment, even if refusal will lead to death. It has been held that it is irrelevant whether the reasons for refusal are 'irrational, unknown or non-existent'[1]. Courts are less likely, however, to allow parents to make decisions of this kind about treatment for their children. They have consented to treatment for minors in a number of cases in the face of opposition from parents.

1 *C v K (inherent powers)* [1996] 2 FLR 506.

5.168 Parental opposition to the recommended treatment is often based on the parents' own religious beliefs. Courts are reluctant to accept thi and have frequently overruled parents' refusal to allow the use of blood products or blood transfusions because of religious beliefs[1]. Where medical opinion is clearly in favour of treatment, the court is likely to authorise it.

1 *Re S (a minor) (medical treatment)* [1993] 1 FLR 376; *Re R (a minor) (blood transfusion)* [1993] 2 FLR 757; *Re S (a minor) (consent to medical treatment)* [1994] 2 FLR 1065.

5.169 The other main reason for parental objection to treatment is that in the long term the child will suffer more than if the treatment is not authorised. There is 'a strong presumption in favour of a course of action which will prolong life...[but] account has to be taken of the pain and suffering and quality of life a child will experience'[1]. Where there is conflicting medical evidence, parental views as to what is in the best interests of the child may be of more weight.

1 *Re J (a minor) (wardship: medical treatment)* [1991] 1 FLR 375, per Lord Donaldson.

5.170 These issues have been considered in detail in the 1997 case of *Re T (a minor) (wardship; medical treatment)*[1]. Here, the Court of Appeal considered not only the clinical issues but a 'broad range of environmental factors'[2]. In this case, a child born with a liver defect had undergone an early operation which had caused pain and distress. Without a transplant, substantial future medical intervention and a very high level of care from his mother, the child was unlikely to survive beyond the age of two or three. The local authority applied for permission to bring the child back into the jurisdiction (the child and mother had gone to join the father who was working abroad) and carry out the operation. The judge at first instance held that the mother was being unreasonable in her refusal and that it was in the child's best interests to have the operation.

1 [1997] 1 All ER 906, [1997] 1 WLR 242, CA.
2 Loughrey, J 'Medical Treatment – The Status of Parental Opinion' (1998) Fam Law 147.

5.171 The Court of Appeal found that the judge should have concentrated on the child's best interests, not whether the mother's refusal was unreasonable. Butler-Sloss LJ found that the judge should have assessed the weight of the mother's concern about the benefits of the operation, the danger of failure of the treatment and the possible need for future transplants. In this case an important issue was the view of one doctor that it would be inappropriate to operate without the mother's consent, because the child would need the mother's support for many years to come in order for the treatment to be successful. It was central that: 'this mother and child are one for the purpose of this unusual case and the decision of the court to consent to the operation jointly affects the mother and son. The welfare of the child depends on his mother.'[1] The parents had made a decision in the best interests of their child and the refusal to consent to treatment was upheld.

1 *Medical Treatment – The Status of Parental Opinion* p 148.

5.172 In the case of *Re C (a minor) (medical treatment)*[1], however, the parents of a seriously disabled and dying child were unwilling to agree that her ventilator should be turned off because of their religious beliefs. The child's doctors considered that it was not in her best interests to prolong her life. The court authorised the withdrawal of ventilation from the child.

1 [1998] 1 FLR 384, [1998] 1 FCR 1.

3 Children and blood tests

5.173 The question of consent to blood tests for children will usually arise in the context of a paternity dispute and sometimes in relation to a financial application for a child. Where paternity is in issue, the court may give a direction for the use of blood tests. Samples may then be taken from the child, the mother and the alleged father of the child[1]. Adults and young people over the age of 16 can consent on their own behalf; consent for a child under 16 years of age must be given by the person with 'care and control' of the child[2]. The court has the power to direct blood tests, but cannot compel anyone to give a sample; the court may, however, draw such inferences from the refusal as seem proper[3].

1 Family Law Reform Act 1969, Pt III.
2 FLRA 1969, Pt III, s 21.
3 FLRA 1969, Pt III, s 23.

5.174 Where it appears that the child may be HIV positive, or where there is a contested application for a child to be tested for HIV, the application should be made in the High Court. In the case of *Re W(a minor)*[1] it was held to be in the child's best interest to test the child for HIV where parents had died of AIDS-related illnesses and the court was considering the question of residence.

1 [1995] 2 FCR 184.

5.175 In the widely reported case of *Re C*[1] the London Borough of Camden sought a specific issue order under s 8 of the Children Act 1989 requiring a four-month old baby to be tested for HIV. Her mother had been HIV positive for about nine years; she had breastfed the child since birth despite medical advice that to do so risked transmission of HIV to the baby. The parents refused to agree that the baby should be tested. They did not accept current medical practice and research in the field of paediatric HIV. They argued that HIV tests were inaccurate and misleading and that the baby would not benefit from a test because they would not agree in any event that she should have any HIV-related treatment. Both parents were alternative health care practitioners who argued that their own approach to natural and healthy living offered the best possible option for their child.

1 (1999) Times, 14 September.

5.176 The court was not asked to decide whether the child should receive any medication if she tested positive; the arguments focused on the risk that the child was already infected and that she might become ill in the future. The two consultants who gave evidence insisted that the child should be tested so that if she did become ill she could receive the appropriate treatment. They argued that the parents were denying the child her right to the best available medical care, even though she was apparently healthy at the time of the hearing. All parties agreed that it would be inappropriate for the court to seek to prevent the mother from breastfeeding; such an order would have been impossible to enforce.

5.177 The judge accepted the medical evidence and ordered that the test should be carried out. He accepted the vehemence and sincerity of the parents' views but held that their wishes were outweighed by the benefit to the child of ascertaining her HIV status. At the time of going to press the parents had failed to comply with the order. Their application for permission to appeal failed.

5.178 Although the decision of the court was consistent with the approach in the treatment cases considered in paras **5.167–5.172**, it raised serious issues with regard to the ability of a local authority to encroach upon the autonomy of parents with deeply held but unconventional views, particularly when the local authority does so without having to meet the criteria required for a care or supervision order. Women contemplating an HIV test before or during pregnancy will also need to know that once they have given birth, their choices may be overridden if the doctors treating their child do not agree with their decisions. Many AIDS charities supported the judge's ruling but others were concerned that it might deter pregnant women from being tested and that the problem of paediatric HIV might be driven underground.

F BIBLIOGRAPHY

Batty, D (ed) *HIV Infection and Children in Need* (1993) British Agencies for Adoption and Fostering.

Bedingfield, D *The Child in Need –Children, the State and the Law* (1998) Jordans.

Bor, R and Elford, J *The Family and HIV* (1994) Cassell.

Duke, C and Kovar, Ilya Z 'HIV and the Paediatrician as the Child's Advocate' (1996) *Lancet* Vol 348 July 27.

Faden, R and Kass, N eds *HIV, AIDS and Childbearing Public Policy, Private Lives* (1996) OUP, New York.

Fratter, J 'Positive Options Planning Scheme' in *HIV Infection and Children in Need* (1993) BAAF Ch 7.

Geballe, S, Greundel, J and Andiman, W (eds) *Forgotten Children of the AIDS Epidemic* (1995) Yale University Press.

General Medical Council *Duties of a Doctor; HIV and AIDS; The Ethical Considerations* (1995) GMC.

Hershman, D and McFarlane, A *Children Law and Practice* (1998) Jordans.

Imrie J and Coombes, Y *No time to waste: the scale and dimensions of the problem of children affected by HIV/AIDS in the United Kingdom* (1995) Barnardos.

Loughrey, J 'Medical Treatment – The Status of Parental Opinion' (1998) Fam Law 146.

Mahon, N B 'Public Hysteria, Private Conflict: Child Custody and Visitation Disputes Involving an HIV Infected Parent' (1998) 63 *New York University Law Review* 1092.

Morton, S and Johnson, D (ed) *Children and HIV: Supporting Children and their Families* (1996) The Stationery Office, Edinburgh.

Plomer, A 'Parental Consent and Children's Medical Treatment' (1996) Fam Law 739.

Senak, M S *HIV and the Law – A Guide to our Rights and Challenges* Director of Planning AIDS Project of LA. (1996) Insight Books, Plenum Press NY.

Thorpe, L J 'The Courts and Medical Treatment' (1996) Fam Law 728.

Zantar, R *The Practitioner's Guide to Child Law* (1998).

Chapter 6

Immigration and the right to travel

Wesley Gryk

A INTRODUCTION

6.01 The UK has, relatively speaking, pursued a sensible and commendable approach with respect to the immigration issues arising relating to HIV and AIDS. It has heeded the call of the World Health Organisation, the United Nations, the Council of Europe and various other specialist agencies that the mere fact of being HIV positive should not preclude individuals from being admitted to or remaining in the country, provided that they otherwise qualify under prevailing immigration law and practice.

6.02 This approach is in contrast to that followed by dozens of other countries which have policies refusing the admission of those affected by HIV and AIDS. Such countries are attempting to apply a 'fortress' defence against the spread of the HIV virus. It is their misguided assumption that the attempted restriction of the movement of HIV positive individuals will be an effective measure to prevent the spread of the virus when, in fact, the single most effective strategy is the dissemination of information on how the transmission of the virus itself can be prevented. The United States provides a striking example of this misguided approach. Whilst that country's laws prevent the admission of an HIV positive individual even for purposes of a short visit as a tourist, the rate of HIV infection there far exceeds that of the UK and many other countries which impose no travel restrictions on those affected by HIV.

6.03 An individual's HIV status may, nonetheless, be relevant to his or her right to enter or remain in the UK. The main purpose of this chapter is to outline such situations. It should be stressed, however, that British immigration law is technically complex and important rights can be lost if an individual fails to make a timely or correct application, or fails to file an appeal against a negative decision within strict time limits. Whilst this chapter provides general guidance on the issues which it covers, an individual facing a specific problem should seek expert guidance from a specialised agency or a solicitor with expertise in the field of immigration. The government sponsored 'Legal Help' scheme will enable such advisers to provide guidance without

6.04 This chapter will consider how an individual's HIV status may be relevant at the time of entry to the UK or, subsequently, when making an application to extend one's stay. It will address special situations in which an individual may find it necessary to make an application based purely upon the compelling and compassionate circumstances arising from illness, as well as the particular relevance which HIV status may have in political asylum cases and in the application of the recently announced revised government guidelines relating to the admission of 'unmarried partners' including same-sex partners. The chapter will also review the Home Office's policy with respect to allowing 'carers' to remain to look after those who are ill and, finally, will discuss some precautions which should be taken by British-based individuals contemplating travel abroad to countries with restrictive rules relating to the admission of HIV positive individuals.

B IMMIGRATION CONTROL ON ENTERING THE UK

1 Categories of individuals seeking leave to enter the UK

6.05 The complex system regarding who may enter the UK and under what circumstances is set out in the Immigration Act 1971 (as amended) and in the Immigration Rules[1] laid before Parliament by the Home Secretary as provided for in the Immigration Act. In addition, citizens of European Economic Area (EEA) states (other than the UK and the Republic of Ireland) are governed by European law rather than British immigration law.

1 The current Immigration Rules are HC 395, as amended.

6.06 It is beyond the scope of this chapter to describe in detail the technical labyrinth of the immigration system. Basically, under the system, some categories of individuals are not subject to immigration control under the Immigration Act 1971 and the Immigration Rules. These include 'British citizens' as defined by the British Nationality Act 1981, certain British Commonwealth citizens who fit into a very narrow category of individuals defined as having the 'right of abode' and citizens of the Republic of Ireland travelling to the UK from the Republic of Ireland.

6.07 Similarly, as indicated, citizens of other EEA states do not fall under British immigration law since their movement within the EEA is governed by European law. They can enter the UK to work or seek work and to provide or seek services. Members of their family may also enter the UK even if they themselves are not EEA nationals. Students, pensioners and other categories of EEA citizens also have specific rights of entry. Whilst restrictions on the right of entry by EEA nationals can be imposed for public health reasons, neither AIDS nor any HIV-related illness is listed in the annexe to Directive 64/221, which under art 4 of that Directive comprises the only list of diseases or disabilities justifying refusal of entry. Those individuals not falling under any of the above categories will be subject to the Immigration Act 1971 and the Immigration Rules upon entering the UK. This group of individuals is in turn divided into two further groups, 'visa nationals' and 'non-visa nationals'.

6.08 'Visa nationals' are persons coming from countries listed in an appendix to the Immigration Rules with respect to which the British government has decided that an individual must always obtain a visa (also called an 'entry clearance') from a British Consulate in their country of residence before seeking to enter the UK. The countries with respect to which visas are required tend to be those countries which produce the most political asylum seekers and/or those countries where the level of development is such that the British government is concerned about large influxes of 'economic migrants'.

6.09 'Non-visa nationals' comprise those individuals who do not come from one of those countries with respect to which the Immigration Rules require a visa. Even such 'non-visa nationals', however, may need to obtain a visa beforehand if coming to the UK for certain defined long-term purposes such as marriage, to be reunited with other family members, to set up business or take employment. To make things even more complicated, 'non-visa nationals' may choose to apply for a visa before travelling even if one is not required—eg to come as visitor or student—to ensure that they meet the criteria of admission before travelling. They might do this, for example, if they have previously been refused leave to enter at a British port for some reason.

2 UK policy on the entry of those affected by HIV and AIDS

6.10 For many years, the UK government has maintained a policy that HIV infection (including AIDS) should not in itself be considered justification for recommendation on public health grounds to refuse 'leave to enter' the UK. This policy was first made public when extracts of a letter from the Chief Medical Officer to port medical inspectors was quoted in the *New Scientist* of 6 July 1991 and subsequently reconfirmed by the Department of Health.

6.11 The position has been most fully set out by the government in a set of guidelines entitled *AIDS and HIV Positive Cases* produced in August 1995[1]. Paragraph 2.1 states the basic premise:

> 'The fact that a person is suffering from AIDS or is HIV positive is not grounds for refusing entry clearance or leave to remain *if the person otherwise qualifies under the Immigration Rules.*'

1 See *Butterworths Immigration Law Service,* paras **D[901]–[950]**.

6.12 Paragraphs 3 and 4 of the guidelines set out the specific approaches to be taken respectively by an Entry Clearance Officer considering granting a visa at a British consulate abroad or by an Immigration Officer when an individual applies for entry at a port:

> '3 *Entry clearance*
>
> 3.1 Applications for entry clearance from persons who disclose that they are suffering from AIDS/HIV may be referred by the ECO [Entry Clearance Officer] to the Home Office via MVD [Migration and Visa Department]. The applicant should fully meet the requirements of the Immigration Rules for the

suggest that the applicant is currently in need of regular medication or treatment, he should provide evidence of his ability to meet the costs of such medication or treatment during his stay. This is in addition to the usual requirements as regards maintenance and accommodation. A person with AIDS/HIV seeking an entry clearance to come to the UK for medical treatment should meet the usual requirements of the medical visitors' rules.

3.2 As explained in paragraph 2.1, the fact that a person suffers from AIDS, or is HIV positive, is not in itself grounds for refusing entry clearance. However, where in any cases it appears that public health may be at risk, advice should be sought from:

Department of Health
International Relations Unit 13
Room 538, Richmond House
79 Whitehall
London
SW1A 2NA
Tel 0171 210 4866

4 *On entry*

4.1 The policy and practice on entry at ports will be to adhere to the provisions of the Rules. Where a passenger is found to be suffering from AIDS, the advice of the PMO [Port Medical Officer] will be sought in the normal way in order to determine whether the passenger can satisfy the Rules. Where a passenger does not qualify, entry is to be refused.'

6.13 The main constraint inherent in this policy is a constraint which applies similarly to all medical conditions. Under certain circumstances, individuals concerned will need to be in a position to demonstrate an ability to pay for any medical treatment which may be required because of HIV-related illness during their stay in the UK. Individuals allowed to stay or legally intending to stay permanently and individuals with 'ordinary residence' in the UK should not be subjected to this condition. 'Ordinary residence' includes not only those intending to stay permanently but individuals who have lived in the UK for a period of not less that one year, work permit holders and various other categories. For a fuller definition of 'ordinary residence', see the National Health Service (Charge to Overseas Visitors) Regulations 1989[1]. See also discussion of the definition of 'ordinary residence' by the House of Lords in *Shah v Barnet London Borough Council*[2] where it is referred to as a person's abode adopted voluntarily and for settled purposes as part of the regular order of one's life for the time being whether for long or short duration[3]. The NHS is currently conducting an internal review of its regulations in this area and the Home Office has advised that it will re-examine its HIV policy once the scope of the NHS review is known.

1 SI 1989/306, as amended by the National Health Service (Charges to Overseas Visitors) (Amendment) Regulations, SI 1994/1535.

2 [1983] 2 AC 309.

3 [1998] 2 All ER 728, CA. A recent Court of Appeal case, however, has challenged this definition and is due to be heard by the House of Lords relating to the interchangeable concept of 'habitual residence' used in the social security regulations. In *Nessa v Chief Adjudication Officer* [1998] 2 All ER 728, CA, the Court of Appeal held that 'habitual residence' could not be acquired on the date of one's arrival in the UK even if it was 'for a settled purpose'.

6.14 An individual may also, of course, be able to demonstrate an ability to pay for necessary medical treatment by showing that he or she comes from a country with a reciprocal healthcare agreement with the UK.

6.15 Provisions relating to the function of medical inspectors at the port and their right to carry out medical tests and examinations of those seeking to enter the UK are set out in Sch 2 to the Immigration Act 1971. In cases where a medical inspector considers that an entrant, subject to immigration control, is likely to require medical treatment during his or her stay in the UK and, further, such an individual is responsible for covering the cost of such treatment, the medical inspector is meant to provide an estimate of the cost of such treatment to the immigration officer concerned so that the decision can be taken whether or not the potential entrant has the means to meet these costs.

6.16 In fact, there appear to have been very few refusals of HIV positive individuals resulting from these procedures. One factor, of course, is that in most cases an immigration officer is unable to determine by visual inspection alone that an individual is HIV positive and therefore referrals to the medical inspector are rarely triggered. Furthermore, individuals affected by HIV are not likely to raise the issue themselves unless they are specifically seeking to enter the UK as a 'medical visitor'[1].

1 See paras **6.17–6.19**.

3 Entering the UK for private medical treatment

6.17 As indicated in paragraph 3.1 in the Home Office's August 1995 guidelines, a person may seek entry clearance (or, with respect to non-visa nationals, leave to enter the UK at a port) as a 'medical visitor' coming specifically for medical treatment. Paragraph 51 of the Immigration Rules sets out the main requirements for admission on this basis:

(a) such individuals must not intend to take employment or otherwise engage in business or study at a maintained school;
(b) they must be able to maintain and accommodate themselves and any dependants without recourse to public funds;
(c) they must be able to meet the cost of their return or onward journey;
(d) if they are suffering from a communicable disease, the medical inspector must be satisfied that there is no danger to public health (but it should be emphasised that HIV positive status and AIDS do not qualify as a 'communicable diseases' for these purposes);
(e) they must be able to show that any proposed course of treatment is finite;
(f) they must intend to leave the UK at the end of their treatment;
(g) they must provide satisfactory evidence of their medical condition, arrangements for the necessary consultation or treatment at their own expense, the estimated costs of such a consultation or treatment, the likely duration of their visit and the existence of sufficient funds available to them in the UK to meet the estimated costs.

6.18 Whilst, ordinarily, a visitor's status cannot be extended beyond six months, the stay of a 'medical visitor' can be extended provided that the conditions in para **6.17** have been met. In addition, individuals seeking to extend leave to remain in the UK on this basis must be able to:

(a) produce evidence from a registered medical practitioner who holds an consultation or treatment and its likely duration and, where treatment has already begun, evidence as to its progress;

(b) show that they have met, out of resources available to them, any costs and expenses incurred in relation to their treatment in the UK thus far; and

(c) show that they have sufficient funds available to them in the UK to meet the likely costs of their treatment and intend to meet those costs.

6.19 With respect to individuals affected by HIV and AIDS who are seeking to take advantage of these rules, perhaps the most important condition to meet is to demonstrate that the necessity for medical advice and treatment will be finite. Since the treatment of HIV and AIDS is, necessarily, ongoing treatment, one would need to demonstrate that the individual concerned is coming for treatment for a particular HIV-related illness or, alternatively, is coming to seek specific discrete advice which could then be implemented abroad by the individual concerned after leaving the UK.

C APPLICATION TO REMAIN BY THOSE ALREADY IN THE UK

1 Categories of individuals

6.20 The strategy followed by individuals affected by HIV and AIDS who are already in the UK and wish to remain here will necessarily vary according to their particular immigration status. Again, the law in this area is complex and specialist advice should be sought regarding individual cases. Some general advice regarding the approach in different categories of cases, however, can be provided.

6.21 It is necessary, first of all, to have a general understanding of the different categories into which individuals may fall. The most straightforward category, of course, is someone who continues to have legal permission to remain in the UK. This would include, for example, someone who has been granted leave to enter the UK at a port for a set period of time and that period has not yet expired. Alternatively, the individual, after having been granted leave to enter at a port, might have sought further leave to remain from the Home Office and still fall within the period of that leave to remain.

6.22 In two other categories of case, the Home Office may have reached a determination that an individual is in the UK illegally and may seek to take enforcement action. In the first of these, the individual concerned will have remained in the UK beyond the time period granted by the immigration officer at the port granting leave to enter or the Home Office official granting further leave to remain. In such cases, the individual will be deemed an overstayer and will be subject to deportation.

6.23 In a further category of case, the Home Office may have reached a determination that the individual concerned had entered the country illegally by, for example, making misrepresentations in obtaining a visa or to the immigration officer, by presenting false documentation or by evading immigration control altogether. In such cases, the Home Office could designate the individual an illegal entrant and seek to issue removal directions against him or her.

6.24 It should be noted that different procedures relate to the deportation of overstayers and the removal of illegal entrants. For present purposes, these need not be described in any detail but the legal rights—particularly appeal rights—attached to each vary considerably, with a decision to deport attracting a formal right of appeal and no such right attaching to the removal of an illegal entrant. In any event, this scheme is likely to be amended under the terms of the Immigration and Asylum Bill 1999, which, while not yet enacted into law at the time of writing, provides in its present form for this distinction between deportation and removal to be abolished in many cases as of October 2000.

6.25 A final category consists of those individuals said to be in the UK on temporary admission. The vast majority of these individuals are persons pursuing applications for political asylum. This category also includes people who have been refused entry to the UK but have been temporarily admitted for a short period of time for compassionate or practical reasons. Essentially, an immigration officer granting an individual temporary admission is saying that the individual may physically enter the UK for the time being but that he or she has not been legally recognised as having entered the country. A form (IS 96) is issued to the individuals concerned indicating that they have temporary admission and setting out the address where they must continue to reside and other conditions which must be met.

2 Applications by individuals legally in the country

6.26 Individuals who have current leave to enter or remain in the UK are in the strongest position in terms of applying for further leave to remain. The Immigration Rules set out in detail the particular bases on which such individuals may apply to extend their stay in the UK and, provided that any such application is made while the individual's stay remains legal, there are likely to be appeal rights in the event of a refusal. As already quoted in para **6.11**, the Home Office's August 1995 guidelines make clear that:

> 'The fact that a person is suffering from AIDS or is HIV positive is not grounds for refusing…leave to remain *if the person concerned otherwise qualifies under the Immigration Rules.*'

6.27 An individual affected by HIV and AIDS who is legally in the UK and wishes to stay here should, therefore, logically consider all the potential options available under the Immigration Rules and, if one is applicable, make an application under the rule. There is no need to raise the issue of HIV in such an application (unless, of course, that application is made under the 'medical visitor' rule described in paras **6.17–6.19**).

6.28 Even in cases where there appears to be no applicable category in the Immigration Rules under which an individual may apply for further leave to remain in the UK, those affected by HIV and AIDS in such cases may consider making an application 'outside of the Rules' for 'exceptional leave to remain' in the light of the particular compelling and compassionate circumstances of their situation. Paragraph 5.1 of the Home Office's August 1995 guidelines specifically provides for such applications:

> '5 *After entry*
>
> 5.1 Any application for leave to remain where there is evid[illegible]
> AIDS/HIV is a factor should normall[illegible]

the Immigration Rules. However, in some cases there may be strong compassionate circumstances which justify the exercise of discretion outside the Rules even though treatment is provided on the NHS.'

6.29 Any such application, which should be lodged on Home Office form FLR(O) with the information required by that form, should also be accompanied by comprehensive documentation regarding the compassionate nature of the particular case. Paragraph 5.2 of the Home Office guidelines specifically provides that a doctor's report should be included, confirming that the individual has AIDS or is HIV positive, the life expectancy, the nature and location of treatment being received and fitness to travel if required to leave the country. This doctor's report should set out as fully as possible: the individual's condition; serious illnesses already suffered; and the frank prognosis of the individual's long-term prospects. It may also be appropriate to set out the individual's CD4 count and viral load at relevant times in the individual's treatment, including at the time of diagnosis, at their lowest point and following the administration of combination therapy or other treatment.

6.30 In cases where the individual is receiving combination therapy or other treatment, the short- and long-term effects of withdrawing treatment from the patient should be explained in full and documented. To the extent that the doctor is aware of the non-availability of such treatment in the patient's home country, this too should be set out. If possible, the application should include firsthand information from that country regarding the availability there of the treatment which the patient is receiving. If the treatment is very expensive, evidence should be produced that an individual in the situation of the applicant could not afford the treatment if returned to the country and, therefore, would effectively be unable to continue such treatment.

6.31 In some cases, it may be relevant to demonstrate that, whilst the necessary drugs are available, the necessary medical personnel resources are lacking to monitor their administration, effectiveness and possible side effects. Specialist organisations such as the Advice Centre of the Terrence Higgins Trust can be approached for such information in the first instance. If they are unable to provide specific information, they may be able to provide leads as to agencies, hospitals, etc in the applicant's home country which may be in a position to offer relevant information. Embassies, almanacs and other sources of general factual information may be able to provide statistics about the average earnings of citizens of the applicant's country in order to demonstrate the infeasibility of paying for whatever treatment is available. It is extremely important to document assertions about the availability of treatment as fully as possible. Letters from others aware of the applicant's case such as social workers, friends and relatives may also be appropriate for submission to the Home Office to draw attention to compassionate factors in the case. They may helpfully address issues such as the availability of care, support and accommodation in the UK and contrast this with what the applicant's situation would be if they were returned home. These are points which may bring the applicants within the ambit of the European Convention on Human Rights by demonstrating that they would face 'acute physical suffering' if returned to their home country[1].

1 See paras **6.50**ff.

6.32 Paragraph 5.3 of the Home Office's August 1995 guidelines provides that the Home Office itself may seek information from the diplomatic post in the country concerned regarding the availability of treatment for AIDS in the applicant's own country. The information received through this process is of widely differing quality and reliability and should be challenged vigorously if it falsely presents too optimistic a picture of the availability of treatment in the home country.

6.33 Paragraph 5.4 of the guidelines sets out, somewhat ambiguously, the test to be applied by the Home Office in considering the grant of exceptional leave in such cases:

> '5.4 In many cases the medical facilities and treatment available in the person's country of origin will be substantially less advanced than those available in the UK. This is likely to be true as regards any serious illness and does not in itself constitute grounds for allowing someone with AIDS/HIV to remain. However, there may be cases where it is apparent that there are no facilities for treatment available in the applicant's own country. Where evidence suggests that this absence of treatment would significantly shorten the life expectancy of the applicant it will normally be appropriate to grant leave to remain.'

6.34 These guidelines were drafted prior to the widespread use of combination therapy and, indeed, in paragraph 2.1 state that 'treatments [for AIDS] are unable to extend a person's life expectancy significantly.' This situation has, of course, changed since the development of combination therapy. In those cases, therefore, where an applicant is receiving combination therapy and would not be able to continue receiving such therapy in his or her home country—either because of its total non-availability or because of its impossibly prohibitive cost—the application should arguably be successful in the light of the guidelines' suggestion that it will 'normally be appropriate to grant leave to remain' where 'this absence of treatment would significantly shorten the life expectancy'.

6.35 The Home Office has in fact repeatedly been willing to grant exceptional leave to remain in the UK in such cases where applicants have been able to demonstrate that, effectively, they will be unable to continue their present treatment if returned to their home country and the effects of this are likely to be a significant shortening of their life expectancy. In this regard, the doctor's prognosis regarding the effects of withdrawal of combination therapy or other treatment will be particularly important. In some cases, a doctor may be able to provide an opinion not only as to the resumption of the deterioration of the applicant's physical condition upon withdrawal of the treatment but, further, address the issue that, in some cases, the fact of starting combination therapy and then withdrawing it may in fact leave an individual worse off than if he or she had never commenced the treatment. This would be an important point to make if backed up by medical opinion.

6.36 One potential pitfall in the guidelines also needs to be addressed. Paragraph 5.4 of the guidelines states that it will normally be appropriate to grant leave to remain when the absence of treatment would significantly shorten the life expectancy of the applicant in those 'cases where it is apparent that there are *no facilities* for treatment available in the applicant's own country'. The question arises, therefore, what approach would be taken in those cases where, in the home country, palliative available to ease the physical suffering of a patient but combination therapy or other life-prolonging treatments are not available. It would seem an absurd result if, in such cases, discretion were not to be exercised on a compelling and compassionate basis with respect to individuals whose life expectancy was to be significantly shortened if returned, just because some palliative treatment was available. The fact that the Home Office has indeed allowed applications in a number of such cases indicates that informed decision-makers there have been prepared to grant exceptional leave to remain in those cases where applicants can demonstrate no *effective* facilities for continuing treatment of an individual.

6.37 There are two interesting additional features included in the Home Office's August 1995 guidelines relating to the granting of such exceptional leave to remain. First of all, in paragraph 5.5, the guidelines indicate that caseworkers, in deciding whether to refuse an application, should '...be aware that allowing time for appeals etc the medical picture may look very different by the time enforcement is being considered.' In such cases, where deterioration of the individual's condition is likely and, therefore, the individual may either be unfit to travel or may have only a few months to live, the suggestion is that a positive decision should be taken.

6.38 In fact, in the not too distant past—before the widespread advent of combination therapy and its resultant effect in prolonging life—an applicant was most likely to be successful in obtaining exceptional leave to remain in the UK where he or she could demonstrate that life expectancy was very short. Applications made by those who had already suffered HIV-related illness and whose immune systems were most severely compromised were most likely to be successful. Not surprisingly, the Home Office was most willing to show compassion in those cases where the ultimate burden on the resources of the UK was likely to be relatively small because of the short life expectancy of the individual concerned.

6.39 As in so many other areas relating to HIV, the advent of combination therapy—carrying with it the potential of individuals being able to lead relatively ordinary lives for many years—changes the picture of how individual cases should be approached when making representations to the Home Office. Of course it remains highly relevant in preparing such representations if it can be demonstrated that an individual's life expectancy is short. In most cases today, however, the argument to be made will be that refusal to grant exceptional leave to remain to an individual will result in the withdrawal of necessary life-prolonging treatment, thereby radically reducing the life expectancy of an individual who, if allowed to continue to remain, might well survive for many years.

6.40 At the same time, advisers making such applications must be sensitive to the controversial issue that the successful resolution of such cases necessarily entails a commitment by the UK to provide continuing medical and other support for applicants and their families over a long period of time. From the presentation point of view, this ties in with a second interesting additional feature included in the Home Office August 1995 guidelines. The guidelines note, in paragraph 5.6, that '[c]ases involving AIDS/HIV are emotive and have the potential for considerable publicity.' The guidelines go on to suggest that such publicity may not only be negative if the Home Office takes uncompassionate decisions but, equally, that there may be 'adverse publicity if it became clear that we were routinely permitting anyone with AIDS or who was HIV positive to remain here to receive treatment at public expense.' The guidelines require, therefore, that all such cases be referred to Senior Executive Officer level for decision.

6.41 Obviously, those advising applicants for exceptional leave because of their health must be aware of the emotive nature of the issues involved. The reality is that there are tens of millions of individuals affected by HIV around the world. Neither the UK nor any other country can begin to assume the burden of providing treatment for massive numbers of individuals unable to obtain such treatment in their own countries. In making individual applications, therefore, it is helpful to stress any compelling and compassionate circumstances which indicate that the case is an exceptional one with unique characteristics making it particularly meritorious. Cases, for example, where an applicant has come to the UK for another purpose and then been caught unawares by a medical crisis are more likely to be considered sympathetically by the Home Office than cases where an individual appears to have come to the UK specifically to take advantage of the National Health Service. Considerable thought needs to be exerted in drafting tactful and persuasive representations to the Home Office in individual cases which take into account such sensitive issues.

3 Cases where enforcement action is being considered

6.42 The August 1995 guidelines apply specifically to applications for leave to enter at a port and for further leave to remain to the Home Office. They do not address specifically the policy to be followed by the Home Office with respect to cases where an individual is an overstayer or an illegal entrant and where deportation or removal is being considered.

6.43 The existence of specific guidelines relating to such 'enforcement cases' became known during the course of a judicial review action in 1998 when the Terrence Higgins Trust, representing an applicant, was served with a copy of a document entitled *Enforcement action in AIDS and HIV positive cases*. The document is dated January 1996 and signed 'IS (Enforcement), Enforcement Policy Group'. The formulation included in this document is similar to the August 1995 guidelines and, perhaps, even slightly more positive:

> '2 *Policy*
>
> The general IS(E) [Immigration Service (Enforcement)] policy is that enforcement action may be pursued in relation to persons with full blown AIDS or who are HIV positive unless the medical evidence available is sufficient to satisfy the Department that the person is not fit to travel and/or their life expectancy would be significantly shortened if they were removed or deported.
>
> 3 In many cases the medical facilities and treatment available in the person's country of origin will be substantially less advanced that [sic] those available in the UK. This does not, in itself, constitute a ground for allowing someone with AIDS/HIV to remain. It is, however, a factor which should be taken into account since enforcement action may be inappropriate in the

facilities for treatment in the country to which he/she would be removed.'

6.44 These guidelines suggest that enforcement action may not be appropriate where the individual's 'life expectancy would be substantially shortened'. There is again a reference to situations where there are 'no facilities for treatment in the country', but the placement of this statement in the enforcement guidelines makes it more ambiguous than in the August 1995 guidelines.

6.45 In any event, those representing an individual facing deportation or removal and who is affected by HIV or AIDS should, as set out above, endeavour to put together the strongest possible package of supporting documentation confirming the compelling and compassionate factors in the particular case, including information relating to the applicant's health status, the treatment which he or she is receiving, and the non-availability of such treatment in the applicant's home country.

4 Asylum seekers and others on 'temporary admission'

6.46 Paragraph 4.1 of the August 1995 guidelines, quoted at para **6.12**, makes clear that an immigration officer deciding whether or not to grant leave to enter to an individual must base a decision on the Immigration Rules. If the applicant does not meet the terms of the rules, including in appropriate cases the ability to pay for medical treatment, the guidelines indicate that the applicant 'is to be refused'. This means that the various compassionate factors cited elsewhere in the guidelines relating to those who apply for further leave to remain in the UK are not meant to be applied to those seeking leave to enter the country.

6.47 This creates a difficulty for those individuals affected by HIV and AIDS who are in the UK on a temporary admission status and who, therefore, as described at para **6.25**, are not, from a legal viewpoint, deemed to have entered the UK. By far the largest relevant group in this category are those political asylum seekers who apply for asylum on arrival at the port. Ordinarily, such political asylum applications take years to resolve and, in the meantime, individuals concerned are granted 'temporary admission' to the UK. This means that they are not granted legal leave to enter the country but remain in the ambiguous position of being physically but not legally present. However, not all political asylum seekers fall within this category. It is possible for an individual to come to the UK and be admitted legally in one capacity or another and then, subsequently, to apply for political asylum. Such individuals would be entitled to have any subsequent application for exceptional leave to remain on a compassionate basis considered under the terms of the August 1995 guidelines as well as under the basis outlined below.

6.48 With respect to asylum seekers affected by HIV, another set of Home Office guidelines[1] set out important criteria on the basis of which such individuals may be allowed to remain in the UK exceptionally.

1 Asylum Directorate instructions relating to the granting of 'exceptional leave' apparently issued in July 1998 although only referred to publicly by the Home Office in the context of a judicial review action in late 1998.

6.49 These instructions outline the criteria to be applied in deciding whether or not an asylum applicant unsuccessful in pursuing a claim for political asylum should be granted exceptional leave to enter or remain in the UK. Paragraph 2.1 of the guidelines sets out the 'eligibility criteria' and states inter alia:

> 'ELE/R [exceptional leave to enter or remain] *must* be granted to asylum applicants if they fall under one of the following criteria:
>
> ♦ Where the 1951 UN Convention requirements are not met in the individual case but return to the country of origin would result in the applicant being subjected to torture or other cruel, inhuman or degrading treatment... For example:
>
>   • Where there is *credible* medical evidence that return, due to the medical facilities in the country concerned, would reduce the applicant's life expectancy and subject him to acute physical and mental suffering, in circumstances where the UK can be regarded as having assumed responsibility for his care. In cases of doubt, a second opinion should be sought from a credible source.'

6.50 It should be noted, first of all, that the language of this provision is mandatory. It states that exceptional leave to enter or remain *must* be granted in such circumstances. This provision clearly was put into place by the Home Office as a response to the European Court of Human Rights' decision in *D v United Kingdom*[1]. That case related to a citizen of St Kitts whom the UK was proposing to return to his home country after serving a sentence for a drug-related offence. During the course of that sentence, however, it was discovered that he had AIDS and that his life expectancy was very short. The court found that his removal to St Kitts would constitute a breach of art 3 of the European Convention on Human Rights which provides that 'No one shall be subjected to torture or to inhuman or degrading treatment or punishment.' This finding derived from the court's appraisal of what would happen when the sophisticated treatment he was receiving in the UK was withdrawn from him and he was returned to a country where no effective treatment or care could be guaranteed.

1 (1997) 24 EHRR 423.

6.51 The court, in paragraphs 52 and 53 of its decision, at page 428, stated:

> 'The abrupt withdrawal of these facilities will entail the most dramatic consequences for him. It is not disputed that his removal will hasten his death. There is a serious danger that the conditions of adversity which await him in St Kitts will further reduce his already limited life expectancy and subject him to acute mental and physical suffering. Any medical treatment which he might hope to receive there could not contend with the infections which he may possibly contract on account of his lack of shelter and of a proper diet as well as exposure to the health and sanitation problems which beset the population of St Kitts. While he may have a cousin in St Kitts, no evidence has been adduced to show whether this person would be willing to or capable of attending to the needs of a terminally ill man. There is no evidence of any other form of moral or social support. Nor has it been shown whether the applicant would be guaranteed a bed in either of the hospitals on the island which according to the Government

> In view of these exceptional circumstances and bearing in mind the critical stage now reached in the applicant's fatal illness, the implementation of the decision to remove him to St Kitts would amount to inhuman treatment by the respondent State in violation of Article 3.'

6.52 The limits of the exceptional leave guidelines were recently tested in the High Court in the case of *R v Secretary of State for the Home Department, ex p M*. Again, the subject of the case was an asylum seeker convicted of a serious offence, indecent assault on an 11-year-old girl. He was a Ugandan national in his forties who, at the time of initial refusal of exceptional leave was HIV positive, and then during the course of the case went on to receive a full AIDS diagnosis.

1 Case No CO 4975/98 (23 July 1999, unreported).

6.53 The Home Office's position in refusing to grant him exceptional leave was that it accepted that the applicant's life expectancy would be reduced if returned to Uganda but that such removal would not 'subject him to acute physical and mental suffering', the second relevant requirement set out in the guidelines. Substantial evidence was produced by the applicant's representatives to show that, in the absence of combination therapy and other treatment in Uganda, he would suffer severe illness, pain and distress. Evidence was also adduced that there was no hospice care available in Uganda and that there were no close family members to look after him if he were returned there.

6.54 Sullivan J found that the initial decision taken by the Secretary of State, based on the information available to him at that time, 'may well have been within the range of responses that was open to a reasonable decision-maker'. He pointed out that 'the application of immigration policy to persons with AIDS/HIV positive entails making hard choices'. After reviewing the further evidence submitted, however, the judge found that the proposed removal to Uganda would constitute 'a very substantial interference' with the applicant's art 3 rights and, arguably, with his rights under art 2 of the European Convention guaranteeing the 'right to life'.

6.55 He offered some specific guidance as to how paragraph 2.1 of the guidelines relating to exceptional leave should be interpreted:

> 'I do not underestimate the difficulties faced by the Secretary of State in dealing with cases such as this. For the reasons set out in the letter of 6 January, compassion has to be tempered with realism, but that does not justify an unduly restrictive approach to the criteria set out in paragraph 2.1 of the policy. The words should be given their ordinary and common-sense meaning. It defies common sense to suggest that the applicant would not be subjected to acute physical and mental suffering, if he were returned to Uganda, in the light of the medical evidence to which I have referred.
>
> Returning an applicant to a country where conditions are such that his life expectancy will be considerably shortened and where he will suffer a great degree of physical and mental suffering is, on the face of it, a very substantial interference with that applicant's human rights.

I would, therefore, expect to find substantial justification for the proposition that the applicant's case does not fall within paragraph 2.1 of the exceptional leave to remain policy.'

6.56 Similarly strong language was used by an Immigration Appeal Tribunal chaired by Mr Care in the recent case of *Asiimwe*[1]. The Tribunal in that case endorsed a recommendation made by an adjudicator that the applicant, a Ugandan woman with AIDS, should be granted exceptional leave. It cited the fact that withdrawal of her treatment would cause very rapid deterioration in her health, that she would not be able to afford medication necessary to maintain any reasonable quality of life and that, in order to survive, she would have to return to her own tribal area where there would be little or no treatment available and she would be shunned by her fellow villagers. The Tribunal stated that it was 'hard to imagine' how the appellant's removal to Uganda could be reconciled with the UK's obligations under art 3 of the European Convention.

1 (18692) (8 September 1999, unreported).

6.57 The success in each of these cases was largely dependent on the production of high quality medical and other documentation demonstrating the medical effects which would follow from the individual's removal and, further, demonstrating the extent of 'acute physical and mental suffering' which would result. These are, therefore, points which should be addressed in every application for exceptional leave to enter or remain based upon an applicant's HIV status.

6.58 Another important issue touched upon by the High Court in *R v Secretary of State for the Home Department, ex p M* is whether asylum seekers may base successful applications for political asylum on the fact that they have a 'well-founded fear of persecution' on being returned to their home country specifically because of their HIV status.

6.59 The key legal issue relevant to this question is whether HIV status can be interpreted to define a 'social group' for purpose of the 1951 Convention Relating to the Status of Refugees. Under that Convention, only those individuals who can demonstrate a 'well-founded fear of persecution' for certain set reasons, including membership of a 'social group', fall within the Convention definition of 'refugee' and, therefore, are entitled to protection. Sullivan J did not reach this issue in *R v Secretary of State for the Home Department, ex p M* even though one of the points raised in the appeal was the refusal by the Immigration Appeal Tribunal to grant the appellant leave to appeal against a Special Adjudicator's dismissal of the case, citing the fact that: 'The Tribunal does not accept that those suffering from AIDS constitute a social group under the Convention'. The High Court felt it did not need to address this issue since such a question 'will become academic if the applicant is granted exceptional leave to remain'.

6.60 It seems relatively certain, however, that in future appropriate cases, people who are HIV positive will be deemed to constitute a 'social group'. This is in the light of the extremely important decision by the House of Lords, in *Shah and Islam*[1], which post-dated the Immigration Appeal Tribunal's refusal of leave in *R v Secretary of State for the Home Department, ex p M*[2]. In *Shah and Islam*, which related specifically to the issue of whether 'women in Pakistan' constituted a social group but also separately addressed the issue of whether gay men and lesbians could do so (in both cases deciding affirmatively), it was held that the key factor in defining a 'social group' should be an 'unchangeable characteristic' and, in particular, stated that there should be no additional requirement of 'cohesiveness, co-operation or interdependence'[3].

1 [1999] 2 WLR 1015.
2 Case No CO 4975/98 (23 July 1999, unreported).
3 [1999] 2 WLR 1015, per Lord Hoffman at 1031.

6.61 In order to base an application for political asylum successfully on such a definition, one would of course need to demonstrate the fact that individuals affected by HIV would indeed face persecution in their home country because of their status, either at the hands of their government directly or at the hands of other forces without the government providing adequate protection.

6.62 A key to making such a successful application would be the collection of credible information confirming the existence of such persecution. Aside from the usual sources of information such as Amnesty International, Human Rights Watch, the Refugee Legal Centre Documentation Centre and the United Nations High Commission for Refugees, a specialised collection point for such documentation is:

International Gay & Lesbian Human Rights Commission Asylum Project
1360 Mission Street #200
San Francisco
CA 94103 USA
Tel 001 415 255 8680 Fax 001 415 255 8662

This organisation produces country bundles for a relatively modest fee relating not only to the situation of gay men and lesbians but also of those affected by HIV and AIDS.

D OTHER SPECIAL CATEGORIES OF APPLICATION

6.63 There are two categories of application provided for by special Home Office guidelines outside the ambit of the Immigration Rules which may have particular relevance to those affected by HIV and AIDS. These are the guidelines relating to 'common-law and same-sex relationships' (unmarried partners) and the guidelines relating to 'carers'.

1 Unmarried partners

6.64 In October 1997, the Home Office for the first time enacted a concession under the terms of which the foreign common-law or gay partner of a UK-based person could apply for entry clearance or leave to remain in the UK based upon the couple demonstrating a relationship 'akin to marriage' which had subsisted for at least four years. The terms of this concession were amended in June 1999, reducing the qualifying period from four years to two years. The terms of the concession are found in the Immigration Directorate's Instructions, chapter 8, annex Z. They need to be read alongside the instructions on how the concession should be interpreted and applied. Both the concession and the instructions can be accessed on the Home Office website[1].

1 www.homeoffice.gov.uk/ind/hpg.htm. The full text of the concession is reproduced in *Butterworths Immigration Law Service* at **D[1021]**.

6.65 The concession applies to both same-sex couples and heterosexual unmarried partners where there is a legal impediment to their marriage (such as the impossibility of obtaining a divorce). The foreign partner may be seeking to join or remain with a British citizen, an EEA national residing in the UK or any other person who has indefinite leave to remain in the UK or falls into one of a number of categories of limited leave to remain which lead to indefinite leave to remain. The concession extends to the foreign partners of persons granted asylum in the UK.

6.66 The central requirement of the concession is that 'the partners have been living together in a relationship akin to marriage which has subsisted for two years or more'. Instructions require that the term 'living together' be applied very strictly and, in essence, a couple must be able to demonstrate that they have in fact been cohabiting for at least 18 of the previous 24 months. The instructions specify that 'short breaks apart would be acceptable for good reasons such as work commitments, looking after a relative which takes one partner away for a period of up to six months where it was not possible for the other partner to accompany and it can be seen that the relationship continued throughout that period by visits, letters, etc'.

6.67 The concession further requires that 'there will be adequate accommodation for the parties and any dependants without recourse to public funds in accommodation which they own or occupy exclusively' and that 'the parties will be able to maintain themselves and any dependants adequately without recourse to public funds'.

6.68 If an individual is outside of the UK and wishes to take advantage of the concession, he or she is required under the terms of the concession to apply for entry clearance from abroad. In cases where an individual is already legally in the UK, however, it is possible to apply for further leave to remain under the terms of the concession.

6.69 The Home Office has in the past been prepared to exhibit flexibility in applying the requirements of the concession in those cases where one or both members of a couple are affected by HIV. For example, if the British-based partner is already receiving public funds in his or her own right, because of HIV-related illness, the application should not fail if it can be shown that there will be no additional recourse to public funds by allowing a foreign partner to enter or remain in the UK. Yet even in those cases where foreign partners may not be able to demonstrate an ability to support themselves, the Home Office may be prepared to exercise discretion.

6.70 Similarly, in cases where the requisite period of cohabitation has not yet been met, it may well be worthwhile making an application prematurely citing the compelling and compassionate circumstances of the case.

6.71 Finally, it should be noted that the Immigration Directorate's Instructions specifically provide that, where compelling and can be demonstrated, an individual who has arrived in the UK without entry clearance based on the concession may be granted leave to enter the UK if it can be demonstrated that the other requirements of the concession have been met. This has been applied, for example, to grant leave to enter the UK to a failed asylum seeker on temporary admission in the light of a long-term same-sex relationship with a British-based partner who had become seriously ill due to HIV-related illness.

2 Carers

6.72 In August 1998 a new policy on 'carers' was announced permitting 'applications from persons here in a temporary capacity seeking leave to remain to care for a sick relative or friend who is suffering from a terminal illness such as cancer or AIDS'[1].

1 Immigration Directorate's Instructions, Chapter 17, s 2.

6.73 The Instructions provide that each such application will be considered 'on the individual merits of the case' and they make clear that this is meant only as 'a temporary capacity' and that once alternative arrangements have been made or if the patient should die then the 'carer' will be expected to return home.

6.74 A differentiation is made in the Instructions between caring for a sick or disabled 'friend' or 'relative'. Applications to care for a 'friend' should normally be refused. Leave to remain may be granted for a period of three months in such cases, however, in an emergency (eg where the patient has suddenly fallen ill and there is insufficient time to arrange a permanent carer or where there is nobody else in the UK to whom the patient can turn). The Instructions provide that an extension of further leave in such cases would not be given unless there are 'wholly exceptional circumstances'.

6.75 The Instructions provide that 'it will normally be appropriate to grant leave for three months' to care for a sick or disabled relative although 'on the strict understanding that during this period arrangements will be made for the future care of the patient by a person who does not require leave to remain outside the Immigration Rules.' Factors to be considered in connection with such applications include the type of illness or condition, the type of care required, care which is available and the long-term prognosis.

6.76 Applications for further leave to remain must be accompanied by a number of documents set out in the Instructions including a letter from registered medical practitioner, a letter from the local social services department, if involved, evidence that alternative arrangements are being explored and full details of the patient's family in the UK and previous care arrangements, as well as evidence of the applicant's circumstances, both in his or her home country and in the UK. Given the stringent nature of these requirements, they are relatively rarely used. At the same time, lodging an application can be considered even when it does not fall squarely within these guidelines. Where compelling and compassionate circumstances exist, the Home Office is often prepared to exhibit flexibility. In cases, for example, where the patient is a child, a strong argument can be made for long-term continuity of a single carer since medical evidence can be produced demonstrating enhanced adherence to a particular drug regime by a child being looked after by a single carer.

E THE RIGHT TO TRAVEL

6.77 As reflected in the very beginning of this chapter, the policy followed by the UK with respect to the admission of those affected by HIV and AIDS is much more liberal than those pursued by dozens of other countries which maintain border restrictions relating to the entry of HIV positive people.

6.78 The approaches taken by different countries vary enormously in the degree of their stringency. They are also subject to change. Some countries require proof of a recent negative HIV test simply for purposes of coming as a tourist whereas others impose such a requirement only with respect to those planning to take up residence. With respect to many such countries, however, stated limitations on the entry of HIV positive persons are in fact only invoked if and when immigration officers come to discover that someone seeking entry to the country is HIV positive.

6.79 The National Aids Manual includes a section setting out information on countries imposing HIV-related restrictions on travellers and the Advice Centre of the Terrence Higgins Trust may also be able to provide such information. Another possible source of information is the embassy of the country concerned although, obviously, in making enquiries, individuals should not provide details of the identities of the persons proposing to travel.

6.80 HIV positive individuals contemplating travel to a country which imposes such restrictions obviously need to reflect carefully before travelling. Obviously, one relevant factor to take into consideration is whether or not their HIV status may come to the attention of immigration authorities because of drugs which they are carrying known to be used for the treatment of HIV-related illness. Even if such individuals look perfectly healthy and, therefore, are not likely to be identified as HIV positive by an immigration officer, a problem may arise if a routine inspection reveals the presence of such drugs. In such a case, individuals concerned may find themselves in the unpleasant situation of being detained, treated in a discriminatory fashion and, ultimately, unceremoniously removed with a trip intended as a holiday completely spoiled. It is important, therefore, that anyone contemplating such travel weighs the risks involved.

6.81 In the worldwide context, the policies of the UK, whilst far from perfect, are much more realistic and commendable than those exhibited by many other governments. Unfortunately, all too many of these other governments, whilst seeking to erect barriers at their borders, do very little to carry out the public education and other steps which could prove genuinely effective in preventing the spread of the HIV virus amongst their population. Some quiet satisfaction can be taken from the fact that the UK has followed a more enlightened policy in this regard.

Chapter 7

HIV and criminal law

Angus Hamilton

A TRANSMISSION OF HIV

1 Transmission of HIV as a criminal offence

7.01 In June 1992, there was an outcry in the British press over the alleged behaviour of a young HIV positive haemophiliac, Roy Cornes. It was suggested, although never verified, that he had, following an HIV positive diagnosis, deliberately sought to infect a number of women, who were unaware of his status, with the virus through consensual, but unprotected, sexual intercourse.

7.02 The alleged facts of the case prompted wide consideration of whether there were any criminal charges which could have been brought in such circumstances. The preoccupation of the press with the concept of controlling the 'irresponsible' person with HIV meant that other issues, such as the press portrayal of HIV as an infection which was of no risk to heterosexuals and the responsibility of any couple to engage in safer sex practices, were largely ignored. However, there remains the possibility of criminal charges being brought in similar circumstances in the future and that possibility must, therefore, be considered.

7.03 There are a number of late 19th-century authorities on the question of whether the knowing or reckless infection of a sexual partner with a venereal disease constitutes rape or indecent assault on the basis that concealment of the defendant's health status constitutes a fraud on their partner and, consequently, the fraud vitiates the partner's consent. Consensual sexual contact would thereby become non-consensual.

7.04 In the case of *R v Bennett*[1], the defendant had sex with a girl of 13. He was infected with a venereal disease but did not tell the girl this. She contracted the disease and Bennett was subsequently convicted of indecent assault. Because of her age, the girl could not have been regarded as consenting in any event, even if Bennett had not been infected. Despite this, the case appears to have been decided on the basis that Bennett's concealment of his health status from the girl was held to constitute a fraud and the fraud to vitiate the girl's consent.

1 (1866) 4 F & F 1105, followed in *R v Sinclair* (1867) 13 Cox CC 190.

7.05 However, in the later case of *R v Clarence*[1], the analysis in *Bennett* was disapproved. In *Clarence*, the defendant was, to his knowledge, suffering from gonorrhoea and had intercourse with his wife without informing her of his condition. As a result, she, too, contracted gonorrhoea. The defendant was, at first instance, convicted of offences under ss 20 and 47 of the Offences Against the Person Act 1861.

1 [1886–90] All ER 1335.

7.06 The Court of Crown Cases Reserved overturned the convictions and held:

> 'That consent obtained by fraud is no consent at all is not true as a general proposition either in fact or in law. If a man meets a woman in the street and knowingly gives her bad money in order to procure her consent to intercourse with him, he obtains her consent by fraud, but it would be childish to say that she did not consent.'

1 [1886–90] All ER 135 per Wills J.

7.07 The court held that the concept of a fraud vitiating consent could only apply to a fraud as to the nature of the act (for example, pretending that an act of sexual intercourse was a surgical operation[1]) or, possibly, to a fraud as to the identity of the person involved.

1 *R v Flattery* (1877) 2 QBD 410.

7.08 *Clarence* also considered whether the transmission of an infection could amount to an assault per se. The majority held that it could not. An infection was analysed as a kind of poisoning lacking in the 'immediate and necessary connection between a cut or a blow and the wound or harm inflicted'[1] that an assault requires.

1 [1886–90] All ER 135, per Stephen J at 143.

7.09 The court in *Clarence* appears to have been influenced too by the principle that a man cannot 'assault' his wife in the context of sexual activity. This is no longer good law—see the speeches in the House of Lords in *R v R*[1].

1 [1992] 1 AC 599.

7.10 It is submitted that the definition of assault adopted in *Clarence* is rather particular. Assault is more ordinarily defined 'as an act by which a person intentionally or recklessly causes another to apprehend immediate unlawful personal violence or to sustain unlawful personal violence'[1].

1 See, for example, *R v Kimber* (1983) 77 Cr App Rep 225 at 228.

7.11 If this definition is considered, it is rather more difficult to see why the transmission of an infection cannot amount to an assault per se, although a great deal would depend on the interpretation of 'violence'. It is well established that 'violence' includes the application of only slight force. Certainly, in his dissenting judgement in *Clarence,* Hawkins J expressed the view that 'wilfully to place his diseased person in contact with hers without her express consent amounts to an assault'[1].

1 [1886–90] All ER 135 at 148.

7.12 There may also be questions arising from the particular wording of s 20 of the Offences Against the Person Act 1861. This states that it is an offence to 'unlawfully and maliciously wound or inflict any grievous bodily harm upon any other person, either with or without any weapon or instrument.' The term 'assault' is not, therefore, used in the provision. Instead, the concept of 'infliction of harm' is used. These words also appear in s 23 of the Offences Against the Person Act 1861, which actually deals with the administration of poison.

7.13 Section 23 provides:

> 'Whosoever shall unlawfully and maliciously administer to, or cause to be administered to or taken by any other person any poison, or other destructive or noxious thing, so as thereby to endanger the life of such person, or so as thereby to inflict upon such person any grievous bodily harm, shall be guilty of an offence, and being convicted thereof shall be liable...to imprisonment for any term not exceeding ten years.'[1]

The majority in *Clarence* considered the transmission of an infection to be similar to poisoning.

1 Offences Against the Person Act 1861, s 23.

7.14 The meaning of 'infliction of harm' was considered in *Clarence* and it was held that the meaning of the word 'inflict' suggested an immediate and necessary connection between the accused's conduct and the harm suffered by the victim[1], and that, consequently the transmission of an infection could not constitute the 'infliction' of harm. It is respectfully submitted, however, that the analysis here is seriously at fault. Stephen J refers in his judgment in *Clarence* to poisoning not constituting an 'infliction of grievous bodily harm' because, amongst other reasons, the provisions of s 24 of the Offences Against the Persons Act 1861 make no mention of the term. Section 24 renders it an offence to administer a poison 'with intent to injure aggrieve or annoy'. However, as previously mentioned, s 23 of the Act, which appears not to have been considered in *Clarence*, but which also deals with poisoning, does explicitly refer to poisoning resulting in the 'infliction of grievous bodily harm'. This tends to suggest that poisoning and therefore, arguably, the transmission of an infection can constitute an 'infliction of harm'.

1 [1886–90] All ER 135, per Stephen J at 143.

7.15 Thus, even if the transmission of a potentially fatal infection cannot be seen as an assault per se, it is difficult to see how it cannot be construed as an infliction of grievous bodily harm, which would bring the knowing or reckless transmission of the HIV virus within the terms of s 20 of the Offences Against the Person Act 1861.

7.16 If this analysis is correct, then further problems may arise as a result of the Court of Appeal's ruling in *R v Brown*[1]. This case involved the conviction of a number of men for offences under ss 20 and 47 of the Offences Against the Person Act 1861. The men had engaged in consensual sadomasochistic activities which had resulted in minor injuries to some of the participants.

1 (1992) 94 Cr App Rep 302. The decision of the Court of Appeal was upheld in the House of Lords by a 3:2 majority on 11 March 1993. The case was the subject of an unsuccessful appeal to the European Court of Human Rights.

7.17 The Court of Appeal, upholding the ruling of the court below, stated:

> 'It is not in the public interest that people should try to cause, or should cause, each other actual bodily harm for no good reason...What may be "good reason" it is not necessary for us to say.'

7.18 It is inconceivable that a court would view the transmission of the HIV virus as ever being in the public interest. It is possible therefore to envisage a situation in which a couple had engaged in sexual intercourse knowing that one of them had HIV with the result that the uninfected partner contracted the virus too and as a result criminal liability arose despite the knowledge and consent of both parties.

7.19 There was, however, in *Clarence*, a general acknowledgement by the majority of the expediency of their ruling. For, if the transmission of a venereal disease in the circumstances of that case was an offence, then why not the transmission of lesser infections through everyday social contacts? In short, the court was anxious not to open the floodgates to a series of speculative criminal prosecutions. The majority also acknowledged the difficulty in the courts seeking to enquire into the exact details of the negotiations and courtship that occurs before two people embark upon a sexual encounter—and certainly such enquiries would be necessary if the courts sought to intervene in such situations. In short, *Clarence* afforded an illustration of 'the futility of trying to teach morals by the application of the criminal law to cases occupying the doubtful ground between immorality and crime'[1]. Those words and that analysis are surely just as relevant a hundred years on. The current uncertainty of the law may either discourage a prosecution in the circumstances of the Roy Cornes case or may provoke a lengthy test case[2].

1 [1886–90] All ER 135, per Wills J at 138.
2 For an alternative analysis of the potential criminal liability arising for the transmission of HIV see Bronitt, S 'Spreading Disease and the Criminal Law' [1994] Crim LR 21.

7.20 No such test cases have yet been brought. When cases of assault involving HIV have been brought they have involved an allegation of a discrete assault which also involved the transmission of the virus. See paras **7.31–7.34** for transmission by violent act. It is perhaps worth mentioning here that the author has also seen a suggestion that a prosecution might be brought under s 3 of the Sexual Offences Act 1956 in respect of a deliberate transmission of HIV[1]. Section 3 provides:

> 'It is an offence for a person to procure a woman, by false pretences or false representations, to have...sexual intercourse in any part of the world.'

1 Guardian, 24 June 1992.

7.21 The suggestion is that someone who, presumably by silence, represents themselves as being healthy when in fact they are carrying HIV might fall foul of this provision. The provision of course only protects women. It is submitted that the proposition that the use of this section might be appropriate in HIV cases is flawed because it rests upon the proposition that silence might amount to ' false pretences or false representations'. It is submitted that this cannot be correct.

represented himself as being healthy, for example by saying 'I am not HIV positive', whilst knowing this be untrue.

7.22 The uncertainty as to whether the deliberate transmission of HIV alone constitutes a criminal offence should be ended if the government implements proposed legislation on the issue. In a paper published in November 1993[1] the Law Commission argued for a change in the law so that the intentional or reckless transmission of HIV and other infections would be clearly criminalised.

1 Law Com 218 *Legislating the Criminal Code: Offences Against the Person and General Principles* (November 1993).

7.23 The Commission's starting point was that the analysis of the law as stated in *Clarence* was correct and that no person could be prosecuted for the 'simple' transmission of HIV. 'Simple' is used in the sense of a transmission that does not entail an act of violence such as stabbing with a syringe or biting.

7.24 The Commission, admitting that they were influenced by the then public outcry over deliberate or reckless infection of others with life-threatening conditions, including HIV, proposed a definition of 'injury' which would include the intentional or reckless inflicting of illness or disease. The Commission presented a draft bill for consideration which included new offences of intentionally or recklessly causing injury or serious injury to another person. The definition of 'intentionally' proposed by the Law Commission is as follows:

> 'A person acts intentionally with respect to a result when either it is his purpose to cause it or, although it is not his purpose to cause it, he knows that it would occur in the ordinary course of events if he were to succeed in his purpose of causing some other result.'

The definition of 'recklessly' proposed by the Law Commission is:

> 'A person acts recklessly with respect to a circumstance when he is aware of a risk that it exists or will exist and with respect to a result when he is aware of a risk that it will occur, and it is unreasonable, having regard to the circumstances known to him, to take that risk'

7.26 On 15 December 1992, the then Home Secretary gave a written answer to a parliamentary question, to the effect that he had no plans to introduce legislation on the particular issue of the deliberate transmission of HIV[1]. Despite this, the Labour government elected in May 1997 seemed more than willing to accept the Commission's proposals, although, after representations from various groups including the Terrence Higgins Trust, the actual proposal adopted was that only the intentional transmission of an infection should be criminalised and not the reckless transmission.

1 216 HC Official Report (6th series) written answers, col *102*, 15 December 1992.

7.27 In 1998, the government published a draft Offences Against the Person Bill which contained a proposal that criminal liability for the transmission of disease should be limited to the case in which a person 'deliberately transmits a disease intending to cause a serious illness'. The definition of 'intentionally' adopted by the Bill is the same as that proposed by the Law Commission. The first limb of the definition is 'a person acts intentionally with respect to a result when either it is his purpose to cause it' is arguably unproblematic. The second limb: 'a person acts intentionally with respect to a result when although it is not his purpose to cause it, he knows that it would occur in the ordinary course of events if he were to succeed in his purpose of causing some other result'—is far less so.

7.28 In particular, is the 'other result' referred to any other result or another criminal result? Thus, if a man throws a brick at a window with the intention of hitting someone standing on the other side he could be said, under the Law Commission definition, to intend the breakage of the window as it an inevitable part of the brick-throwing. In this scenario, both 'intended' events—hitting the person and breaking the window are criminal. What, however, of a couple, one of whom (a man) is HIV positive and the other (a woman) knows, who decide to have unprotected sexual intercourse in order to try for a baby. If the female partner becomes pregnant but also contracts HIV would the male partner be criminally liable under the Law Commission's definition of 'intentionally'? It is not his purpose to transmit the virus but it may be said to occur in the ordinary course of events (unprotected sexual intercourse) designed to produce another result (pregnancy). Here we have mixed results in the sense that one result (conception) is clearly not criminal while the other, the transmission of HIV, possibly is.

7.29 Arguably, what the Law Commission is proposing is a concept of primary purpose or result and secondary (but nonetheless obvious) purpose or result.

7.30 The actual proposal from the government is to criminalise the deliberate transmission of a disease intending to cause a serious illness. Deliberate is presumably used in the sense of 'intentional'. The additional intention is to cause a serious illness. 'Intention' thus appears twice in the same phrase. However, applying the concepts of primary and secondary purpose mentioned above might still render the male partner in the previously outlined scenario criminally liable. His principal purpose is neither to transmit the virus nor to cause serious illness, but it might be argued that these were the secondary but nonetheless obvious results. The status of the draft bill and its proposed legislative timetable are unclear at the time of writing.

2 Transmission by 'violent' act

7.31 This may occur, for example, when the victim is stabbed with a syringe or, possibly, bitten. Understandably, the confirmed transmission of the virus is likely to be considered an aggravating factor in determining the sentence to be passed. This may be so even where transmission is threatened by an assailant but does not occur, because of the certain distress caused to the victim having to wait three months for an HIV antibody test.

7.32 The second proposition—that fear of the virus may be an aggravating factor affecting sentence—has been mitigated to a considerable extent by the judgment in *R v Malcolm*[1] (a rape case). Here, it was held that the victim's fear of contracting AIDS can factor in a case where there is a valid reason for such a fear. The natural fear of any rape victim that she might have contracted AIDS is not an aggravating feature meriting an increased sentence.

1 9 Cr App Rep (S) 487, CA.

7.33 Persons who have been placed at risk of contracting HIV, including those who have been the subject of an assault by an HIV positive person, are occasionally offered post-exposure prophylaxis (PEP) treatment. Such treatment can have extremely unpleasant side-effects. It remains to be seen whether having to endure such treatment will be considered as an aggravating feature of sentence.

7.34 It is also worth noting that there is sometimes a considerable exaggeration of the risks of HIV transmission involved in particular acts. Particular examples are spitting and biting. These are not high risk in terms of HIV transmission. Any suggestion that they are should be countered by detailed medical information or evidence. One of the best practical resources for information about methods of transmission and a good starting point for gathering such information is the National AIDS Manual published by NAM publications.

3 Transmission by non-violent but unlawful sexual activity

7.35 This may occur, for example, during unprotected anal intercourse between two men at least one of whom is under 18[1]. Again, failure to use a condom or otherwise engage in acknowledged safer sex practices is seen as an aggravating factor, even when the virus is not actually transmitted.

1 The age of consent is due to be lowered to 16 by government legislation. See the Sexual Offences Amendment Act 1998.

B DISCLOSURE OF HIV STATUS

1 Disclosure of HIV status at a police station

7.36 For solicitors who advise on the telephone or who attend detainees at a police station a question may arise as to whether an HIV positive detainee should disclose their status to the police. In some circumstances, the decision may be taken away from the detainee—for example, if another person at the scene of the arrest discloses the fact to the arresting officers, or if the arrested person has medication on them from which an HIV positive status can be inferred.

7.37 A detainee may be eager to disclose their status if they need access to medication. On arrival at a police station all medication and indeed most other property will be removed from the detainee. Access to medication will not be permitted without the sanction of a divisional surgeon. It is generally inadvisable for an HIV positive detainee to disclose their status to the police. In the first place, experience has shown that HIV positive detainees may be treated less considerately during the course of their detention. Second, adverse inferences relating to the alleged offence for which the person has been arrested may be drawn—for example, if a man has been arrested for an alleged offence of sexual misbehaviour and discloses that he is HIV positive he may suffer an attitude of 'Oh well, he must be gay and must therefore have committed the offence'. Third, it used to be and may still be routine police practice for an individual's HIV status to be recorded on the police national computer (PNC).

7.38 This practice has been a source of considerable disquiet, since it means that HIV positive people who have come into contact with the police and whose status have been ascertained—not necessarily with their consent—can be readily identified. When there are regular calls for controls on 'irresponsible people with AIDS', it is clear why the central recording of 'criminals or semi-criminals' who are HIV positive causes so much concern. In mid-1991, there were press reports[1] that the police in Cleveland took the recording of detainee's HIV status one step further by displaying photographs of people suspected of being HIV positive on a police station notice board.

1 Independent, 15 June 1991.

7.39 The practice of recording HIV status on the PNC was the subject of a complaint in 1992 by, amongst others, the Terrence Higgins Trust to the Data Protection Registrar (DPR)—the public official who is responsible for the regulation of the storage and use of personal data (information about living individuals) on computer. The basis of the complaint was that the information was excessive and irrelevant and therefore held in breach of the Fourth Data Protection Principle[1] under the Data Protection Act 1984.

1 The Fourth Data Protection Principle provides that: 'personal data held for any purpose or purposes shall be adequate, relevant and not excessive in relation to that purpose or those purposes'.

7.40 The registrar, in his eighth annual report, concluded :

> 'It appears to me that there is a small, but foreseeable, risk of infection with HIV or AIDS which could arise in connection with policing activities. Accordingly, I am satisfied that, in general, the holding of a factual warning signal, including an indication of HIV or AIDS status in the PNC conviction records, is neither excessive nor irrelevant to policing purposes.'

7.41 In practice, an individual's HIV status should have no relevance at all to their arrest or detention. The police should already have in place procedures to reduce the risk of contracting infections during arrest and detention without such procedures being dependent upon ascertaining the detainee's health status. Furthermore, even if such procedures are not implemented, the information that an individual is HIV positive invariably becomes available after a 'risk' situation has passed. For example, if the police are dealing with someone injured and bleeding after a fight or road accident it is very unlikely that personal details sufficient to carry out a PNC check and ascertain health details will be obtained until after the immediate emergency has passed.

7.42 For these reasons, the Terrence Higgins Trust, amongst others, made further representations to the DPR after the publication of his eighth annual report arguing against permitting the police to record individual's HIV status on the PNC. These representations were instrumental in achieving a change of view on the part of the registrar, who in his ninth annual report stated:

> 'I have reviewed the position which I took last year. The new factor is that there is now a firm policy on procedures, which should be adopted by police forces, to avoid the risk of HIV infection. Once these procedures are in place, whilst I would look at the facts of each particular case, the holding of HIV markers would seem to be irrelevant. Such markers would also possibly be excessive in view of the danger that they may encourage a false sense of security. This might undermine the hygiene procedures and put police officers at risk.
>
> I have concluded that I should hold to my original view until there has been sufficient time for the necessary training and education activities for police officers to be put in place...I would expect an early development of the required courses and materials.'

7.43 In his tenth annual report published in July 1994 the registrar indicated that such training should have been completed by December 1993 and expressed some impatience with those police forces that were still retaining HIV markers on the PNC. The registrar indicated that he might be obliged to take action if the retention of such information persisted as he regarded it as a breach of the Fourth Data Protection Principle.

7.44 This matter has not been fully resolved. The first appointed registrar, Eric Howe, who tackled this issue, has been replaced by Elizabeth France. Her appointment marked the disappearance from the registrar's annual reports of updates on the HIV 'markers' issue. The last indication was that police forces were complying with the registrar's requirements.

7.45 The 1984 Act will be replaced in 1999 by the Data Protection Act 1998. This still contains a principle that 'personal data shall be adequate, relevant and not excessive in relation to the purpose or purposes for which they are processed'[1] which is virtually identical to the relevant provision under the 1984 Act.

1 Data Protection Act 1998, Sch 1, Pt 1.

7.46 In the situation where a detainee wishes to disclose their HIV status with a view to obtaining access to medication it is recommended that the detainee be advised to request the attendance of the divisional surgeon, explain the circumstances to them, insist that they treat the disclosure of HIV status as confidential and ask them to authorise access to medication. As a matter of practice divisional surgeons routinely disclose information about a detainee's health to the police and indeed an officer may be present or nearby when the examination is carried out. However, divisional surgeons are not, despite their common title of 'police doctors', employed by the police, but are independent general practitioners, and as such, it is submitted, subject to the same rules of confidentiality as if they were the detainee's own doctor. If a detainee specifically forbids disclosure, therefore, this will serve to remind the doctor of the duty of confidentiality and to emphasise the possible disciplinary consequences if disclosure occurs.

7.47 One final note of caution needs to be sounded with respect to advising an HIV positive detainee at a police station and trying to ensure that their status is not needlessly disclosed. Very few telephone conversations between a detainee and their advising solicitor are confidential and, indeed, many outgoing telephone lines from a police station are routinely taped. Consequently, such matters should not be discussed over the telephone but only during a personal attendance at the police station.

2 Disclosure of HIV status during criminal proceedings

7.48 A defendant's HIV status is a factor that is potentially relevant in all prosecutions. It may be directly relevant to the commission of the alleged crime—for example, inadequate state benefits or financial support have, on more than one occasion, been the impulse for the commission of an offence of dishonesty.

7.49 Furthermore, the HIV status of a defendant may provide grounds, particularly in less serious cases, for an approach to the Crown Prosecution Service (CPS) to see if they will deal with the defendant either by withdrawing the charge altogether or by coupling such a withdrawal with a non-conviction option such as a bind-over or a caution.

7.50 It is of course fundamental that the defendant consents to and co-operates with such an approach, or indeed any disclosure of their health status (for example for the purposes of mitigation) which may take place during criminal proceedings. It is advisable for information relating to HIV status to be volunteered by the defendant rather than asked for. If sought, the questions should be qualified with an explanation as to how the disclosure of the information may assist the client and an assurance that the questions need not be answered if that is the client's wish.

7.51 As mentioned in paras **7.36–7.47**, HIV status may, unfortunately be established during criminal proceedings without a defendant's co-operation and consent, for example when a search is conducted at a police station and medication or a medical appointment card is discovered, which indicates that the detainee is HIV positive. This information is then likely to be recorded on the detainee's custody record. In such a case the proper course is to establish with the client whether any further, beneficial, use can be made of the information.

7.52 Having established HIV status and the client's informed consent to disclosure, the next consideration is whether disclosure is likely to be of benefit to the client—that is, whether it is likely to lead to the discontinuance of the prosecution and the avoidance of a criminal conviction. Such a resolution is less likely where the offence is serious or indeed where the defendant is, relatively, healthy.

7.53 It is also important to take into account the nature of the alleged offence and the possible ignorance of the prosecutor with whom a defence lawyer will deal. The latter factor is, of course, quite unpredictable. For example, where the allegation is one of sexual misbehaviour, disclosure may have the wholly undesirable result of encouraging rather than discouraging a prosecution on the basis that the defendant's behaviour may have transmitted the virus and put others at serious risk. This is an attitude that has been displayed in cases of alleged sexual misbehaviour even where the activity complained of is not capable of resulting in HIV transmission. An attempt can, of course, be made to counter such attitudes by providing the prosecutor with more realistic information, but this type of prejudice and misinformation is not easy to tackle.

7.54 The CPS has certain criteria to consider in establishing whether to charge a potential defendant or to proceed with a prosecution. These are set out in the Code for Crown Prosecutors which is published on behalf of the Director of Public Prosecutions[1]. These criteria place an obligation on the prosecuting authorities to consider, amongst other points, the defendant's health and also whether the pursuit of a prosecution may lead to the worsening of the defendant's state of health. The latter consideration is important given that it is well established that stress can result in a deterioration in the health of a person who is HIV positive. The criteria explicitly state that more weight should be given to such factors in less serious cases—especially where the defendant's health is likely to lead a court to impose a purely nominal penalty if the prosecution is pursued.

1 See, inter alia, *The Law Society Gazette* 23 July 1986.

7.55 An approach to the prosecuting authority suggesting that, through reasons of health, a prosecution ought not to be continued should be in the form of a letter referring the prosecutor to the criteria relied on and any additional points of assistance relating to the particular defendant (age, previous good character, etc). The letter should be accompanied by a medical report confirming an HIV positive diagnosis, describing the defendant's current state of health and treatment and, if the supervising doctor is willing, expressing the likely adverse effect of continuing the prosecution. On the issue of confidentiality, it is important to state in the letter that the information disclosed about the defendant is not to be passed to any other party under any circumstances.

7.56 The approach will either be met with a refusal to halt a prosecution, an agreement to do so (possibly coupled with a bind-over) or a request for further information (clarification of the defendant's state of health or, in exceptional cases, a request for an independent medical examination). If the initial approach is met with a refusal, it is always worth considering a further appeal later in the proceedings, especially if there have been developments in the defendant's state of health which can be attested to in a further medical report. Further approaches will, of course, only be possible if the case is continuing for some time and not , for example, being dealt with by way of a guilty plea at the first hearing.

3 A defendant's HIV status as a point of mitigation

7.57 If there seems to be no possibility of the prosecution discontinuing the case, then the material gathered for the purposes of making the relevant representations to the CPS can be used, in the event of a guilty plea or conviction, for the purposes of mitigation. There is a strong, but encouraging, distinction between the regular experience of practitioners who are presenting details of their client's HIV status as a point of mitigation and the few Court of Appeal authorities on the relevance of a defendant's HIV diagnosis.

7.58 The general experience is that sentencing judges and magistrates are prepared to give considerable weight to the consequences of an HIV or AIDS diagnosis for either the defendant or their partner in terms of the likely impact on their life expectancy and quality of life and, as a result, to reduce substantially the 'usual ' penalty. It must be mentioned at this point that although the HIV status of a defendant's partner can be relevant for the purposes of mitigation it does not appear to be a point which the CPS are obliged or ready to take into account in considering whether to drop a case or not.

7.59 There are three leading Court of Appeal authorities which specifically consider the relevance of an HIV diagnosis as a point of mitigation. First, *R v Moore*[1], in which the appellant pleaded guilty to two counts of burglary and asked for three other offences to be taken into consideration. The burglaries were carefully planned attacks on substantial houses and involved the theft of property worth over £40,000. The appellant had been diagnosed in 1986 as HIV positive and the lower court apparently found that there was a likelihood that he would develop AIDS within about two years. The Court of Appeal accepted that his treatment would be more difficult in prison, but Lord Lane CJ ruled as follows:

> 'We....are asked in this case to mitigate the penalty of five years' imprisonment imposed upon the appellant because this man is HIV positive and it is suggested, but not based upon any medical evidence apart from second hand evidence via the defendant himself, that his life expectancy may thereby be diminished. As I say, we have no medical evidence as to the length of life expectancy.
>
> Nevertheless, assuming that such evidence does exist, we do not consider that it is the function of this court to base its decision upon possible medical considerations of this sort. ...We do not know what the future may hold with regard to medical science and medical expertise. We do not know what he future may hold with regard to this particular appellant. If the time should come when it is no longer possible, for practical reasons, or for reasons of humanity, to hold this appellant in prison because of his physical condition, then that is the job of the Home Office...[i]t is not for this court.'

1 (1990) 12 Cr App Rep (S) 384.

7.60 A very similar line was taken by the Court of Appeal in *R v Stark*[1]. In this case, the defendant pleaded guilty to possessing heroin with intent to supply. The defendant had been in possession of 27 grams of heroin ...

street value of £2,500. He was sentenced to four years' imprisonment. Before the Court of Appeal, it was emphasised that the appellant had been diagnosed as being HIV positive some time previously and, more recently, AIDS had developed. His life expectancy was estimated at between one to two years. It was accepted that his condition made life in prison 'particularly hard'. The court was asked to reduce the sentence to allow the appellant to be released and to die with dignity, but declined to do so, holding that the appellant's record clearly indicated that there was a grave risk that the appellant would continue to traffic in drugs as long as he would be able to do so. As in *Moore*, the court held that it was not their function to manipulate a sentence in such circumstances—it was a matter for the exercise of the royal prerogative of mercy.

1 [1992] Crim LR 384.

7.61 The third authority also called, rather confusingly, *R v Moore*[1] confirmed the approach taken by the Court of Appeal in *Stark* and held that it was not for the court 'to alter an otherwise proper sentence to achieve a desirable social end'. The latter part of that phrase possibly reflects a more compassionate view of the appellant's circumstances and certainly the court directed that all the medical reports before them should be forwarded to the prison authorities to effect a consideration as to whether the royal prerogative should be exercised in the appellant's favour. In this case the appellant had pleaded guilty to possessing a class A drug with intent to supply—84 grams of heroin. The appellant had been diagnosed as HIV positive but had not received an AIDS diagnosis. He was sentenced to five years' imprisonment which was reduced, on appeal, for reasons other than his health, to three-and-a-half years.

1 (1993) 15 Cr App Rep (S) 97.

7.62 The earlier *Moore* might be excused on the basis of ignorance about the medical issues involved. Certainly, Lord Lane emphasised the rather surprising lack of professional medical evidence before the court. The decisions in *Stark* and the later *Moore*, however, were reached after the court heard medical evidence. Given this series of decisions it is difficult to argue that the cases should be confined to their own particular facts although in *Stark* it is clear that the concern of the court was to 'control' a defendant who, despite his illness, was continuing to offend and who had already had one previous prosecution for drugs offences halted on the grounds of his illness.

7.63 These Court of Appeal authorities do not appear to be being followed by the lower courts and it may be that other, more general, sentencing guidelines are being applied. There are authorities, for example, that urge leniency where it can be established that an offence was committed in circumstances of severe emotional stress[1], or where an offence of dishonesty is committed as a result of severe financial difficulties[2]. The courts may also take into account any physical disability or illness which would subject the defendant to an exceptional degree of hardship if sent to prison[3] and the possibility that a defendant may be placed in a segregation unit under r 43 of the prison rules if imprisoned[4]. This latter point may be of significance to an HIV positive defendant at risk of imprisonment as such a person is likely to be segregated if their health status is known to the prison authorities.

1 *R v Law* (24 April 1975, unreported), CA.

2 *R v Oakes* (4 November 1974, unreported), CA; this was a case of the defendant's partner's overspending causing the financial difficulties.
3 *R v Herasymenko* (12 December 1975, unreported), CA.
4 *R v Holmes* (1979) 1 Cr App Rep (S) 233, but note the conflicting decision in *R v Kirby* (1979) 1 Cr App Rep (S) 214.

7.64 The courts will generally not take into account the possible adverse effects on immediate family if a defendant receives a custodial sentence[1]. This would appear to cause difficulties with mitigation for a defendant who is the partner or carer of a PWA or HIV positive person. However leniency is shown where a custodial sentence would clearly cause an unusual measure of hardship. For example, *R v Renker*[2], where the defendant was the carer of a child with leukaemia or *R v Halleth*[3] where the defendant was the sole surviving parent of a child with kidney disease.

1 *R v Ingham* (3 October 1974, unreported), CA.
2 (29 June 1976, unreported), CA.
3 (1982) 4 Cr App Rep (S) 178.

C HIV AND PRISONS

7.65 It was not until 1987 that a training programme was implemented that was designed to give prison staff clear information about HIV in relation to their work. Prior to this, information had been provided on a very localised basis.

7.66 The Prison Medical Service (in England and Wales) had adopted the policy of labelling the files of prisoners known to be HIV positive with 'VIR' (viral infectivity restrictions). The VIR system was originally designed to protect against infection from the Hepatitis B virus. Labelling a prisoner with a VIR status permits a wide range of restrictions to be imposed including housing a prisoner in a single cell, requiring them to share with a similarly diagnosed prisoner or segregating them in a hospital wing. Testing for HIV is not compulsory in prison but there has been evidence of inmates known to be either gay or drug users being placed on a VIR regime until agreeing to be tested. If the test is negative then they will be removed from the VIR regime.

7.67 In 1989, a policy document was issued by the prison department which indicated that prisoners with HIV who were well should be allowed to participate in normal prison regimes. However evidence suggests that this advice was largely ignored with HIV positive prisoners being routinely barred from physical activities and work. Segregation was (and still is) routinely justified on the basis that HIV positive inmates require protection from other prisoners. There is also colloquial evidence to suggest that HIV positive prisoners routinely have their confidentiality breached by prison officers or medical staff disclosing their status to other inmates.

7.68 Questions have also been raised about the quality of medical treatment available to HIV positive inmates. Prisoners can be moved fairly regularly between different prisons and such moves may affect continuity of treatment which can be crucial where modern combination therapies are being used. Medical negligence actions against the Prison Medical Service whilst possible are extremely unlikely—what serving prisoner with HIV would be willing to put themselves in such a vulnerable position?

7.69 It has proved extremely difficult to challenge prison policies with respect to treatment of HIV positive prisoners. Prison life in England and Wales is governed by the prison rules which are made by the Secretary of State under the powers set out in the Prison Act 1952. The legal status of the rules is unclear. A breach of the rules has never been recognised as a ground for judicial redress by the courts. Prisoners therefore have to rely on an assertion of their general rights in order to achieve any redress before the courts. The European Convention on Human Rights in particular, which is about to be adopted in UK law, has provided some prisoners with remedies against questionable treatment whilst in prison.

7.70 Article 3 of the Convention provides that 'no one shall be subjected to torture or degrading treatment or punishment'. 'Inhuman treatment' has been held by the European Court of Human Rights to be treatment that deliberately causes severe suffering, mental or physical[1]. 'Degrading treatment' usually means physical acts, for example interrogation practices. However, it has been held that any act which lowers a person in rank, position, reputation or character can be regarded as degrading treatment if it reaches a certain level of severity[2]. It has been suggested that the segregation or isolation of prisoners with HIV might amount to inhuman or degrading treatment[3] but the issue has not yet been tested. Again, the vulnerability of prisoners who are HIV positive may mean that many will be reluctant to pursue this potential remedy.

1 *Denmark v Greece* (1969); *Ireland v United Kingdom* (1978).
2 *East African Asians case* (1973) 3 EHRR 76.
3 Sieghart, P, *AIDS and Human Rights: A UK Perspective* (1989) BMA foundation for AIDS.

7.71 Potentially the most significant legal development relating to the treatment of HIV positive prisoners is the case brought by 37-year-old former prisoner Glen Fielding who is seeking a judicial review of the refusal by the prison service to supply him with condoms whilst serving his sentence. Mr Fielding was released from Wandsworth prison in 1996 after serving a sentence of four-and-a-half years. During the last two years of his sentence Mr Fielding repeatedly requested condoms from prison medical authorities, but was told that they could not be supplied. Mr Fielding was transferred between prisons many times during his sentence and believes that the principal reason was his repeated requests. The explanation given by the prison authorities for refusing to supply condoms is that it would encourage unlawful homosexual activity. This is on the basis that a prison cell could not be regarded as a private location.

7.72 The Sexual Offences Act 1967 is sometimes seen as 'legalising' gay male sexual activity. It does not do so. Rather it decriminalises such sexual activity within a very small window. The conditions for legality are that any such acts are in private and both parties have attained the age of 18[1].

1 The age of consent is due to be lowered to 16 by government legislation. See the Sexual Offences Amendment Act 1998.

7.73 'Private' has a particular definition. Section 1(2) of the Sexual Offences Act 1967 provides that an act is not in private when:

(a) more than two persons take part or are present;
(b) the act is in a lavatory to which the public have or are permitted to have access whether on payment or otherwise.

Thus, any group sexual activity between men is automatically unlawful as is activity between two men with another merely observing person. Similarly any activity in a public lavatory, even within a locked cubicle is automatically unlawful. The courts have also given consideration to the question of privacy particularly in relation to outdoor locations which might ordinarily be considered public but where sexual activity takes place late at night.

7.74 In *R v Reakes*[1] R was indicted for committing an act of buggery other than in private and without the consent of his sexual partner. The act took place in an enclosed unlit private yard at about 1 am. There was a gate from a public road into the yard and in the yard was a 'water closet' used by patrons of two neighbouring restaurants and the employees of a taxi service. Someone came to use the WC shortly after the act. R's defence was that the act was done in private and with his partner's consent. The judge directed as to privacy 'you look at all the surrounding circumstances, the time of night, the nature of the place including such matters as lighting and you consider further the likelihood of a third person coming upon the scene'. On appeal, the direction as to privacy was held to be clear and wholly satisfactory. The appellate court rejected submissions that the test of privacy was subjective and that regard should only be had to the moment when the act took place: all the circumstances had to be looked at and considered.

1 [1974] Crim LR 615.

7.75 The direction appears to concede that the public or private nature of a place can vary from time to time. The act done in a public bar or public library would presumably be done in private if it occurred when all the patrons had gone home, the doors were locked and only the two participants were present.

7.76 In the case of *R v Ghik*[1], G was indicted for committing an act of gross indecency with C in a public place: the underground car park at Euston station. The act was alleged to have taken place on stairs inside the NCP at 0035. The station shut at 0100. The case was before the Central Criminal Court and at the end of the prosecution case the defence submitted that the onus of disproving privacy lay upon the prosecution and that there had to be at least some evidence of the likelihood of a third person coming upon the scene. The fact that the place was ordinarily a public place was not conclusive since Parliament, in the 1967 Act, by specifically excluding from its provisions acts done in private in a public lavatory, clearly envisaged that privacy could be found and relied on in other public places.

1 [1984] Crim LR 110.

7.77 Thus, it is submitted, a prison cell or, indeed, another location within a prison may be regarded as 'private' depending upon the likelihood of a third party coming upon the scene. Furthermore, the prison authorities will clearly have a substantial discretion in deciding whether any complaint should be made to the police regarding discovered sexual activity and therefore whether any prosecution should be brought.

7.78 Mr Fielding's application for a judicial review of the refusal to supply condoms was initially rejected by the High Court. At the end of November 1998 the Court of Appeal reversed that decision but declined to expedite the judicial review[1]. Currently, no date has been set for the judicial review hearing. If the application succeeds, it could lead to prisoners being issued with condoms on request. Home Office guidelines on the issuing of condoms are unclear. It appears that there are some prisoners diagnosed as HIV positive who have been supplied with condoms by the prison authorities. However this restricted policy does not acknowledge the risk to prisoners who do not have virus and who engage in unprotected sexual activity.

1 Unreported.

D OUTREACH WORK

7.79 In HIV-related health promotion, there is a perceived need to target certain groups, for example intravenous drug users, gay men who make use of public lavatories or 'cruising grounds' for the purpose of sexual contacts or women engaged in prostitution, who may be most in need of the information. As well as providing health information, outreach workers may also wish to provide more practical help in the form of contraceptives or needle exchanges. There is a concern that such work should not fall foul of the criminal law.

1 Counselling by telephone

7.80 It is an offence under s 43 of the Telecommunications Act 1984 to send by means of a public telecommunications service a message that is 'grossly offensive or of an indecent, obscene or menacing character'. A prosecution under this provision might technically be possible if it was felt that advice, or counselling, relating to safer sex as given by counsellors to members of the public over the telephone was 'obscene', but it is very difficult, given the one to one nature of counselling, to envisage a complaint ever arising to provide grounds for a prosecution.

7.81 It is an offence under the Sexual Offences Act 1956 to aid, abet, counsel or procure an act of anal intercourse (buggery) between two men or a man and a woman. or an act of gross indecency (for example, oral sex) between two men. The Sexual Offences Act 1967 only permits such acts between consenting males over the age of 21 in private[1].

1 An amendment to the Criminal Justice and Public Order Bill 1994 passed by the House of Commons on 21 February 1994 will, if the Bill is passed, lower the age of consent for gay male sexual activities to 18 years of age.

7.82 If counselling or outreach work is confined to advising the likely participants as to how to perform these acts more safely, it is difficult to see how such counselling might be viewed as the promotion or encouragement of such behaviour. Again, from a practical point of view, it is also difficult to envisage who the complainant to found a prosecution might be.

2 Outreach work with sex workers

7.83 Understandably, outreach workers who liaise with male and female prostitutes may be involved in the provision of condoms to their clients. Whilst it is extremely difficult to envisage the distribution of condoms as placing the outreach worker at any practical risk of investigation or prosecution for a criminal offence, the carrying of condoms by male or female prostitutes can increase the risk of prosecution for them. This factor should be carefully considered by condom providers and it may be considered appropriate to advise the recipients about the risks.

7.84 The carrying of condoms by an individual is, by itself, clearly not sufficient to establish one of the several criminal offences associated with prostitution—for example, soliciting[1]. However the carrying of condoms has been used by the police as corroborative evidence to support an allegation before the courts that an individual is operating as a prostitute. Such strategies have been the subject of attacks by, amongst others, the English Collective of Prostitutes, as it discourages the carrying of condoms by prostitutes and consequently encourages the practice of unsafe penetrative sexual intercourse.

1 Section 1 of the Street Offences Act 1959 for women and s 32 of the Sexual Offences Act 1956 for men.

7.85 As a result of such lobbying, the Metropolitan Police Service indicated, at the end of 1993, that they would not seek, in the future, to rely on the carrying of condoms by women accused of prostitution as evidence in such cases.

7.86 In police prosecutions of brothels, gay saunas and the like, the presence and availability of quantities of condoms and even safer sex literature[1] on the premises has been used as evidence to indicate that unlawful sexual acts and/or prostitution are taking or are intended to take place. Using the presence of condoms and safer sex material as evidence in this manner is likely to lead to sauna and brothel managers restricting the availability of such items on their premises with the consequent increased risk of the spread of infection.

1 Safer sex literature was seized by the West Midlands Police in their raid on the Greenhouse gay sauna near Birmingham in January 1994.

3 Counselling intravenous drug users and establishing needle exchanges

7.87 Very similar analyses to those adopted in the preceding section regarding the 'risks' to safer sex counsellors in providing such information and condoms can be applied to situation of those counselling intravenous drug users and providing clean needles through needle exchanges.

7.88 It is very difficult to envisage such counsellors or providers as being at risk from a criminal prosecution. Even as a matter of academic argument it is hard to see how a possible charge of aiding and abetting an offence under the Misuse of Drugs Act 1971 of possession of prohibited drugs could be sustained since the connection between the counselling or needle provision and the possession is arguably impossible to establish. Furthermore, hypodermic needles are specifically excluded from the provisions of the Misuse of Drugs Act 1971 which make it an offence to supply drugs paraphernalia[1].

1 Misuse of Drugs Act 1971, s 9A.

7.89 It is an offence to incite another to commit an offence under the Act[1], but arguably the provision of a clean needle to an existing drug user cannot be viewed as an additional incitement and in any event public policy criteria should operate to prevent a prosecution in such circumstances.

1 Misuse of Drugs Act 1971, s 19.

7.90 It is also an offence for the managers and occupiers of premises knowingly to permit the supply of drugs at the premises although it is not an offence to permit their intravenous consumption[1]. Managers of needle exchanges should, arguably, still have policies prohibiting drug possession, use and supply on their premises. People attending needle exchanges may be placing themselves at risk of police investigation for drugs offences and those involved in establishing such exchanges may need to take steps to try and ensure security and anonymity.

1 Misuse of Drugs Act 1971, s 8.

Chapter 8

Personal finance and HIV

Ivan Massow

A INTRODUCTION

8.01 The financial problems facing people who are diagnosed HIV positive are clearly very different from those of others who fall ill. As soon as the diagnosis is made, a wide number of financial options disappear. This is especially true of the various types of health and life assurance. It is one of the ironies of insurance that those who need it most are denied it.

8.02 Another big problem for people who are HIV positive is planning. HIV is one of the most unpredictable diseases known. Some people will die shortly after diagnosis while others are still alive and at work 15 or 20 years after contracting the virus, without a single symptom.

8.03 In addition, new drugs and technology could affect the future of the carrier. This makes planning for the future very difficult. Should one fail to take one out and then fully recover (or become a long-term survivor of HIV), he or she may end up very poor in retirement. Alternatively, they may pay into a pension and watch the pension fund provide almost nothing because tax legislation will not allow a personal pension fund to be commuted for cash.

8.04 One of the greatest needs of those who are HIV positive is to ensure they have sufficient income. This may not be apparent at first, but it usually becomes so. A large number of people with HIV are able to continue working for almost the entire duration of the infection, either because the virus has little or no physical effect or because the nature of the person's work allows them to make up periods of absence. However, in many cases the trauma of the diagnosis itself is enough to lead to ill-health.

8.05 Much depends on each individual's way of dealing with the illness. Some may cope by throwing themselves wholeheartedly into their jobs, others may prefer to take time out to come to terms with the way their lives have changed. But, no matter how the disease is dealt with, it is certain that bills will keep arriving even though an individual's income may have dried up. In some cases even more money may be needed to cover the cost of, say, adapting the home or moving house. Some employers may be willing (indeed, some will be contractually bound) to cover all or part of a sick employee's salary for a while, but this is unlikely to continue for the whole period of ill-health.

8.06 In a nutshell, for a person who becomes HIV positive, there are very few options available. The main problems are as follows:

(a) Health insurance cannot be obtained, and in any case, it wouldn't pay out if one became ill because nearly all health insurers exclude HIV.
(b) Income protection policies cannot be obtained and, again, they don't cover HIV.
(c) The government requires individuals to insure their mortgage interest premiums against the possibility of falling sick and having to leave work. However, once again these policies do not pay out if they are HIV positive.
(d) Travel insurance is very difficult to obtain, often restricting those with HIV to travel within countries with reciprocal institutionalised health services (basically around Europe).
(e) Mortgages become difficult to get, especially via a bank, because affordable life cover or, in general, *any* life cover is impossible to arrange for people who are HIV positive.
(f) Inheritance tax planning is practically impossible because the life companies will not issue whole of life contracts. As many people with HIV are gay and cannot legally marry, their partners will usually lose out heavily as a result of their deaths.
(g) Business people with HIV are stifled because they are unable to arrange key person insurance or to cover themselves in accordance with any lending institution requirement.
(h) Pension funds will often not pay out to partners and the government's review criteria and transfer rules make it impossible to help people to transfer into a plan that will pay out in the event of death.
(i) People who are HIV positive who are hoping to cash in their pensions are likely to be sold annuities on 'standard mortality rates'. As such, they are only ever likely to receive from their pensions a small percentage of the amount originally invested within the annuity.
(j) The Inland Revenue, although happy to see a pension fund of a personal pension pass to a beneficiary free of tax on death, does not allow the individual with a terminal disease access to the pension fund prior to death (although company pension schemes can grant such privileges when the individual has less than a year to live).
(k) Critical illness cover is difficult to arrange and excludes HIV.

These are just some of the financial problems facing someone with HIV. In this chapter some of the few solutions will be outlined.

B PERMANENT HEALTH INSURANCE

8.07 Most medical insurance and permanent health insurance (PHI) taken out during the last few years will exclude treatment for HIV-related illnesses. Even medical complaints that are obviously nothing to do with the disease are bound to be caught up in such a general exclusion. The only exception may be policies that were taken out earlier than 1987 when insurance companies were less concerned about HIV, most of which have been retrospectively altered to exclude the disease.

8.08 In any case, if someone has a PHI policy that is a few years old, it should be checked out. If there is no specific HIV exclusion, make sure there is also nothing there that allows the insurer to change the terms of the policy without prior warning. Several companies include such a clause, and use it as a let-out from HIV-related claims.

8.09 Although an insurance company may reserve the right to change some terms and conditions of a policy, the 'permanent' in the PHI name means that once the policy has been started it cannot be cancelled—regardless of how the policyholder's health or lifestyle changes. The only exception may be where the policyholder takes up a new occupation, which is more dangerous than the last. However, some companies have started selling short-term and reviewable PHI policies in order to get round the 'permanent' obligation.

8.10 The heavy claims experience of some health insurers has caused them to clamp down on claims. One or two have even employed 'medical' staff whose job is to monitor the condition of those who are already receiving payments from them. If the company doctor believes that an individual is able to work in spite of the illness—regardless of the opinion of an independent doctor—then the claim may be disallowed. An independent financial adviser should be able to identify the companies with a history of treating claimants in this way.

1 PHI for those in HIV/AIDS 'high risk groups'

8.11 Given that most established permanent health insurance still does not cover HIV, there is little that can be done to provide cover if someone has already contracted HIV. However, as a consequence of the perceived HIV risk to insurers, insurance companies very often continue to send intrusive questionnaires asking specific sexuality-related questions. Even those who are honest about their sexuality, test negative for HIV, and are healthy will often be refused cover.

8.12 The main people subjected to this form of discrimination are gay men. While being gay does not always exclude a person from being covered and some companies will offer 'standard rates' to gay clients, it can complicate matters when a claim is made.

8.13 Several state benefits are available to those who are unable to continue working, but these can often prove inadequate. The basic statutory sick pay is available for up to 28 weeks and usually too small for most people to survive on.

2 Medical expenses insurance

8.14 Medical expenses insurance is the best known and most widely used type of cover. In return for a regular premium, the holder gains relatively quick access to a range of private hospital services. Sometimes the insurance company owns these services, but mainly it just pays the bill. The types of policy available are many and varied, mainly because of increased competition are HIV positive. In addition, those in so-called HIV high risk groups may not be covered for HIV.

3 Exclusions

8.15 In addition to HIV, general exclusions under both PHI and medical expenses insurance include illnesses caused by alcoholism, drug addiction, self-inflicted injury, or childbirth. Certain dangerous occupations may also be excluded or subject to special terms. Many companies also run 'simplified underwriting' schemes where they simply exclude pre-existing illness. Naturally, once again, HIV will disqualify a person from cover, as will a range of other illnesses.

8.16 Some insurers are prepared to offer a moratorium with certain illnesses: if an individual has not needed treatment for five years or so, he or she may effectively be granted a clean bill of health. The only proviso is that for two years the pre-existing illness, and anything related to it, will not be covered. The difficulty here is in defining which illnesses are connected. An insurer may happily provide cover to a person who had a heart attack six years ago, but with an exclusion for heart disease during the first two years of the policy term. But if during the first two years a claim were made because of high blood pressure, this could well be deemed to be related to the pre-existing illness and the claim disallowed.

4 Group PHI

8.17 The vast majority of private health plans are funded by employers as a perk. There are very few providers who offer HIV cover for groups: UNUM, Canada Life and others. However, this cover may be prohibitively expensive.

5 Accident and sickness

8.18 Accident and sickness insurance is in some ways similar to PHI. The main difference is that the policy is renewed every year, which makes it generally less attractive than PHI. If an individual's health deteriorates or he/she makes a claim, the insurance company can alter the terms of the contract at the renewal date. It may increase the premium, or even cancel the policy completely. Accident and sickness insurance, unlike PHI, can be arranged to provide a specific amount of cover. The premium cost can be weighed against the amount of insurance required. As with PHI, the benefits can be deferred for a while, reducing the premium cost further. Once again this cover excludes HIV.

6 Critical illness insurance

8.19 Critical illness insurance (sometimes known as 'dread disease insurance') is yet another health insurance option. Once such a policy has been taken out, if the holder gets one or more of a range of specified illnesses the policy will pay out a lump sum. This money is tax-free and can be put to whatever use is desired. For example, it can supplement income during recuperation, or if home alterations would make life easier, the money can be used for that. The types of illness covered are much the same across the range of insurance companies selling critical illness benefit. The list normally includes heart attacks, cancer, renal failure, heart bypass surgery, strokes, organ transplants and several others.

8.20 The problem for gay people, and others in HIV at risk groups, who are thinking of buying this type of insurance is that it is invariably attached to a life assurance policy. Even when purchased alone, it very often involves lifestyle questionnaires and the possibility of higher premiums or exclusion.

8.21 On the whole, critical illness cover rarely includes cover for HIV. The one or two insurance companies that consider HIV to be a critical illness will pay up only if the claimant can prove that the infection was the result of a 'needle-stick injury' (an accidental jab with an HIV-infected syringe, usually affecting doctors and nurses). Again, it is important to find out from an independent adviser which companies have a better attitude than others towards people in AIDS high risk groups.

AIDS as a critical illness

8.22 Remarkably, critical illness insurance is the only area of the personal insurance market where cover against AIDS is available. At least one provider includes the disease on its list. Unfortunately, a claim can only be made under limited circumstances: the infection must have been contracted through no 'fault' of the claimant's, and several other people must have been infected at the same time. This aims to include all but those infected by blood transfusion, but with updated blood screening techniques this is now an unlikely event.

8.23 The wording of such policies is to a certain extent open to interpretation, and it would be interesting to see whether there are circumstances where HIV sexually transmitted between willing partners could result in a claim. These are often potential challenges to the refusal of cover.

7 Tax treatment

8.24 For policies that do pay out, permanent health and critical illness insurance is now paid free of income tax.

C LIFE ASSURANCE

8.25 Although almost every life assurance product on the market will payout if someone dies of an AIDS related illness when it the past if there is no exclusion clause, if a person is HIV positive now they will not qualify for life assurance of any kind.

8.26 In addition to people with HIV being refused life cover, there is also a knock-on effect for people who fall into, so called, AIDS high risk groups, such as gay men. These people are also generally refused cover or, at the very least, have their premiums increased (loaded). It is not unusual to see a 'lifestyle' related hike in premiums of 600% for gay men purely because of the supposed AIDS risk, although the industry standard is 250%.

1 Cash surrender of insurance policies and selling the death values (viaticating)

8.27 If an individual already has a life assurance policy that is at least a few years old, there is a chance that it will have an accrued value. Even a pure life assurance policy, one that normally has a value only when the insured person dies, can sometimes be turned into cash by arranging a 'viatical settlement'.

(i) Cash surrender

8.28 An endowment policy, the type of policy, which has an investment element, can simply be cashed in with the insurance company it was bought from. The amount that the policyholder will get back will depend on a number of factors such as the length of time he/she has owned the policy and how much bonus has been added. In some cases, especially with policies that are only a few years old, there may be no cash surrender value at all. This is because during the early years of a policy, especially with the poorer quality insurers, most of the contributions may have been used to pay the life company's charges.

8.29 When the policy does have a cash surrender value, that value could be less than the total amount that the applicant has paid in, even if the time is fairly close to the policy's maturity date. This is because insurance companies frequently apply penalties to policies that are cashed in early. Also, from a tax viewpoint, policies have to be in force for at least ten years for the proceeds to be paid free of tax. If the individual surrenders the policy in less than ten years, he/she may be landed with a tax bill.

8.30 In spite of the possible drawbacks, there is no harm in asking the insurance company to tell the policyholder how much his or her policy is worth. But if surrendering an endowment policy appears to be a poor option, there are alternatives.

(ii) Auctioning an endowment policy

8.31 Many types of insurance policy have an inherent value. For endowment policies this is the maturity value plus the death benefit; for whole-of-life policies it is the death benefit only. A growing number of investors are starting

to see that buying a second-hand policy can be extremely profitable. They agree to pay the policyholder a cash sum, and take over any remaining premium payments. In return they will receive the tax-free cash payout at the end of the policy's term. Auctions of such policies are held regularly, and usually secure more cash for the policyholder than a cash surrender would. A financial adviser will be able to suggest several reputable auction houses. Before deciding to auction a policy however, it may be worth looking at whether the death value has a greater value by:
(a) selling the death value; or
(b) taking accelerated life cover (terminal death benefit).

2 Selling the death value (viaticating)

8.32 This is a variation on the above theme, and is a way of raising cash on a pure life policy or which otherwise would have no value until the day the policyholder dies or on an endowment where the surrender value may be much lower. Instead of buying the investment value on the policy, the investor buys the life cover. The policyholder is paid a cash sum by the investor who, in turn, makes a claim against the insurance company when the policyholder dies.

8.33 The idea of a complete stranger having a financial interest in someone's death may sound like a plot for a thriller, but in fact it can be an excellent way of raising money just when an individual who is ill needs it most—even though he/she is likely to be telephoned regularly to see whether or not the policy holder is still alive. The buyer takes over any regular premium payments and the policyholder is paid between 50% and 80% of the sum assured.

8.34 For example, in the UK, this service is offered by a company set up in 1992 called Life Benefit Resources, which buys most types of life policy from those diagnosed as having a life expectancy of two years or less. At the time of writing, the company was looking at the viability of pushing this limit up to three years. It claims to have paid out an average 69.4% of the insurance value of policies it has bought so far.

8.35 Since the introduction of the new combination therapies and their enormous success in keeping people alive, companies offering a 'viaticating' service have become more reluctant to take on people who are HIV positive. Although they will still offer a settlement where the individual is ill and not responding to the new therapies, these cases are quite rare, as the drug trials have been very successful.

(i) Accelerated life cover (terminal death benefit)

8.36 For those who are diagnosed as terminally ill, more and more companies are prepared to pay out life assurance claims before the policyholder dies. This makes sound business assurance paying out before the policy holder dies is an attractive add-on benefit for those looking for cover, and it adds nothing to the cost of the policy other than the prospect of paying out slightly earlier.

8.37 If a client has a life assurance policy, this possibility should be looked at carefully before approaching a viatical company. Even if there is nothing in the policy booklet to indicate that they will pay out upon the discovery of a terminal illness, some insurers will agree to make this payment on a one-off basis if approached. There is nothing to be lost by trying and nothing to worry about if a client's HIV status is revealed to an insurer in doing so. Providing a policy was effected legally and using full disclosure, it remains completely valid and cannot be cancelled by the insurer.

D TYPES OF LIFE COVER

1 Whole-of-life assurance

8.38 Whole-of-life assurance is the most basic type of life assurance, and is most commonly used to plan for inheritance tax (or death duty, as it used to be called).

2 Term assurance

8.39 Term assurance is probably the most common type of life assurance. It has the same with-profits and without-profits alternatives as does whole-of-life, but with much more besides. Instead of providing life cover for the rest of the policyholder's life, term assurance covers a specific period. This has two advantages. First, it is cheaper than whole-of-life because the insurance company is taking a smaller risk. If, for example, with a 20-year life policy there is a good chance that the insurance company will never have to pay out. Second, it means that your cover can be taken out when it is needed most. In everyone's life there are times when their financial responsibilities are greater than at others. Those with mortgages or who have dependants will want to make sure their commitments are met after they die. But the level of such commitment is unlikely to remain at the same level throughout one's life. At some point, for example, one's mortgage will be paid off. Because of its range of possible applications, there are various types of term assurance designed to meet certain needs.

Decreasing term assurance

8.40 Decreasing term assurance is usually used to insure loans—especially mortgages. Even for those who feel they have no need for life assurance, lenders frequently make loans conditional on its purchase. Sometimes, as with a mortgage, a lender will insist that the policy be assigned to it. This means that the lender will hold on to the actual policy document and the borrower will only receive a copy. If the borrower dies during the policy term, the proceeds from the policy will automatically be used to repay the loan. Anything left over will be paid to the estate.

8.41 Decreasing term assurance differs from other types of term assurance because the level of cover it provides gradually reduces. This makes it best suited to loans where the regular repayments consist of interest plus a portion of the loan itself. With these, the amount owed steadily reduces from the first repayment to the last. So the level of insurance cover required clearly reduces as well. Although there is nothing to stop one buying a term assurance contract to do the job, it would be more expensive than a decreasing term policy and would add to the overall cost of the loan.

3 Family income assurance

8.42 Family income assurance is another type of term assurance contract. In spite of its name, it can be useful whether or not one has a family. It is broadly the same as any other term assurance except that instead of paying out a cash lump sum it provides the holder's dependants with a regular tax-free income after his or her death. With some policies, income payments will continue for a specified period no matter when someone dies during the term of the policy. There is a cheaper version, effectively based on a decreasing term assurance, with which if an individual dies during the term of the policy, income will still be paid but only until the date the policy was due to finish. This, again, can be a useful cost-cutting measure if there are specific liabilities to cover.

4 Convertible and renewable assurance

8.43 As with whole-of-life products, term assurance can also be fairly flexible. For some people it may not be so easy to predict how their future insurance needs may change. Rather than be locked into a policy with a specific term and cover they may prefer a more flexible approach. Convertible and renewable policies can provide this.

(i) Convertible assurance

8.44 Convertible term assurance allows the policyholder to switch to another type of policy with the same company at any time during the term—usually without requiring any further evidence of health or lifestyle. There are, however, several restrictions on how this option can be used.

(ii) Renewable assurance

8.45 Renewable term assurance policies are usually convertible too, but also include an option to renew the policy at the end of the term without further evidence of health. The renewal periods tend to be quite short—about five years—and such policies often carry the same age restrictions as convertible plans.

5 Some add-on benefits

8.46 For a while during the 1980s there was a trend towards selling life assurance with what was called a guaranteed insurability option. This gave policyholders the right to increase their life cover further medical evidence. Like several other 'add-on' benefits, it became increasingly available on policies other than the flexible varieties mentioned above. There are still some companies prepared to offer it, but because of the AIDS risk the trend is no longer upwards.

8.47 Another typical add-on benefit with many life policies is waiver of premium. Very often, for either health or financial reasons, people find it difficult to continue paying the premiums on a life policy. Waiver of premium can take two forms. Either the insurer will allow the insured to stop paying premiums for a limited period without reducing the level of cover or, under some circumstances, it will waive the premiums altogether. Without the waiver there are two main risks. Either the policy could be cancelled, or the benefits could be reduced to match the total level of premiums paid into the plan. Unfortunately, waiver of premium does not cover HIV.

6 Key-person (often known as key-man) insurance

8.48 People with HIV/AIDS who are in business may have different life assurance needs from individuals. Often, when the nature of the business makes two individuals financially dependent on each other, some type of cover is needed to ensure that if one business partner dies the other will not lose money. It is only under these circumstances that individuals who are not related to each other can cross-propose life policies. This means that instead of having a policy where the owner and the beneficiary are the same person, one person can own a policy insuring another person's life. Naturally, where the individual whose life is sought to be insured is HIV positive, no matter who effects the policy, the insurer will not grant cover.

E LIFE ASSURANCE SAVINGS PLANS

1 Endowment policies

8.49 The most common form of savings policy is the endowment, usually used to back interest-only mortgages. As with many insurance contracts, the premium paid is pooled with other policyholders' money in the insurance company's life fund. It is then invested on the policyholders' behalf by the fund manager into relatively safe gilts and bonds, although some funds have moved towards more volatile equities.

8.50 As a with-profits fund grows, bonuses are added to the initial sum assured on the policy in the same way as for with-profits, whole-of-life, and term assurance policies. The difference here is that, instead of paying out on death, the policy pays out on maturity. If the money is invested for more than 10 years this payout will be free of any income tax or capital gains tax and will not affect any other tax allowance.

8.51 Understandably, the premiums for this type of policy are a lot higher than for straightforward life cover. Their efficiency has also been called into question during recent years. During the boom years of the 1980s, endowment plans were extremely popular mainly because they were safe investments providing a better return than the bank or building society. The only drawback was the lack of access to one's money. Few people worried about this until bonus rates started to fall at the beginning of the 1990s.

8.52 Although it is possible to arrange cover for people in AIDS 'high risk' groups such as gay men, people who are HIV positive will not receive cover. However, it has been known for insurers to provide a policy with a 'debt' against it equal to the life cover. This means that the policy pays out in the event of death with one hand and takes back the cover with the other hand.

2 What to expect if an HIV positive person attempts to arrange life cover

8.53 Most single men risk being weeded out for closer inspection when they apply for insurance, particularly if they live with another single man. So too is anyone previously infected with a sexually transmitted disease or anyone who has visited a part of the world with a high level of HIV infection, like Africa or Southeast Asia.

8.54 The ABI have substituted the wording, 'Have you ever had an HIV test?' for 'Have you tested positive for HIV/AIDS?'. Although this seems like an improvement, insurers will often ask single men the former question on their 'lifestyle' questionnaire and, even if the test was negative, the company will consider it an indicator of a high-risk lifestyle rather than a sign of how safe the client is as a risk. If someone is HIV positive, his or her proposal will be turned down outright.

8.55 Depending on the individual insurance company, there are a number of ways they might react to any of these answers. In most cases the applicant will be sent a lifestyle questionnaire. These nasty, intrusive forms ask more direct questions about one's sexual activity and general lifestyle, including specify questions about homosexuality, bisexuality and sometimes numbers of sexual partners.

8.56 Depending on the applicant's answers and the attitude of the insurance company chosen, there are a number of possible outcomes. Even without being HIV positive, the applicant may be refused life cover altogether. This could also result in the applicant's name being added to the Impaired Lives Register, which could prevent him or her from applying for insurance from another company. Even if one manages to avoid this list, with any life assurance applications he or she makes elsewhere the question will inevitably be asked as to whether he or she has ever been refused insurance.

8.57 The good news is that there are companies now that will insure gay men and other 'high risk' groups. The bad news is that they will probably be expected to stump up a higher than usual premium. This 'loading' can be up to 250% more than the premium paid by a heterosexual man of similar age and fitness.

8.58 The only way of avoiding these problems completely is not to bother with life assurance at all, however this is not a practical solution. Even those who feel no particular urge to buy life assurance will chapter, pensions, loans, mortgages, healthcare, savings, and various other types of financial instrument can all include at least an element of life cover.

8.59 Lying on a proposal form is not at all recommended, although many gay men have done it simply to obtain mortgages and pensions. In fact it can prove to be an absolute minefield. Even if the client can pass the application stage without being given away by his/her doctor, one can be certain that the insurance company will be extremely cautious before paying out. If the applicant dies, even from something totally unrelated to AIDS, and the insurance company finds that he or she was less than honest on the proposal form, it will probably refuse to pay out.

F PENSIONS

1 The pensions revolution

8.60 State-funded pension schemes—which, until 1988, formed the backbone of most people's retirement planning—depended on there being a high proportion of people in work relative to those drawing their pension.

8.61 That situation is gradually being reversed in the UK and other developed nations, as governments find it more difficult to make ends meet. The rate at which the proportion of older people in the UK is increasing led to calls for dramatic changes in the way pensions are funded. The alternative, it was claimed, would have been a failure to pay the pensions people expected, or tax increases to cover the shortfall.

8.62 Making other pension arrangements, either through a company scheme or a personal pension, is essential. And the sooner one starts, the better: the longer there is to build up a retirement fund, the bigger the pension will be. Starting early means the cost of funding an adequate pension will take a much smaller portion of income than if one starts later.

8.63 For someone who is HIV positive the problem of how to fund his or her retirement is compounded by the high proportion of pension schemes run by insurance companies. Personal pensions, which may be based on life assurance products, could be especially problematic for obvious reasons. Even if an individual with HIV is offered a contract with waiver-of-premium benefit with HIV excluded (wavier of premium undertakes to cover the premium payments on your pension if you become too ill to work), the client would need to be very careful. Regardless of the exclusion, questions about HIV are still asked and the contract would still be refused.

2 State pensions

8.64 The most basic retirement provision is the state retirement or 'old-age' pension. Anyone who pays National Insurance (NI) contributions is entitled to one. State pensions are not geared to the individual's own earnings during his or her working life, but—as a rule of thumb—are about 20% of national average earnings. To qualify, one must have been credited with National Insurance contributions for about 90% of one's working life. For this reason, during long periods of absence from work, one should if possible sign on as unemployed even if one does not need Income Support Benefit. Once registered with the Department of Social Security, the necessary credits will continue to be made until the individual finally signs off.

8.65 The basic pension increases each year in line with the Retail Prices Index. Even if an individual makes other arrangements, the basic pension should still be part of the picture. The right to receive it is unaffected by other pensions held, and it can be a useful little extra on retirement. Like other state pension benefits, it can be drawn in any EC country.

3 SERPS

8.66 The State Earnings Related Pension Scheme, or SERPS, was introduced in 1978. Like the old-age pension, it aims to provide 20% of average earnings. The difference is that this is 20% of the individual's own earnings, rather than 20% of the national average. Entitlement is based on the level of National Insurance contributions made and on an average of the person's income.

8.67 It is SERPS that the government says it is having trouble funding, and the percentage of income it is able to cover is gradually reducing. Those who have paid National Insurance contributions for most of their working lives and will be retiring before 2009–10 can expect to receive up to 25% of their best 20 years' average earnings. After that year, the rate will be 20% of the total earned during the entire working life. This will deliver significantly less than the present system.

8.68 SERPS provides only a regular income. None of it can be taken as a lump sum, and there is no way of getting to it before the normal retirement date. However, it is possible to postpone SERPS payments benefits can be delayed for up to five years, and will grow slightly during that time. Self-employed people have never been eligible for SERPS contributions or benefits, and have had to look to the private market to fund their retirement.

4 Should someone with HIV take a pension?

8.69 Pensions represent a huge and very complicated issue for people with HIV. This is one of the many areas of financial advice where there are often no clear-cut answers to the many problems that exist. For example, how can someone who is HIV positive decide whether to take out a pension where, by and large, if they need to take an early pension due to ill health, the pension will inevitably be small? The problem is that pensions are not insurance contracts, but simply glorified savings vehicles with lots of tax relief. As such, if someone has been only saving for a few years, it is unlikely that he or she will have built up a significant enough fund to provide a realistic pension.

8.70 The next problem is that, although insurers may increase the premiums of those who are in AIDS 'high risk' groups by as much as 600% per annum, even though the individual is not HIV positive, when it comes to paying annuities even to those will full blown AIDS, the insurers often choose to asses

8.71 As such, the level of pension given will be the same as any other young person trying to buy an annuity to cover a long and full life. In reality, especially before the advent of the new combination therapies, someone with a diagnosis sufficient to qualify for an ill-health pension, had on average a two-year life expectancy. Other than any tax free lump sums that may have been available from the pension policy, the policyholder is only likely to receive between 5–7% of the pension fund for every year they live. Given a two-year prognosis, this means that the insurers will pocket the remaining 86%.

8.72 As discussed later in this section, there are now 'short life annuities' operated by specialist outlets. However, these are very rare and complicated to apply for.

8.73 The problems for people with HIV/AIDS, however, don't stop here. Quite frequently people with HIV or AIDS are gay men and this causes a double set of problems. Because pensions are written under discretionary trusts, it can be difficult to ensure that any accrued benefits which may be payable on death go to the partner, even before the pension has started to be paid.

8.74 This issue has caused brokers who provide advice in the field a great many problems. The government's pension transfer policy has had very sweeping implications which makes it practically impossible for brokers to transfer funds from pensions which will not pay out to same-sex partners or schemes that won't provide a 'short life annuity', if the other transfer conditions are not perfect. In brief, the receiving scheme must be able to provide an equivalent or better pension for the client and a notional spouse and children, even though the client has no spouse or children and will never live to retirement.

8.75 As a result, brokers have had to accept the cost of expensive audits and pension reviews on old cases where the individuals were HIV positive and gay and could not receive the desired benefits from their original pension scheme. It is suggested therefore, even though such a transfer is much better in theory for the client, that it is more bother than it is worth.

G PERSONAL PENSIONS

8.76 There are essentially two types of personal pension today:

(a) the old-style s 226 'personal pensions', which cannot be offered any longer (although many people do still have them); and
(b) the modern day personal pension plans, sometimes referred to as PPPs, which arrived as recently as 1988.

The two pensions are, in essence, very similar. However, the new style plan can be contributed to by an employer, has slightly lower tax-free cash at retirement and is designed to be easier and simpler to understand.

8.77 Apart from filling the gap for those who were not otherwise covered by SERPS or by company schemes, personal pensions were introduced to encourage people to make their own pension provision. The government hoped that this would relieve the pressure on the public purse, and that people would be considerably better off in retirement. National Insurance contributions are not reduced, they are merely rebated unless one enters a company scheme. The contracting-out incentive for opting out is 1% for people aged over 30.

8.78 Personal pension plans are sold mainly by insurance companies, building societies and banks. They are of a type known as money purchase schemes. The individual's contributions, limited to a stated maximum, are invested on his or her behalf in a tax-free fund. Over time the contributions build up, and—if the fund's manager is doing a good job—will have grown substantially by the time of retirement, which with personal pensions can be anywhere between the ages of 50 and 75. The money is then made available to fund one's retirement.

8.79 The level of the pension contribution naturally depends on how well the investment grows, the term until retirement, and how much is required at retirement. For someone who is HIV positive, these can be very difficult questions to answer.

1 Life cover

8.80 At the moment, no pension company offers people with HIV life cover, unless they are lucky enough to have it automatically included in an employer's pension policy without medical questions (some of the larger occupational plans do this). However, for those who are not HIV positive, an additional 5% of gross income can be used to fund a life assurance element within the personal pension. This can ensure that a lump sum is paid to an estate if the policy holder dies before a given age, to a maximum of 75. The inclusion of life assurance cover in a pension also means that contributions attract tax relief at the highest rate.

8.81 If someone already has pension life cover before diagnosis of the virus, this policy should be maintained at all costs. However, it is vitally important to make sure that this payment goes to the person for whom it is intended (especially important in the case of someone who is in a same-sex or unmarried relationship). If the pension plan manager will not allow the policyholder to make this clear on the contract, have it confirmed with a trust. That way one can ensure that the partner or any dependants have the benefit of the cash, even if there is a likelihood of some infighting from hostile relatives about who is to receive the money.

2 Using pensions to benefit partners and dependants

8.82 There may be a situation where an individual is working, and takes a dim view of his or her prognosis and as such has never really considered pensions but wants to save to assist a dependant after the individual's death. The best advice, usually, is still to take out a pension. People with children or other dependants and who want to save to provide a lump sum in the event of death would ordinarily consider a building society account or an ISA to put money into a pension scheme and name the child as the beneficiary in the event of death. This way, contributions receive full tax relief at the individual's highest rate, contributions grow in a tax-free environment and the pension fund is payable as a lump sum to the dependant free of inheritance tax.

8.83 The largest benefit for people who set up a pension plan as a savings vehicle for dependants is that arrangements set up years ago for people who believed their life expectancy to be very short, now look more and more likely to be used as a proper pension for the clients themselves. Fortunately, the new drug trials are breathing new hope for life into an otherwise depressing prognosis. In the circumstances, failing to put money into a pension could mean, if the drug trials are successful and new drugs are discovered, that individuals could find themselves retiring without benefit. In addition, psychologically speaking, the effects of continuing with life as normal and working towards retirement is believed by many to be a positive step towards prolonging healthy living.

8.84 Ironically, although company pension plans can make lump sum payments equivalent to the amount in the pension fund to individuals with less that a year to live, the Inland Revenue has blocked this on personal pension plans. It seems perverse that a person could save hard into a pension for many years and build up a cash fund which, when he or she really needs it and is about to die, can't be accessed, so that benefits must be relied on instead.

3 Expression of wishes

8.85 Regardless of how a pension is arranged, whether through a company scheme or a private pension plan, it is important for the individual to complete an Expression of Wishes form. This is to try to ensure that if the individual dies before receiving a pension, the full fund of money that has accrued to pay for it will pass to whoever he or she wants to have it. On death, pension benefits from occupational pension schemes fall outside the estate, and are likely to end up with the wrong people if specific wishes have not been expressed; there is even a risk that the insurance company will hang on to them. Pension benefits from a personal pension plan, however, are considered to be part of the deceased person's estate, so with these an Expression of Wishes form will be needed only if no will exists.

8.86 However, the Expression of Wishes form can be overridden by the pension company. If the contributor has asked that the fund be passed to a gay partner, the insurance company may decide that an ex-wife or child has prior claim. Even if no such relatives exist, the company may refuse to pay the fund to a same-sex or unmarried partner. To overcome this, the individual needs to talk to an independent financial adviser who has successfully negotiated an agreement with a quality pension company whereby it will honour the express wishes of the insured.

4 Waiver of premium

8.87 Many pension plans (and life assurance policies) offer waiver-of-premium benefit for those who are too ill to continue working. While this does not provide any cash, the pension or assurance policy will continue accruing benefits—at least for a while. Unfortunately, newer plans have an HIV exclusion clause and old plans have usually been changed retrospectively to avoid potential claims. As with all modern income protection plans, this exclusion means that even if you are disabled after being hit by a bus, an insured person may be prevented from making a claim if he or she is HIV positive.

5 Company pensions generally

8.88 Company pensions continue to exist despite the pensions revolution. There are two basic types:
(a) contracted-out money purchase schemes; and
(b) defined benefits schemes.

Defined benefit schemes are usually better for people with HIV because the early retirement provisions can often be greater and they don't rely on funds performing well in order to get a substantial annuity. However, most people do not get the choice unless they work for very large organisations.

6 Company pensions for people with HIV

8.89 People in occupational pension schemes are often well served when they are HIV positive. Frequently, there are good early retirement provisions, life assurance benefits and sometimes widows' and dependants' benefits. Under occupational pension rules the trustees can also pay out an individual's entire portion of the pension fund if he or she has a reduced life expectancy (usually where the terminal prognosis is little more than a year). However, early retirement or getting the value of the fund paid as a lump sum, requires the individual to explain the illness to his or her employer—something many HIV sufferers may not feel comfortable about.

7 Death in service benefit

8.90 A particular advantage for people who are HIV positive is the death-in-service benefit the Inland Revenue allows pension schemes to pay. If a person dies before he or she is due to retire, a maximum of four times the final salary can be paid to the estate, together with a refund of all of the individual's personal contributions with interest. This is not usually subject to the typical restrictions life companies impose on gay men or people with HIV for life assurance. In addition, such schemes can continue paying up to two-thirds of an individual's pension entitlement to any dependants. Whether or not a death-in-service benefit can be directed towards a partner may depend on the wording of the scheme's contract. The problem is that most people don't die in service. The virus usually makes work too difficult in the last two years or so of its development and the individual is forced to leave work or retire. When someone leaves service, the death in service benefit would normally be lost and the life cover disappears.

8 Transfers

8.91 The main disadvantage with company schemes, as compared with personal pensions, is their lack of portability. A personal pension is unaffected by job changes. Those in a company scheme need to be aware of how changing jobs may alter their pension entitlement. There are two alternatives: the contributions and years of service which have been put into a company scheme can be either left where they are or transferred, depending on which suits the individual's circumstances best. Much depends on the pension situation of the new job.

8.92 Every employer has to allow an employee to transfer his or her accrued pension rights if desired, provided he or she has been a member of the scheme for two years or more and left service after 1 June 1986. In the past there have been examples of company schemes being awkward about providing a transfer value, but now they are compelled by law to do so. The transfer value will probably be subject to administration costs. These need to be examined closely to ensure they do not destroy the advantage of transferring in the first place. Transferring pension schemes is very complicated, and needs specialist advice.

9 Maxwell and the Goode Committee

8.93 The case of the Robert Maxwell employees who retired to find that their company pension funds had been 'borrowed' caused a public uproar. The Goode Committee, which was formed by Peter Lilley, the then Secretary of State for Social Security, and chaired by Professor Goode, set out to make recommendations to restore public confidence in occupational pensions.

8.94 The Goode Committee recommended, among other things, that pension legislation be simplified and that legislation be introduced to clarify employers' obligations. The Committee also recommended that the valuation of company pension funds by actuaries be tightened up, with greater controls on the appointment of the pension fund trustees who are responsible for the investment of the funds. Additional restrictions on the future 'borrowing' of funds were also recommended, with a restriction on self-investment of company funds to 5%.

10 Additional Voluntary Contributions (AVCs)

8.95 Far from overfunding their company pensions, most UK employees are contributing well below the amount they need to secure a full pension. Figures from the National Association of Pension Funds show that only 1% of employees are contributing the maximum 15% of their income permitted for company schemes. On average, employers deduct 5 or 6% of employees' earnings to contribute to the fund. Those who want to put more in have to do so themselves by funding Additional Voluntary Contributions (AVCs).

Unfortunately, people only seem to realise this when they are nearing retirement, and then, concerned about the amount of pension they are due to receive, they seek to make up lost years of contributions. Consequently, the majority of people making AVCs are within five to ten years of retirement. There are signs that younger employees are beginning to make AVCs, but this is still very limited.

8.96 Only 10% of employees are taking advantage of AVCs and many people who are HIV positive think that this type of planning goes too far. The fact that they are already in a pension scheme is enough for them. However, for those with a less pessimistic outlook and poor history of pension contributions, AVCs should still be considered.

11 Self-Invested Pension Plans

8.97 There are two types of self-invested plan, one for individuals and one for companies, which are much the same as for the standard schemes described above. Self-Invested Personal Pensions (SIPPs) are the individual version, and Small Self-Administered Schemes (SSASs) the company version. Each of these allows the investors to decide how the money they pay into the scheme will be invested.

12 Self-Invested Personal Pensions

8.98 With SIPPs, the limits on contributions are the same as with any other personal pension. The £87,600 earnings cap applies too. To build a SIPP fund, almost any investment can be included. There are, though, some notable exclusions: endowment policies, unlisted shares, commodities, foreign currency, residential property, and, for directors, shares in one's own company. A financial adviser should be able to suggest a number of companies that offer SIPPs.

8.99 There are only one or two disadvantages in doing this. Having a business's property tied in with one's pension benefits could cause problems when one decides to retire, especially if this is earlier than expected—and it proves difficult to sell the property. If the company cannot afford to buy it, things can become complicated.

(i) Company employees

8.100 For those who are employees of a company rather than directors, the restriction on one's own company's shares does not apply. Provided the company concerned is a listed company, a SIPP can buy as many of its shares as desired. As with any pension fund investment, profits are free of all tax. The charges made by the SIPP manager vary depending on how much work there is to do. Even when the manager does nothing more than provide the legal framework, certain charges are likely to be incurred. Individual charges will be made on particular deals where assets are either brought into or taken out of the scheme.

(ii) Hybrid schemes

8.101 SIPPs that are run by an insurance company are sometimes slightly different from otherwise fully self-invested schemes. They are known as hybrid schemes. Part of the scheme has to be invested in the insurance company's own funds. Different companies make various demands about how big this level should be. The thing to bear in mind is that an insurer only allowing you to invest in its own fund is offering not a self-administered scheme, but a standard personal pension operating under a different name. An insurance fund element can be useful in reducing costs. Quite often several of the administration charges that would normally be charged separately are taken care of in the insurance element, and can make the SIPP cheaper than its fully self-invested rivals.

13 Small Self-Administered Schemes

8.102 Small Self-Administered Schemes (SSASs) are a type of executive pension plan. They provide pension benefits for the directors of small to medium-sized companies. Specialist advice is recommended.

14 Executive pension plans

8.103 Executives and directors have several options open to them when making pension arrangements. Where no company scheme exists but the employer is prepared to make contributions, a personal pension plan seems an obvious choice. The 17.5 to 40% of gross income that can be paid into a personal pension plan will provide a respectable pension.

8.104 Executives and directors have a slight advantage here. Although employee contributions into executive pension plans (EPPs) are restricted to 15% of salary, there is no restriction on the amount your company can pay. Instead, a limit of two-thirds of final salary is placed on the eventual pension. This will also benefit directors who have chosen to take relatively small salaries, but are taking further income in the form of dividends from invested profits. While this arrangement will mean that a portion of the director's income will be free of NI deductions, the disadvantage is that the Inland Revenue will not include dividend income as part of one's yearly salary. The final two-thirds salary received as a pension will then be smaller than if the full amount received as payment were classed as salary.

8.105 With some EPPs, the members are able to act as the scheme's trustees. In other words, they are responsible for the way the fund is operated. For same-sex partners in business this has the advantage of allowing them to decide the rules of the scheme, and makes it easier to ensure that partners are treated fairly. Trustees can also have control over how the fund is invested (as with SSASs).

H ANNUITIES

8.106 Annuities are sold by life companies and provide a regular income in return for a lump-sum payment. Although anyone with available cash can buy an annuity, they are most commonly associated with money purchase pension schemes. With personal pension plans and some company pension schemes, the investor will be paid a lump sum when he or she dies. While up to 25% of this can be used in whatever way the pensioner wants, the rest of it must be used to buy an annuity. If someone is unwell with HIV, it may be possible to get an enhanced annuity rate by applying to a 'short life' or 'impaired life annuity' provider.

8.107 Insurance companies offering personal pension plans will also be able to offer an annuity, but for someone who is ill, their rates will usually not be as good as those offered by an impaired life annuity provider. For someone who isn't ill, it must be remembered that even 'standard' annuity rates vary, so before choosing one should ask an independent financial adviser which companies are offering the best rates[1]. There are several types of annuity, offering different benefits. One type may be better suited to the individual's circumstances than another.

1 As already noted, the list may not include the company the pension plan was bought from.

Tax

8.108 Although there are tax benefits attached to the way a pension fund is built up, the individual will be liable for income tax on income from his or her annuity. This can be mitigated in two ways.

(a) Entitlement to personal tax allowances on income continues after retirement. Up to the age of 65, this will be the same as for those still in employment. After 65, tax-free earnings are enhanced by special age allowances.

(b) The second way income tax liability is reduced in retirement is by the way annuities are treated for tax purposes. A portion of whatever income is bought with the pension fund is deemed by the Inland Revenue to be part of the original investment. So this portion of income is tax-free. Liability rests only with the part of income considered to be the profit on the original investment. Even if one lives long enough for the annuity to have paid back all of the initial capital, the Inland Revenue will continue to view part of that income as returned capital.

I MORTGAGES

8.109 In personal finance terms, mortgages are relatively straightforward: a mortgage lender will lend someone who is credit worthy the money required to purchase a property. However, for people with AIDS or even people in 'high risk groups' (such as HIV), this simple transaction can become very complicated. The problems begin when a lender makes one of two possible demands.

(a) It may insist that the loan is secured with a life assurance policy in the borrower's name with all benefits assigned to the lender. Should the borrower die while the loan is outstanding, the proceeds of the policy will be paid directly to the bank, building society, or finance house making the loan.
(b) Types of loan repayment vehicles (such as endowments) automatically include life cover. As already discussed, the problem for people with HIV or for gay men is that because endowments are based on life assurance, and that the insurer is likely to refuse to cover them.

1 Raising a mortgage

(i) The self-employed

8.110 The self-employed must demonstrate their income by presenting their accounts, usually for at least the previous three years. Those without enough of a trading history could have problems unless they find one of the rare lenders prepared to take an accountant's word about their current earnings and future potential. Being self-employed can be a particular problem if an accountant has successfully whittled down his client's tax bill by offsetting various expenses against it. While this is useful for tax saving, it does make earnings appear low on paper. Many self-employed business people who proudly boast of paying hardly any tax are incredulous at the attitude of most lenders to their 'official' earnings, but they should really not be so surprised. Their best hope is to put their hefty tax savings aside for a deposit on a property.

(ii) Non-status mortgages

8.111 By building up a large enough deposit, an individual could become eligible for a non-status loan. As with all loans, their availability depends largely on current market conditions. Unlike the position with more basic mortgages, non-status lenders demand no proof of your ability to repay the loan. This would seem perfect for someone who is retired due to HIV and who is hoping to move home, re-mortgage their own property for more cash or purchase a new property from scratch.

8.112 The catch is that they usually demand a deposit of at least 25% of the property's value, and usually 30%. However, even for those who can raise the deposits there are still some further problems:
(a) Although non-status mortgages do not require proof of income, they do often require applicants to be either registered as self employed or self employed.
(b) Most/all non-status mortgage providers require life cover.
(c) The interest rates on non-status mortgages are usually quite high.

(iii) Indemnity policies

8.113 A lender prepared to lend more than 75% of the value of a property will usually demand the one-off payment of an indemnity insurance premium.

Some lenders have waived this requirement now and some will add this to the loan. Naturally, regardless of HIV status, those lenders without this additional cost (which averages out at about £1,000) represent better value providing that the interest rates are just as competitive.

8.114 One's ability to buy this type of cover is unaffected by HIV status or sexuality. Indemnity insurance comes into play only if a property is repossessed. If lenders are unable to recoup all of the money owed to them, insurers will make up the difference.

2 Types of mortgage

8.115 Exactly which type of loan one opts for depends on the individual's particular needs. Some types are more appropriate to people with HIV or AIDS than others.

(i) Repayment mortgage

8.116 The repayment mortgage is the basic home loan. The lender pays an advance and the borrower repays the loan at regular intervals over a specified term—usually 25 years. Each regular repayment is made up of interest on the loan plus a portion of the loan itself. In the early days of the mortgage, each repayment is mostly interest with only a tiny portion of capital. This balance gradually changes over the term until, towards the end, most of each repayment is capital and only a small part is interest. In this way the amount owed gradually reduces over time.

8.117 Repayment mortgages became less popular with the arrival of new forms of home loans. Now, though, they are enjoying something of a renaissance following some of the bad experiences people have had with other types of mortgage.

8.118 For people with HIV, the problem with repayment mortgages is that lenders expect the loan to be covered by some form of life assurance, usually a decreasing term policy. With such a policy, the amount of life cover gradually reduces over the period of the mortgage, and should mirror the amount of money owed to the lender at any one time. If the borrower dies, the policy will pay off whatever is left of the mortgage.

8.119 In addition, there are other problems with repayment loans for people with HIV.

(a) The repayment is being made directly to the provider but, as mentioned above, hardly any of the loan is being repaid. If the individual were to fall ill and require cash, the 'repayment element' is not available to, say, turn into income because it has been repaid to the building society. Quite simply, it would have been better to have only paid interest to the lender and put the rest of the cash into a savings vehicle of some type. This leaves all options open for the future.

(b) The DSS only covers mortgage interest – not repayments. If the individual only has an 'interest' liability to the building society and falls ill, it is unlikely that he or she will fall into arrears and suffer credit problems in the future.

(ii) Endowment mortgages

8.120 Endowment mortgages are now the most popular type of mortgage, and account for roughly 70% of the total mortgage market. There are two elements:
(a) the loan; and
(b) an endowment policy from an insurance company.

Endowment mortgages are often cheaper than repayment mortgages, and no matter how many times one moves there is no need to keep renewing the term of the loan. This is because the endowment that will eventually pay back the loan can be transferred between mortgages.

8.121 Although there has in recent years been a lot of bad publicity about endowment mortgages, they work well providing a good provider with a good contract is selected. The problem for someone with HIV who does not already have an endowment, is again that it will be impossible to arrange one because of the life assurance aspect contained within the policy. It is impossible to remove this life assurance without rendering the policy 'non-qualifying' for tax relief on maturity.

(iii) Investment-backed mortgages (PEPs/ISAs and pensions)

8.122 Investment mortgages (interest only) are similar to endowment mortgages in that the monthly repayments are divided into two parts: interest on the loan and a regular contribution to a savings plan which will eventually be used to repay the lender. These can work very well for someone who is HIV positive.

8.123 Once again, someone with HIV will still have to ensure that the lender doesn't insist on life cover. But beyond that, applying for a mortgage should be no more complicated than for someone who is not HIV positive and not in an HIV high risk group.

8.124 The problem with a mortgage backed up with an investment is that a stock market crash just before cashing the plan in could leave the borrower short of the amount needed to pay off the loan. There is also the risk that a new chancellor might abolish or change existing policies.

(iv) Pension mortgages

8.125 Pension mortgages provide another way of building up tax-free benefits to pay off an interest-only loan. Those paying into a personal pension can take up to 25% of their total fund on retirement as a tax-free lump sum, excluding the protected rights proportion of the fund. (Protected rights are the equivalent of the state pension benefits funded by National Insurance contributions). By running a personal pension alongside a mortgage, part or all of this money can be used to repay the loan. This can be extremely cost effective. Depending on one's age, the percentage of net relevant earnings (the total taxable income) that can be paid tax-free into a personal pension ranges from 17.5–40%. All income and capital gains on the pension fund itself are also free of tax.

8.126 Pension mortgages can be very good for people who are HIV positive because they:

(a) Encourage individuals to make pension contributions which, otherwise, they may not have felt necessary. This is very important if the individual then goes onto survive the virus, as is now looking more and more likely.
(b) Build up a tax free lump sum which is payable on death and which could be used to help a partner or dependant in the event of death.
(c) Allow the individual to benefit from income tax relief on contributions and enjoy tax free growth on the fund.

8.127 Although a pension mortgage answers many of the concerns that someone with HIV may have, once again there are two major pitfalls.

(a) Many mortgage providers, even if they would not ordinarily insist on life cover, usually do require life cover for pension mortgages. Given this, extra effort should be made to ensure that life cover is not required.
(b) Many pension companies will not pay the death benefits to same-sex or unmarried heterosexual partners under an 'expression of wishes' declaration. This is because, on the whole, pensions are set up under a discretionary trust. The applicant should check that the pension provider is happy to pay out to a same-sex partner if this applies and/or set up a dedicated trust.

Chapter 9

Preparing for death

Steve Deutz

A INTRODUCTION

9.01 This chapter is about advising the client with HIV on the preparation of wills and other legal documents which will enable the client to retain control over his or her property and medical treatment both during his or her lifetime and after death. It will also cover the advance refusal of medical treatment.

9.02 The assumption behind this chapter is that the reader is already fully familiar with will drafting and that detailed explanation of the general law relating to this is not required. In relation to testamentary documents, therefore, this chapter will concentrate on the particular and additional issues, both practical and legal, which are relevant to advising the client who is HIV positive. This chapter will then look at other matters which the adviser should, as a matter of course, raise with the client who is HIV positive who has, in the first instance, sought advice and assistance simply about the preparation of a will. These are, principally, the living will and the enduring power of attorney (EPA).

9.03 It is important to keep a balance between advising the client on the steps which she or he can take to retain control over their affairs, whilst not overwhelming them with information and legal forms. Confusion can easily arise in the mind of the client as to which document does what: the will disposes of their property after death; the EPA concerns their property and affairs whilst they are alive; the living will is concerned only with their medical treatment.

9.04 As far as wills are concerned, there are matters which are relevant to the preparation of wills for all people with HIV: delay in completing the work, and the capacity of the client to give instructions and to execute the will. Then there are other matters which are particularly relevant to the two communities in the UK which have, to date, been most affected by HIV, namely gay men and African people. There will therefore be some reference also to the matters which affect these two groups and of which the adviser should be aware.

B WILLS

9.05 Most people do not make a will. In the absence of a will a person's property will devolve in accordance with the provisions for intestate estates set out in the Administration of Estates Act 1925, as amended.

9.06 The order of distribution set out in the act was based on the average will filed at the probate registry before 1925 and is confined to spouses, children and blood relatives. Unmarried partners, which, of course includes same-sex partners and friends, are therefore excluded. The Act makes no provision for the appointment of guardians for children, and no means for communicating wishes regarding funerals.

9.07 One of the most frequently heard reasons not making a will is the belief that wills are only made by those who have considerable assets. Other reasons are superstition, ignorance or the understandable reluctance to have to think about dying. Campaigns by the Law Society to increase awareness may change attitudes but in the meantime it is sometimes necessary to work hard to persuade people that there are very good reasons why they should make a will.

1 Legal Aid

9.08 If cost is a factor, then the adviser should remember that in certain circumstances wills can be prepared free under the Legal Aid Board advice and assistance scheme.

9.09 First of all a client must qualify financially. In all circumstances a client's disposable capital has to be assessed. The maximum disposable capital for a person with no dependants is £1,000 for the year beginning April 1999 and increases if there are dependants. If however, the client is in receipt of income support, income-based jobseeker's allowance, family credit or disability working allowance they will qualify automatically on income although capital still needs to be assessed as above. The maximum disposable income limit is currently £83 per week as calculated according to legal aid regulations. The income and capital of same-sex partners is not aggregated when carrying out these calculations.

9.10 If the client qualifies financially he or she will be entitled to assistance in the preparation of a will if he or she qualifies under Regulation 4 of the Legal Advice and Assistance (Scope) Regulations 1989. That is, he or she must be someone who is:

(a) aged 70 or over; or
(b) blind (or partially sighted), deaf (or hard of hearing) or dumb, or who suffers from mental disorder of any description, or who is substantially and permanently handicapped by illness, injury or congenital deformity; or
(c) a parent or guardian within the meaning of s 87 of the Child Care Act 1980 of a person to whom any description in (b) applies, where the client wishes to provide in the will for that person

(d) the mother or father of a minor who is living with the client where the client is not living with the minor's other parent and the client wishes to appoint a guardian for that minor under s 4 of the Guardianship of Minors Act 1971 (now the Children Act 1989).

9.11 These categories are set out in the Claim 10 form and the category relied upon needs to be ticked. By signing the Claim 10 form the client confirms that this information is correct.

9.12 The limits of financial eligibility are low, but so long as the client qualifies financially, many clients with symptomatic HIV infection will be able to certify that they are permanently handicapped by illness and so can rely on the second category to obtain free advice and assistance.

9.13 If the client does not qualify for free advice and assistance for a will under the scheme then there are other possibilities. For example, the Terrence Higgins Trust, through its paid staff and volunteers, provides a free wills service for people with HIV living in London. Home and or hospital visits can be arranged and, in emergencies, clients can be seen the same day.

2 Taking instructions

9.14 As stated in para **9.02**, it is assumed that the reader is familiar with the process of advising on the preparation of wills. However, it is worth remembering the need to take extreme care to avoid future liability either for breach of contract or negligence. In the case of *Ross v Caunters*[1] a solicitor failed to advise a client that the spouse of a beneficiary could not witness his will and then, when the will was returned to him, failed to check that the will had been properly attested. The solicitor was held liable to the beneficiary whose gift was invalidated as a result. Megarry J said:

> 'A solicitor who is instructed by his client to carry out a transaction that will confer a benefit on an identified third party owes a duty of care towards that third party in carrying out the transaction, in that the third party is a person within his direct contemplation as someone who is likely to be so closely and directly affected by his acts or omissions that he can reasonably foresee that the third party is likely to be injured by those acts or omissions.'

1 [1980] Ch 297.

9.15 In general terms, the solicitor must ensure that he or she has taken full and detailed instructions from the client and given the correct advice. This means, in particular, that the solicitor has the client's own instructions; that others have not unduly influenced those instructions; that the client understands the will and that it is in accordance with the client's instructions; and that the client has capacity.

9.16 To avoid any suggestion of undue influence the client should be seen on his or her own. When a client is seriously ill, perhaps with only hours to live, it is not easy to ask a partner to leave the room whilst instructions are taken, but this should be attempted wherever possible. An explanation that it is necessary to see the client alone to ensure the validity of the will is usually sufficient.

9.17 To ensure that the client understands the will it is advisable to provide a written clause by clause explanation of the effects of the will in plain English, although again this is unlikely to be possible in an emergency. A full attendance note should be taken of the instructions received and the explanation given.

3 Delay

9.18 As stated in para **9.14**, the case of *Ross v Caunters*[1] established that a solicitor has a potential liability in the tort of negligence to the intended beneficiary. In the case of *Smith v Claremont Haynes & Co*[2] a solicitor was found liable to an intended beneficiary when as a result of the solicitor's unreasonable delay in preparing the will the testator died before he could execute it.

1 [1980] Ch 297.
2 (1991) Times, 3 September.

9.19 What an unreasonable delay is will depend on the facts of the case. In the case of *Smith v Claremont Haynes & Co*[1] the court found that the solicitor might reasonably have been expected to be aware of an element of urgency in the preparation of the will by reason of the intended testator's state of health.

1 (1991) Times, 3 September.

9.20 In *White v Jones*[1] Lord Browne-Wilkinson said:

> 'I would hold that by accepting instructions to draw a will, a solicitor does come into a special relationship with those intended to benefit under it in consequence of which the law imposes a duty to the intended beneficiary to act with due expedition and care in relation to the task on which he has entered.'

1 [1995] 2 WLR 187 at 214.

9.21 The solicitor who is preparing a will for a person with HIV, being aware of the client's condition, must act expeditiously in preparing the will and having it executed. As stated elsewhere, this might mean preparing the will at the time the instructions are given.

9.22 If the solicitor is reliant upon standard will clauses then he or she should, of course, take them to any meeting with a client in hospital so that a handwritten will can be executed straightaway. A typed version can always be prepared later if time permits.

4 Capacity

9.23 Any testator must have testamentary capacity when making the will for it to be valid. In the case of an emergency will, perhaps made in hospital on the testator's deathbed, the question of the person's real and relevant one. It is certainly a fear of some people that their relatives will use any means possible to challenge their will and disputing their capacity is a possible battleground for such a dispute.

9.24 The case of *Banks v Goodfellow*[1] set out a three-limb test for establishing testamentary capacity. The testator must understand:
(a) the nature of the act and its effects;
(b) the extent of the property of which he is disposing; and
(c) the claims to which he ought to give effect.

1 (1870) LR 5 QB 549, QB.

9.25 It is for the lawyer to turn the client's wishes into the legal language of the will itself. However, the testator must broadly know what the will is doing. Likewise he or she must know broadly the extent of the property of which he or she is disposing.

9.26 As for the third test, the testator simply needs to be able to consider the people to whom he or she might leave his or her property, even if he or she decides, having given the matter some thought, that he or she will not after all leave them anything. A standard will checklist serves as a useful prompt in establishing capacity.

9.27 The relevant time for the testator to have capacity is when the will is executed: ie signed and witnessed. The case of *Parker v Felgate*[1] established a rule that the will may be valid in the case where the testator has lost capacity by the time he or she comes to execute the will provided that:
(a) the testator had capacity when he or she gave his instructions;
(b) the will is prepared in accordance with those instructions; and
(c) the testator was capable of understanding and did understand that he or she was executing a will for which he or she had previously given instructions.

1 (1883) 8 PD 171.

9.28 The person propounding the will has the burden of proving that it is valid but there is a presumption that a will which looks rational was executed by someone with testamentary capacity. The onus then shifts to those who attack it to show that the person did not have capacity. The solicitor should always make very full and detailed notes of his or her attendance on a client while taking instructions. In addition, if capacity would appear to be an issue, every effort should be made to seek the assistance of medical staff.

9.29 In the case of *Re Simpson*[1] Templeman J said:

> 'In the case of an aged testator or a testator who has suffered a serious illness there is one golden rule which should always be observed, however straightforward matters may appear, and however difficult or tactless it may be to suggest that precautions be taken: the making of a will by such a testator ought to be witnessed or approved by a medical practitioner who satisfied himself of the capacity and understanding of the testator, and records and preserves his examination and finding'.

1 (1977) 121 Sol Jo 224.

9.30 Experience shows that however sensible such a course may be, most hospitals have rules against their medical staff witnessing a patient's will. A doctor may be willing to make a statement detailing the patient's medical condition however, and this should be kept on file.

9.31 In the end, the decision of capacity is a legal one and it is the solicitor's responsibility to establish it. The three-stage test set out in para **9.24** should be applied in all cases. If the client is found to lack capacity then the only way that a will can be made is through the Court of Protection.

5 Possible claims of others

9.32 In addition, the issue of the claims of others needs to be dealt with in the context of possible claims under the Inheritance (Provision for Family and Dependants) Act 1975. The Act allows a court to make orders for the provision of a spouse, former spouse, child, child of the family or dependant out of the estate. Consideration of this Act in the context of advising a disappointed client is given in paras **9.54–9.61**.

9.33 In the process of preparing the will the solicitor must have regard to the possibility of such claims arising. This means taking detailed instructions from a client on his or her relationships and the existence of someone who may fall into one of the categories set out in s 1(1) of the Act. The solicitor should not fall into the trap when advising gay or lesbian clients of assuming that they are not married or have not been married or that they are without children.

9.34 If a potential applicant under the Act is identified, then the solicitor needs to be able to advise on the strength of any application and its likelihood of success. In this situation, the solicitor should advise the client to prepare a statement explaining that in his or her will he or she has not made any financial provision for a particular person and then setting out the reasons, with reference to the matters which the court will take into account for the purpose of assessing reasonable financial provision. Such a statement will be admissible in any proceedings under the Inheritance Act 1975 by virtue of s 21 which states that a statement made by the deceased whether orally or in a document or otherwise shall be admissible under s 2 of the Civil Evidence Act 1968 as evidence of any fact stated in it. It is advisable to set out these reasons in a separate document kept with the will, rather than recorded on the face of the will itself as the will becomes a public document after the grant of probate.

9.35 Despite having good reasons for making a will, people still leave it to the last minute and this is often the case for people with HIV. The solicitor who regularly advises clients must be ready for hospital visits and must be ready to prepare a will for someone who might have only hours to live. This can be distressing and taking instructions in this situation extremely difficult. A certain amount of advance work can alleviate the problems to a certain extent: for example, obtaining the client's full name and address and other relevant details from a nurse. Medical staff can also give their opinion on the client's capacity to make the will. However, all information obtained from third parties still needs to be checked with the client and it is for the solicitor to satisfy himself or herself that the client has capacity.

9.36 It is important not to underestimate quite how little clients, whatever their condition, understand about making a will. If the will is not being made in an emergency it can be helpful to talk over the basics of a will with a client on the telephone, and possibly to send them information, before the appointment. This way the client will have had a chance to think about the various matters that need to be considered beforehand.

9.37 If the client has made a will before and the adviser is discussing their situation on the telephone, the adviser needs to talk about revoking the existing will. Advice needs to be given to the client on the consequences of dying intestate as compared with the provisions contained in the existing will. If the client wants a new will because their current will leaves everything to a now ex-partner then immediate revocation may be a good idea. However, if the alternative prospect of everything being left to an estranged parent is even worse, then revocation will not be a good idea. This is a gamble for the client and the solicitor must be able to show that the client was advised.

6 Guardians

9.38 A common reason that parents with young children have for wanting to make a will is to make provision for the future care of their children. The issue of HIV and children is considered elsewhere in this book and reference should be made to chapter 5 for a detailed consideration of the matter. As stated in para **9.10**, a single parent who wishes, by means of a will, to appoint a guardian for a minor living with him or her may be entitled to have the will prepared free under the Legal Advice and Assistance Scheme.

9.39 The relevant legislation for the appointment of guardians is contained in s 5 of the Children Act 1989. A guardian may be appointed by the court, by a person with parental responsibility for the child, or by a guardian. The rules on the effectiveness of an appointment made by a parent are dependent on a number of factors at the time of the death of the person making the appointment. If a parent is the only person with parental responsibility for the child, then that person's appointment will take immediate effect. If the other parent has parental responsibility for the child then the appointment will be postponed until the other person has died. If, however, the appointment is made by someone with a residence order for the child then the guardianship will take effect but parental responsibility will be shared with the other parent.

9.40 It is difficult for the adviser in this situation to provide the certainty which the client will probably seek: for example, a single mother may make an appointment now, which will later prove of limited value if the child's father later acquires parental responsibility. Whatever appointment is made, the role of the courts in determining the upbringing of children can never be excluded and the wishes of the mother, even if she is dead, will carry weight in the proceedings. So even if the client cannot be advised now about exactly what will happen in the event of her death, the adviser can ensure that her wishes and views are so clearly recorded that they will be considered by the court in any future litigation.

9.41 A client should always be advised to consider whom to appoint as guardian and make the appointment in accordance with s 5 of the Children Act 1989. This states that a parent with parental responsibility, or a guardian, may appoint another individual to be the child's guardian or take his or her place as the child's guardian in the event of his or her death. Such an appointment needs to be made in writing, dated and signed. In addition, it can be made in a will, so that if the will cannot be signed then it can be signed at the direction of the testator in accordance with s 9 of the Wills Act 1837.

9.42 A person who is appointed a guardian under s 5 of the Children Act 1989 has parental responsibility for the child in question. The ideal is for the guardian to be able to care for the child, although this is not necessary. If there is no one to look after the child, it may fall to social services to provide care, although there are clear advantages to having someone with parental responsibility to look after the child. In this case, it would be up to the guardian to request that the council accommodate the child under s 20 of the Children Act 1989. If necessary, the guardian could bring that arrangement to an end, or could ask someone else to look after the child. Whether a guardianship appointment is made by will or not, the legal consequences are the same. The decision as to which to use is therefore a practical rather than legal one.

7 Funerals

9.43 A number of matters arise in the context of including funeral arrangements in the will. Not surprisingly, it is a matter upon which clients often have strong views whilst being difficult to raise and talk about. The first matter upon which the client needs to be advised is that the responsibility for the disposal of the deceased lies with the executors of the will.

9.44 In the case of *Williams v Williams*[1] it was held: 'A binding disposition of the dead body of the testator cannot be made by will so as to oust the executors rights and duties as to its disposal.' The client can give elaborate instructions for his or her funeral but should be advised that the executor is not bound to carry these instructions out.

1 (1882) 20 ChD 659.

9.45 The second concern that clients often have is who is going to pay for the funeral and how. In *Rees v Hughes*[1] Tucker LJ stated the law to be as follows:

> 'It has long been well settled that where a man dies possessed of property his funeral expenses must come out of that property. In Blackstone's Commentaries...dealing with the powers and duties of an executor it is said: "He must bury the deceased in a manner suitable to the estate which he leaves behind. Necessary funeral expenses are allowed, previous to all other debts and charges". See also *Edwards v Edwards* where Parke B said: "I take the rule to be that the executor is entitled to be allowed reasonable expenses, and if he exceeds those he is to take the chance of the estate turning out insolvent." In *Tugwell v Heyman* and *Rogers v Price* it was held that executors with assets in their hands were liable for payment of funeral expenses even where they had not ordered the funeral.'

1 [1946] KB 517.

9.46 The client must be advised that, whilst the costs of the funeral will be a first charge on the estate, the executor will be bound to arrange a funeral which is in a manner suitable to the estate which is left behind. As against a creditor, an executor will only be allowed to spend an amount out of the estate which is reasonably necessary, bearing in mind the size of the estate. There will be nothing to stop the executor paying for the funeral, or bearing additional costs, out of his or her own money. This is something which the client may need to bear in mind when asking, for example, to have her or his body repatriated.

9.47 One practical reason why it may not be a good idea to include client's funeral instructions in a will, is that the will may go undiscovered. Likewise, if there is a chance that the instructions about the funeral are going to change more frequently than those relating to other terms of the will, it will be better to set out the instructions on a separate document. If these are to be kept with the will, the client needs to be advised not to attach them to the will as this may affect the will's validity when an application for a grant of probate is made.

8 Foreign property and domicile

9.48 There is a possibility that there will be a foreign element in the circumstances or property of the client and the solicitor must be able to identify when such an issue arises. The foreign element will be either the domicile of the client or the location of his property. The issue of a foreign element is complicated and detailed analysis of it is beyond the scope of this chapter but a brief guide to the issues follows.

9.49 If the client is domiciled in England and Wales, and has no foreign property, then it is the internal law of England and Wales which applies. If there is a foreign element, arising from the client having foreign property, or having a domicile outside England and Wales, then the courts will apply private international law to determine which jurisdiction's internal law will be applied. Where foreign property is concerned, private international law distinguishes between immovable property (which is generally land but has a wider definition than realty) and movable property. In general terms, a will of movable property is governed by the law of the testator's domicile and a will of immovable property is governed by the lex situs, the law where the immovable property is situated. As far as testamentary capacity is concerned, for movable property the relevant law is that of the testator's domicile; for immovable property it will be the lex situs.

9.50 The formal validity of the will is governed by the Wills Act 1963, s 1 which states that a will of movable or immovable property is to be treated as properly executed if its execution conformed to the internal law in force in the place where it was executed, or any place where at the time of execution or the testator's death, he or she was domiciled or habitually resident or in a state in which, at either of those times, he or she was a national. Under s 2(1)(b) of the Act a will of immovable property is also properly executed if the execution conforms to the law of the place where the property is situated.

9.51 The essential validity of the will, which covers the validity of the will under the relevant law, is in the case of movable property governed by the testator's domicile at death and for immovable property by the lex situs. As for the law covering construction of the will, this will be presumed to be the law of the testator's domicile at the time of execution of the will. Otherwise it will be covered by the law intended by the testator and the intention can be expressed in the will.

9.52 A person's domicile will always start off as their domicile of origin, being the father's domicile, unless the parents are not married, in which case a person will acquire the domicile of his or her mother. A person can acquire a domicile of choice by taking up residence in another country with the intention of residing there permanently. The domicile of origin is suspended on taking up a domicile of choice and will be revived if the domicile of choice is abandoned and not replaced by another domicile of choice.

9.53 The solicitor will have to first identify the client's domicile. If it is a foreign domicile then the solicitor will be able to make a will which covers immovable property in England and Wales, but will need appropriate advice on the disposal of any other property. If the client has an English domicile and owns foreign property then the solicitor can make a will for the English movable and immovable property but should be careful as far as the foreign property is concerned. The best advice is for the client to have a will prepared by a lawyer from the country concerned. This should cover both immovable and movable property. In short, if there is a foreign element, the solicitor needs either to obtain advice from a lawyer with the relevant knowledge and expertise or advise the client to have another will prepared by a lawyer from the country concerned. The solicitor should be careful to establish whether there is already a foreign will so as not to revoke it by a general revocation clause. If a foreign will is to be made then the client should be advised to copy his or her English will to the other solicitor.

9 The Inheritance (Provision for Family and Dependants) Act 1975

9.54 The Inheritance (Provision for Family and Dependants) Act 1975 applies to all cases where a person domiciled in England and Wales dies after 31 March 1976. It serves to limit the freedom that testators have in disposing of their estate by giving the courts powers to make financial provision out of an estate for certain categories of people.

9.55 To the extent that it deals with events after the testator's death, its detailed provisions will be of limited interest to the client seeking to make a will. Yet the adviser must be aware of the effects of the Act in advising the client on his or her freedom to dispose of his property. The adviser must also be in a position to advise a client who has not been made reasonable provision in a will, or as a result of the rules on intestacy, as the Act will also apply in these cases.

9.56 If a client has been left nothing as a result of intestacy or a will, then it is important to be able to advise on the strict time limits which are imposed on bringing a claim under the Act. Any claim must be made within six months of the date of the full grant of representation and although the court has the power to extend the time limit, the onus falls on the applicant to show special reasons for allowing an application outside the time limit and the court will look very closely at the reasons for the delay[1].

1 See *Re Salmon (deceased)* [1980] 3 All ER 532 and

9.57 The categories of applicants who may apply for an order, because a will or the intestacy rules have not made reasonable provision for them, are set out at s 1(1) of the Act:

(a) the spouse of the deceased;
(b) a former spouse;
(c) a child of the deceased;
(d) a person (not being the child of the deceased) who is treated by the deceased as a child of the family in connection with a marriage to which the deceased was a party; or
(e) any person (not being a person included in the foregoing paragraphs) who immediately before the death of the deceased was being maintained wholly or partly by the deceased.

9.58 The Law Reform (Succession) Act 1995 added a further class of possible claimants where the deceased died after 1 January 1996, namely a person other than a spouse or former spouse who has lived with the deceased as husband and wife in the same household for at least two years immediately before the death. This category has, through the term husband and wife, deliberately excluded same-sex couples who will still have to rely on s 1(e) of the Act.

9.59 If the court is satisfied that an applicant is from one of these categories, then the court needs to decide whether the provision made is reasonable. In the case of a surviving spouse the court's approach will be similar to that of a court in dealing with matrimonial assets on divorce. In all other cases, the court will consider whether the will or the intestacy has made such financial provision as it would be reasonable in all the circumstances of the case for the applicant to receive for his maintenance[1].

1 Inheritance (Provision for Family and Dependants) Act 1975, s 1(2)(b).

9.60 The test, in both cases, is an objective one so that the court will look at all the circumstances of the case and not just the facts as known to the deceased. This makes it impossible to guard completely against an application, but the adviser, in preparing a will, should explain the terms of the Act and check with the client where there are any persons who may have a claim under the Act as amended by the Law Reform (Succession) Act 1995. If there are any possible claimants then a detailed note should be made of the testator's reasons for not making provision in his will for a particular person. If the reason is good, the court will take it into account. The reason should not go on the face of the will.

9.61 Once the court has decided that reasonable provision has not been made it must decide whether to make an order and then what order to make. The Act sets out guidelines for the court to consider in determining these matters. For the adviser of people with HIV, many of whom may be gay men, the issue will most probably arise in the context of same-sex relationships.

C ENDURING POWERS OF ATTORNEY

9.62 The living will form serves to provide an element of control for a patient over his or her medical treatment. An enduring power of attorney (EPA) is another important tool for the client with regards to his financial and personal affairs for that time when he or she may be unable to deal with those himself or herself.

9.63 Before going into detail on this point, for the client who is perhaps dependent on state benefits and has few assets, there may be simpler solutions to the problems of sorting financial affairs when he or she has lost capacity than creating and registering an EPA.

9.64 A client on benefits can nominate another person to collect his or her benefits on his or her behalf. This process of nomination can take place at the time of making the claim or any time thereafter. Otherwise the solution is to create an enduring power of attorney.

9.65 An ordinary power of attorney is a document in the form of a deed created by a person (the donor) who gives to another (the attorney) the power to act on his or her behalf in the running of his or her financial affairs. The power lasts until the donor revokes it or until the donor loses mental capacity.

9.66 The enduring power of attorney avoids the problem of loss of mental capacity. The enduring power of attorney was created by the Enduring Power of Attorney Act 1985. Provided that the donor has capacity at the time the power is created and that the power has been registered, it will remain valid after the donor has lost capacity.

9.67 The increased chance of a loss of capacity in someone with HIV means that it is necessary to advise on creating an enduring power of attorney. The power is created by a form governed by the Enduring Powers of Attorney (Prescribed Form) Regulations 1990. As printed forms are available from law stationers, it is suggested that these are used to avoid the possibility of error. Although the use of the form makes the creation of the power itself straightforward enough, this does not mean that the client can simply be given the form and allowed to complete it.

9.68 The form itself is divided into three parts:

(a) **Part A** contains information about using the form. This information, as well as the notes in the margins in the other two sections are part of the form, and when the form is signed the donor confirms that he or she has read, or has had read to him the notes in Part A.

(b) **Part B** is to be completed and signed by the donor in the presence of one witness who cannot be the attorney and should not be the client's husband or wife. If the form is signed at the direction of the donor then a second witness is required.

(c) **Part C** is signed by the attorney in the presence of one witness (two if the document is signed at his or her direction) and the donor may not witness, nor may another attorney. If more than one attorney is to be appointed then another sheet in the same form as Part C needs to be completed and signed by each additional attorney and added to the document. In Part C the attorney confirms that he or she understands the duty to apply to the Court of Protection for registration of the form when the donor is becoming or has become mentally incapable.

Capacity of the donor

9.69 There is no test of capacity in the Enduring Powers of Attorney Act 1985 but the matter was considered by the court in the cases of *Re K*[1] and *Re F*[2] in which tests were laid down. The court said that the test was not the same as for capacity to make a will, nor did the donor need to show that he or she had capacity to manage his or her own affairs. The court said that the test was that the donor understood the nature and effect of the document.

1 [1988] Ch 310.
2 [1988] 1 All ER 358.

9.70 The court said that to show that the donor understood the nature and effect of the enduring power, he or she should understand that:

(a) the attorney will be able to take on complete authority over all the donor affairs, depending on any restrictions included in the power;
(b) the attorney will be able to do anything as regards the donor's property which the donor could have done, again depending on any restrictions;
(c) the authority will continue even after the donor has lost mental capacity;
(d) once the donor has lost mental capacity the power can only be revoked with the permission or at the direction of the Court of Protection.

If there is any doubt about the donor's capacity then it is advisable to obtain medical evidence. This can then be produced if, at the time of registration, the court raises a query about the donor's capacity at the time the power was created.

9.71 The form itself allows for the donor to grant the attorney general authority to act on his or her behalf or to limit the scope of the authority in relation to all the donor's property and affairs or just those listed. The donor may wish to limit the authority, perhaps granting control over certain matters to one attorney and others to another. Clearly there is a risk here that certain matters will be left out so great care is required in drafting any limits. Otherwise, it is advisable for the attorney to have general authority to act over all the donor's property and affairs as the idea, of course, is for the attorney to be acting at a time when the donor is incapable of administering any of his or her affairs himself or herself.

9.72 In discussing with the client whether to impose any restrictions on the attorney's powers, the starting point, it is suggested, is that the powers should be as wide as possible. They cannot be extended once the donor has lost capacity. The donor should, of course, trust the attorney and be confident that he or she will carry out the role in a responsible way. The power of the attorney is, in any event, subject to restrictions set out in the Enduring Powers of Attorney Act 1985. For example, there are limits on the making of gifts and the attorney may not benefit him or herself, or others, except in so far as the donor might have been expected to.

9.73 The one restriction the client should perhaps be advised to consider concerns the commencement of the power. The power becomes effective immediately unless such a restriction is included. Such a restriction may be: 'my attorney shall not act unless they have reason to believe that I have become or am becoming mentally incapable'. The use of such a restriction will depend upon why the client is creating the power in the first place. As with the restrictions referred to earlier, the client should be advised that if they do not trust the attorney without such a restriction, then they may have selected the wrong person.

9.74 If any additions or amendments are made to the form they do not need to be initialled as the presumption in the case of a deed is that all alterations are made prior to execution. It may, however, be a sensible precaution to advise the signee and witness to initialise any changes.

9.75 The enduring power of attorney form also needs to be completed by the attorney himself. The attorney must understand that he has a duty to register the form under the Act when the donor is becoming or has become mentally incapable. He must also sign that he understands his limited powers to use the property to benefit persons other than the donor. It would certainly be good practice to ask the client, ie the donor, to return the completed form once the attorney has signed it. In this way the solicitor can check that it has been executed properly.

D LIVING WILLS

9.76 There is no specific definition of the term 'living will' but it is generally held to mean a document which includes a direction about future medical treatment which is to take effect when the patient is unable to communicate. Such directions are also known as 'advance directives'. They are not provided for in statute, although in December 1997 the government issued a Green Paper *Who Decides?*[1] which sought, amongst other things, to place living wills on a statutory footing. A common misapprehension therefore is that they are not legally binding. However, it is now quite clear that an advance refusal of medical treatment is binding at common law, provided that certain conditions, which are referred to later, are met.

1 *Who Decides? Making decisions on behalf of mentally incapacitated adults.*

9.77 The consent of a patient with mental capacity is required before medical treatment is given. Without the consent, the treatment would be unlawful. Where a person lacks the necessary mental capacity, treatment can be given only to the extent that is necessary and in the best interests of the patient. The case of *Re F (mental sterilisation)*[1] refers.

1 [1990] 2 AC 1.

9.78 All adults who have mental capacity are entitled to withhold their consent to medical treatment whatever the consequences for them of not having that treatment. A living will simply seeks to achieve this in advance. It is perhaps important at this stage to consider the issue of euthanasia. Euthanasia is positive intervention to hasten the end of someone's life and is illegal. Indeed, the government made clear in *Who Decides?* that it supported the views of the House of Lords Select Committee on Medical Ethics: 'euthanasia is unacceptable and the Government has no plans to change this position'.

9.79 The case of *Re T (adult: refusal of treatment)*[1] confirmed that a patient can refuse medical treatment

> 'An adult patient who...suffers from no mental incapacity has an absolute right to choose whether to consent to medical treatment, to refuse it or choose one rather than another of the treatments being offered. … This right of choice is not limited to decisions which others might regard as sensible. It exists notwithstanding that the reason for making the choice is rational, irrational, unknown or even non-existent.
>
> But just because adults have the right to choose, it does not follow that they have in fact exercised that right. Determining whether or not they have done so is a quite different and sometimes difficult matter. And if it is clear that they have exercised their right of choice, problems can still arise in determining what precisely they have chosen.
>
> [A] refusal [of consent to treatment] can take the form of a declaration of intention never to consent in the future or never to consent in some future circumstances.'

1 [1993] Fam 95, CA.

9.80 The case established that refusal of medical treatment will be legally binding if it is 'clearly established and applicable to the circumstances'. Three conditions must be met:
(a) the patient must have had capacity at the time the directive was made;
(b) the patient must not have been subject to the undue influence of another person at the time the decision was made; and
(c) the decision was intended to be applicable in the circumstances which have later occurred.

9.81 In the case of *Airedale NHS Trust v Bland*[1] the legal validity of advance refusals of treatment was confirmed. The case also stated that artificial hydration and nutrition are medical treatment for these purposes.

1 [1993] AC 789, HL.

9.82 The test for capacity in this sort of situation was considered by the Court of Appeal in the case of *Re MB (medical treatment)*[1]. The case concerned a pregnant woman whose unborn child was at risk if delivered normally. The woman refused to consent to a caesarian section because she was afraid of the needles which would be used in the process of administering the anaesthetic. She was not opposed to the operation itself. The Court of Appeal held that there was a presumption that every person has capacity until the presumption is rebutted.

1 [1997] 2 FLR 426, CA.

9.83 If the patient has capacity then he or she has complete freedom to withhold consent for whatever reason:

> 'A competent woman who has the capacity to decide may, for religious reasons or other reasons, for a rational or irrational reason or for no reason at all, choose not to have medical intervention, even though the consequences may be the death or serious handicap of the child she bears, or her own death. In that event the courts do not have the jurisdiction to declare medical intervention lawful and the question of her own best interests objectively considered do not arise.'

9.84 The court distinguished irrationality from misperception of reality:

> '...panic, indecisiveness and irrationality in themselves do not as such amount to incompetence but they may be symptoms or evidence of incompetence. The graver the consequences of the decision, the commensurately greater the level of competence is required to take the decision.'

9.85 The court also held that 'a person lacks capacity if some impairment or disturbance of mental functioning renders the person unable to make a decision whether to consent to or to refuse treatment'. So, if a phobia prevents the person from understanding or retaining the information which is given to them and which is material to the decision then they will be held to lack capacity.

9.86 Finally, the court held that whilst someone could rationally refuse to undergo an operation because of their fear of it, that fear may also destroy the capacity to make the decision. The court decided that MB[1] did lack capacity to make a decision because her overriding fear of needles was dominating her thinking and prevented her from considering anything else. The treatment would therefore be lawful.

1 *Re MB (medical treatment)* [1997] 2 FLR 426, CA.

9.87 The form of an advance directive is not important provided the conditions referred to above are satisfied. However, as the British Medical Association Code of Practice *Advance Statements about Medical Treatment*[1] advises: 'there are advantages to recording one's general view and firm decisions in writing'.

1 (May 1995) BMA.

9.88 A number of organisations have prepared living will forms, including the Terrence Higgins Trust (see Appendix III). The form, now in its third edition, was first published in 1992 and since then over 30,000 have been sent out. In its structure, as far as possible, it replicates the legal requirements to ensure that the document is legally binding. Nevertheless, it is the adviser's responsibility, if relying on a standard form, to ensure that the patient understands the legal consequences of the form while appreciating the importance of discussing the medical implications with his or her doctor. The important fact to remember is that the living will is a written record of wishes which may well have been passed to the doctor. That process of discussion and understanding with the doctor is therefore a crucial part of the process. Indeed, the BMA Code of Practice stresses the importance of the process of preparing an advance directive.

9.89 As stated in para **9.81**, artificial nutrition and hydration do constitute medical treatment and could therefore be the subject to an advance refusal. However, palliative care, the provision or basic care and comfort, is not and the BMA Code of Conduct says that as a matter of public policy 'people should not be able to refuse basic care in advance nor instruct others to refuse it on their behalf.' An individual may seek an injunction to enforce a refusal of treatment[1].

1 See *Re C (adult: refusal of medical treatment)* [1994] 1 WLR 290.

9.90 The requirement that the patient has in mind at the time of making a decision the circumstances which have actually arisen is important. The person with HIV will almost certainly be making the living will in the context of that illness. Its refusal of certain forms of treatment might not therefore apply in another situation.

9.91 The living will, once completed, is best copied and distributed to interested parties. Care should, however, be taken as too many copies floating around may cause confusion should the living will ever be redone or amended. The BMA Code of Practice says that a copy should be given to the a person's general practitioner. It also says that 'for chronically ill patients, who are treated by a specialist team over a prolonged period, a copy of the advance statement should be in all relevant hospital files and the GP['s] record'. Storage of the form and notification of its existence remains the responsibility of the patient, however, and there may be good reason why the client does not wish the GP to have the living will form, perhaps because he or she has not disclosed his or her status to the GP. It would be important to discuss this with client.

1 Health care proxy

9.92 In the case of *Re T (an adult) (consent to medical treatment)* Lord Donaldson said:

> 'There seems to be the view in the medical profession that in such emergency circumstances the next of kin should be asked to consent on behalf of the patient and that if possible treatment should be postponed until that consent has been obtained. This is a misconception because the next of kin has no legal right either to consent or to refuse consent'.

9.93 In other words no one can consent to or refuse medical treatment on behalf of an adult who lacks capacity. However, the close relatives of the patient will often be consulted by doctors when treating such a patient. There lies a potential for dispute especially in the case of a same-sex partner.

1 [1992] 2 FLR 458 at 461.

9.94 The Terrence Higgins Trust Living Will[1] form includes a section for appointing a health care proxy to make representations about treatment. The appointment of a health care proxy is probably not legally binding but the law in this area is fluid and a client should always consider making such an appointment provided they are aware of the legal position. As stated above, the wishes of the health care proxy will probably not be legally binding on a doctor. In the absence of an advance directive and capacity the medical staff will be able lawfully to treat the patient in accordance with medical opinion as to the patient's best interests in accordance with the doctrine of necessity see *F v West Berkshire Housing Authority*[2]. The health care proxy will have a role in representing the views of the patient as perhaps set out in the living will, or indeed drawing to the attention of the doctors the existence of the living will in the first place.

1 See Appendix IV.
2 [1989] 2 All ER 545.

9.95 However, in the case of *Re S (hospital patient: court's jurisdiction)*[1], Sir Thomas Bingham MR said:

> 'Where a serious justiciable issue is brought before the court by a party with a genuine and legitimate interest in obtaining a decision against an adverse party the court will not impose nice tests to determine the precise legal standing of that claimant.'

1 [1996] Fam 1 at 18, CA.

9.96 In this case the claimant was a woman 'whose companionship and support S had enjoyed in the years before he became incompetent' . The dispute concerned the standing of the claimant as against S's wife and son. At issue was whether S should be treated in Norway or England. S was a Norwegian citizen and the wife and son lived in Norway and wanted him to return there. The claimant had lived with S for some years in England and she had cared for him there. She was also his attorney under a power of attorney.

9.97 The Terrence Higgins Trust are aware of occasions when disputes have arisen at hospital between close relatives on one side and partners, often same-sex, on the other. The case of *Re S* at least goes some way to confirming that an individual may be have some standing. The appointment of the partner as health care proxy and attorney may be of evidential assistance in the event of a dispute. The client must be fully advised of the limitations of this particular appointment but nonetheless encouraged to complete it.

9.98 Failure to adhere to the binding instructions set out in a living will could amount to a criminal offence or lead to civil proceedings. Many HIV doctors practising in London at least will be used to seeing living will forms and discussing them with their patients. We rarely hear of any problems arising as a result of a doctor's refusal to abide by the wishes set out in the form although this could be for a number of reasons.

2 Conclusion

9.99 The client who is HIV positive is no different from any other client when it comes to the need for a will. Likewise, all clients who come to see a solicitor for a will should be advised on making a living will and creating an enduring power of attorney. However, when it comes to preparing the will of someone with HIV there will be additional matters which the solicitor should be alert for so as to ensure that the client has retained as much control as is possible over his or her affairs both during his or her lifetime and afterwards.

Appendix I

Glossary of medical terminology

amino acid The building blocks from which proteins are made

anaemia Shortage of red blood cells. These carry oxygen to cells of the body

antacid A substance that temporarily reduces the acidity of the stomach; used to relieve indigestion

antibiotic A drug that affects bacteria

antibody A protein substance produced by the immune system in response to a foreign organism

antigen Something the immune system can recognise as 'foreign' and attack

anti-histamine A drug that blocks the effects of histamine, a substance produced in the body which causes some of the symptoms of allergies

anti-oxidant A vitamin, mineral or drug which can reduce the activity of free radicals, the unpaired electrons produced as a consequence of the burning of energy in a cell

anti-retroviral A substance that acts against retroviruses such as HIV

apoptosis A process by which a cell kills itself in response to specific chemical signals within the body

apthous ulcer A small painful ulcer in the lining of the mouth

asymptomatic Having no symptoms

atherosclerosis Hardening and narrowing of the arteries

bacteraemia The presence of bacteria in the blood

bacteria Single celled micro organisms

bacterial Of bacteria

baseline Starting point or value

bile A fluid produced by the liver which is partly a secretion of waste products and partly aids digestion by breaking down fats and assisting the absorption of nutrients

bioavailability How well a drug is absorbed into the

biopsy	A small sample of tissue that can be examined for signs of disease
blood-brain barrier	A name for the body's defence system which makes it hard for many substances in the blood to get into the central nervous system
'buffalo hump'	Fat accumulation on the back of the neck and shoulders associated with lipodystrophy
candidiasis	A disease caused by the fungus Candida albicans. Commonly known as thrush.
catheter	A tube that is implanted with one end within the body and the other remaining outside, to make it easier to get drugs into or waste products out of the body
CD4	A molecule on the surface of some cells onto which HIV can bind. The CD4 cell count roughly reflects the state of the immune system
CD8	A molecule on the surface of some white blood cells. Some of these cells can kill other cells that are infected with foreign organisms
central nervous system	The brain and spinal cord
cervix	The 'neck of the womb' at the top of the vagina
chemotherapy	The use of drugs to treat an illness
cholesterol	A waxy substance known as a sterol, or solid alcohol. Cholesterol occurs in a number of places in the human body, including the brain, kidney, liver and blod. Although it is popularly associated with hardening of the arteries, most cholesterol in the body is actually made by the body, and it is used to produce bile and steroid hormones.
chronic	A long-term condition, as opposed to an acute (short-term) illness
clades	The technical term for the several different sub-types of HIV-1
clinical event	The occurrence of a physical sign or symptom, rather than an abnormality that can only be detected by laboratory tests
clinical outcome	The occurrence of a physical symptom
clinical trial	A research study with people, usually to find out how well a new drug or treatment works in people and how safe it is
CMV	Cytomegalovirus, a virus that can cause blindness in people with advanced HIV
CMV PCR positive	The presence of CMV in a sample, indicating that it is actively replicating
CNS	Central nervous system. The brain, spinal cord and its coverings
codon	A position on a gene

cohort	A group of people who share at least one common factor (such as being HIV-positive) and are studied over a period of time
combination therapy	Using more than one drug at a time
coronary artery disease	A type of heart disease which can lead to angina and heart attack, caused by narrowing of the arteries in the heart
'Crix belly'	Fat accumulation around the stomach associated with lipodystrophy
cross-resistance	The mechanism by which HIV that has become resistant to one drug may also be resistant to one or more different drugs
cryptosporidiosis	Infection with the gut parasite *Cryptosporidium*, causing diarrhoea
cytokine	A natural chemical used to pass signals between cells
cytoxic chemotherapy	Treatment with drugs that kill cells
dementia	Direct effects of HIV infection in the brain, which may cause problematic changes in mental functions, coordination and personality
diabetes	A condition characterised by a raised concentration of sugar in the blood, due to problems with the production or action of insulin
dialysis	A process used to separate substances from a solution. In artifical kidneys, this process is used to separate impurities and waste products from the blood
disease progression	The worsening of disease
DNA	The material in the nucleus of a cell where genetic information is stored
double-blind	A clincial trial where neither the researchers nor participants know who is taking the experimental treatment
early inter-vention	Starting HIV treatment relatively early in the course of the disease
encephalopathy	Disease or infection affecting the brain
enzyme	A protein which speeds up a chemical reaction
epidemiology	The study of epidemic diseases within populations
epithelial	The cells that form the outer layer of the skin
expanded access scheme	A programme that allows access to an experimental drug outside clinical trials for people in particular need
first-line therapy	The drug(s) used when somebody starts treatment for the first time
follicular	Immune cells that trap antigens and trigger other

dendritic cells	cells
gall bladder	An organ connected to the liver which stores bile
gastrointestinal	Relating to or affecting the stomach, gut or bowels
genotype	The sequence of proteins which makes a gene
glucose	The form of sugar found in the bloodstream. All sugars and starches in food are converted into this form in the intestines before they are absorbed
gynaecology	The study of the medical conditions specific to women
HAART	Highly Active Antiretroviral Therapy: a phrase sometimes to used to describe HIV combination therapy with three or more drugs.
haemophilia	An inherited illness in which the blood does not clot unless injections of a blood clotting agent are given
hepatitis	Inflammation or infection of the liver liver An organ involved in digestion of food and excretion of waste products from the body
hyper-amylasëmia	A condition in which blood levels of the enzyme amylase are increased
hyperglycaemia	Raised concentration of sugar in the blood
hyperlipidaemia	High fat levels in the blood
hypersensitivity	An allergic reaction
hypertension	Elevated blood pressure
hyper-amylasëmia	High levels of triglycerides in the blood
hypoglycaemic drugs	Drugs that lower levels of sugar in the blood
immune-modulator	A substance that changes some aspect of the way the immune system is working
immune system	The body's mechanisms for fighting infections and eradicating tumour cells
immuno-suppression	A reduction in the ability of the immune system to fight infections
insulin	A hormone produced by the pancreas which enables the muscles and other tissues to take up sugar from the blood. People with diabetes may need to inject themselves with insulin to enable them to use sugar properly
integrase	An HIV enzyme that the virus uses to insert its genetic material into that of the infected cell
intravenous	Injected into a vein
intravitreal	Injected into the eye
Kaposi's sarcoma	Lesions on the skin and/or internal organs caused by abnormal growth of blood vessels

leukoplakia	A mouth infection caused by Epstein-Barr Virus that can occur relatively early in HIV disease
lipid	A general term for fats in the blood
lipodystrophy	A disruption to the way the body produces, uses and distributes fat
liposomes	Fatty particles in which drugs can be 'wrapped' to reduce their side-effects and target them to particular body tissues and cells
log	Short for logarithm, a scale of measurement often used when describing viral load. A one log change is a ten-fold change, such as from 100 to 10. A two-log change is hundred-fold change, such as from 100 to 1
lymphoma	A type of tumour affecting lymph nodes
lymph nodes	Special areas in the body where white blood cells and other important immune cells are found. Also known as glands
lymphocyte	A type of white blood cell
lymphoid tissue	Tissue involved in the formation of lymph fluid, lymphocytes (a type of white blood cell) and antibodies
macrophage	A white blood cell that roams the body tissues engulfing foreign organisms
MAI	Micro-organisms related to TB which can cause disease in people with advanced HIV
maintenance therapy	Taking drugs for a period of time after an infection has been treated, to stabilise the condition or prevent a recurrence
meningitis	Inflammation of the outer lining of the brain
metabolism	The mechanisms which sustain life, including turning sugar and fat into energy
microsporidiosis	Infection with the gut parasite *Microsporidium*
monocyte	A white blood cell that roams the body tissues engulfing foreign organisms
monotherapy	Taking a drug on its own, as opposed to in combination with other drugs
mutation	A single change in genotype
mycobacteria	The family of bacteria that includes the causes of tuberculosis
nadir	The lowest out of a series of measurements
naive	Never having taken anti-HIV treatments before
named patient basis prescribing	A means of access to an unlicensed drug, in which a doctor requests supplies from its manufacturer for a specific individual
natural killer cells	Cells in the immune system which attack and destroy infected cells or tumour cells. They are called 'natural' because they attack without having to be specifically programmed to detect a certain foreign

neuropathy	Damage to the nerves
neutropenia	A shortage of neutrophils, immune cells in the blood which can attack bacteria and fungal infections
NNRTI	Non-nucleoside analogue reverse transcriptase inhibitors: the family of anti-HIV drugs that includes nevirapine, delavirdine, loviride and DMP-266
NRTI	Nucleoside analogue reverse transcriptase inhibitors: the family of anti-HIV drugs that includes AZT, ddI, ddC, 3TC and d4T
nucleoside	One of the building blocks from which DNA and RNA are made. Nucleoside analogue drugs such as AZT resemble one of these building blocks
nucleoside analogue	A chemical which is similar to one of the parts of DNA or RNA. AZT, ddI and ddC belong to this class of drugs
oedema	An abnormal accumulation of fluid beneath the skin or within a body cavity
oesophagus	The tube leading from the throat to the stomach
OI	Opportunistic infections: specific infections which cause disease in people with damaged immune systems.
open-label	A clinical trial where both the researchers and participants know who is taking the experimental treatment. Opposite of **double-blind** where neither is aware.
oral hairy leucoplakia	A mouth infection that causes white patches on the side of the tongue
pancreatitis	A condition of the pancreas causing servere abdominal pain, shock and collapse which can be fatal even if treated.
PBMCs	Cells with a single nucleus which circulate in the bloodstream
PCP	A form of pneumonia
PCR	Polymerase Chain Reaction, a method of amplifying fragments of genetic material so that they can be detected
peptide	A compound formed by two or more **amino acids**
perinatal	Around the time of birth
peripheral neuropathy	Damage to the nerves in the hands and/or feet, causing symptoms ranging from numbness to excruciating pain
phenotype	Trait or behaviour which results from changes in genotype
phosphorylation	The process by which NRTI drugs such as AZT and d4T are converted within human cells into forms that inhibit HIV
placebo	A pill or liquid which looks and tastes exactly like a real drug, but contains no active substance
plasma	The fluid portion of the blood
PML	Progressive multifocal leukoencephalopathy, an extremely serious brain infection
primary	The first few weeks after infectionss with HIV

infection	
prognostic indicator	Something that helps to reveal an individual's likely outcome, such as the risk of disease progression
prophylactic drugs	Drugs which prevent or delay an illness
prophylaxis	Taking a drug to delay or prevent an illness **primary prophylaxis** the use of drugs to prevent a first occurrence of illness **secondary prophylaxis** the use of drugs to prevent reoccurrence of illness
protease	An enzyme that HIV uses to break up large proteins into smaller ones from which new HIV particles can be made. Protease inhibitors work by interfering with this enzyme
protease inhibitor	Anti-HIV drugs which target the protease enzyme, eg saquinavir, ritonavir, indinavir, nelfinavir
protein	A complex chain of amino acids joined together, which forms the structure of most cells
proviral DNA	The chemical form in which HIV's genetic information is stored within infected cells
psoriasis	A disease in which the skin develops raised, rough, reddened areas
pulmonary	Affecting the lungs
radiotherapy	Treatment using radium or other radioactive matter
randomisation	Process of selecting by chance the treatment that a trial participant will receive
recombinant	Genetically reconstructed
regimen	Drug or treatment combination
replication	The process of viral reproduction
resistance	A drug-resistant HIV strain is one that is less susceptible to the effects of one or more anti-HIV drug because of its genetic make-up
retinitis	Damage to the retina, the light-sensitive surface at the back of the eye
retrovirus	The family of viruses to which HIV belongs
reverse transcriptase	A retroviral enzyme which converts genetic material from RNA into DNA, an essential step in the lifecycle of HIV
RNA	The form in which HIV stores its genetic information
seroconversion	The time at which a person's antibody status changes from negative to positive.
spleen	An organ which produces white blood cells and acts as a reservoir for red blood cells
steroids	Immune-suppressing drugs used to damp down excessive immune responses
stomatitis	Swelling of the mucous membranes inside the mouth
sub-therapeutic	Below the level needed to be an effective treatment

surrogate marker	An indirect indicator of something, such as the treatment effect of a drug
synergy	When two or more drugs produce an effect greater than adding their separate effects
T cell	A type of immune cell which is damaged in the course of HIV disease
thymus	A gland in the chest where cells produced in the bone marrow mature into effective immune system components
topical	Applied directly to the affected area, as opposed to systemic
toxicity	The extent or ways in which a drug is poisonous to the body
triglycerides	The basic 'building blocks' from which fats are formed
trough level	The lowest point to which levels of a drug fall in the blood, between doses
undetectable viral load	A level of viral load that is too low to be picked up by the particular viral load test used
viraemia	The amount of virus in the blood; in other words, another term for viral load
viral load	A measurement of the amount of virus in a sample. HIV viral load indicates the extent to which HIV is reproducing in the body
virologic response	Effect of treatment on viral load
wild-type virus	Virus found in people who have never taken anti-HIV treatments before

This glossary is reproduced by permission of NAM Publications, publisher of the National AIDS Manual, a comprehensive guide to HIV infection, its treatment and prevention, and to AIDS service organisations in the UK and Europe. Call 020 7627 3200 for details, or visit NAM's website at www.aidsmap.com.

Appendix II

Good practice guidelines

We must always be aware of our duty to keep information on clients in the strictest confidence. We can only discuss their case with a third party with their consent. Names of clients should be used as little as possible in the office.

1 CONFIDENTIALITY – GENERAL

(a) Only one appointment should be made at a time. People making appointments should check with the main office diary to try and ensure that. Occasionally, when there is more than one client appointment, we should be extra careful with confidentiality.

(b) All staff should remember to be careful with leaving messages on people's telephone numbers. It is better not to mention Immunity but simply to give a name and suggest that you will call again or they can ring back.

(c) When we write to clients we should not mention their HIV status unless it is particularly relevant. We should use the 'Private & Confidential' stamp to all private addresses and otherwise where appropriate and remember to turn any outgoing post upside down in the outgoing post tray. Check addresses carefully and use sticky label with our address on. If we learn of a letter going astray we should ask that it be returned.

(d) At the end of the day, we should put away and lock all client files.

(e) We should try not to write the names of client names on the outside of files as they are sometimes taken out of the office.

(f) We should remember to shred confidential client information on a regular basis. The message book should be kept out of sight of visitors to the office as should the diary.

(g) Finally, before embarking on litigation, we should consider the question of applying for anonymity orders or similar procedures to protect the client's confidentiality.

2 ADMINISTRATION – POST

(a) All incoming post should be opened by a solicitor and one other person, date stamped (with the exception of original d...

which should clearly not have a stamp on them). All envelopes from the Home Office and the Immigration Nationality Department should be kept with the letters.

(b) If there is any doubt about whether a letter should be stamped or an envelope kept, one of the solicitors should be asked about this.

3 APPOINTMENTS

(a) We should be careful to ensure client confidentiality around appointments at all times.

(b) The interview room should be soundproofed and we should ensure that the client feels comfortable in the room including offering tea / coffee etc.

4 HOME VISITS

(a) Solicitors should be aware that there is a policy to check whether it is likely to be appropriate to visit someone at home. IF the client has been met before and the solicitor feels OK about visiting them at home it is OK to do that. If they have been referred by a doctor or a social worker then the issue of whether it is appropriate should be discussed with those professionals.

(b) If the person self-refers, we should ask them whether we could speak to a doctor or social worker before we do a home visit.

(c) If there is any doubt, the solicitor should ask for someone to go with them if they feel that that is more helpful. They should take the mobile phone in case of any difficulties.

(d) Extra care should be taken with confidentiality during visits to people's homes.

December 1996
Reproduced from Immunity's Good Practice Guidelines.

Appendix III

Enduring Powers of Attorney

ENDURING POWERS OF ATTORNEY (PRESCRIBED FORM) REGULATIONS 1990, SI 1990/1376

SCHEDULE

Regulations 2 and 3

ENDURING POWER OF ATTORNEY

Part A: About using this form

1 **You may choose one attorney or more than one.** If you choose one attorney then you must delete everything between the round brackets on the first page of the form. If you choose more than one, you must decide whether they are able to act:

- Jointly (that is, they must all act together and cannot act separately) or
- Jointly and severally (that is, they can all act together but they can also act separately if they wish).

On the first page of the form, show what you have decided by crossing out one of the alternatives.

2 **If you give your attorney(s) general power** in relation to all your property and affairs, it means that they will be able to deal with your money or property and may be able to sell your house.

3 **If you don't want your attorney(s) to have such wide powers**, you can include any restrictions you like. For example, you can include a restriction that your attorney(s) must not act on your behalf until they have reason to believe that you are becoming mentally incapable; or a restriction as to what your attorney(s) may do. Any restrictions you choose must be written or typed where indicated on the second page of the form.

4 **If you a trustee** (and please remember that co-ownership of a home involves trusteeship), you should seek legal advice if you want your attorney(s) to act as a trustee on your behalf.

5 **Unless you put in a restriction preventing it** your attorney(s) will be able to use any of your money or property to make any provision which you yourself might be expected

to make for their own needs or the needs of other people. Your attorney(s) will also be able to use your money to make gifts, but only for reasonable amounts in relation to the value of your money and property.

6 **Your attorney(s) can recover the out-of-pocket expenses** of acting as your attorney(s). If your attorney(s) are professional people, for example solicitors or accountants, they may be able to charge for their professional services as well. You may wish to provide expressly for remuneration of your attorney(s) (although if they are trustees they may not be allowed to accept it).

7 **If your attorney(s) have reason to believe** that you have become or are becoming mentally incapable of managing your affairs, your attorney(s) will have to apply to the Court of Protection for registration of this power.

8 **Before applying to the Court of Protection for registration** of this power, your attorney(s) must give written notice that that is what they are going to do, to you and your nearest relatives as defined in the Enduring Powers of Attorney Act 1985. You or your relatives will be able to object if you or they disagree with registration.

9 **This is a simplified explanation** of what the Enduring Powers of Attorney Act 1985 and the Rules and Regulations say. If you need more guidance, you or your advisers will need to look at the Act itself and the Rules and Regulations. The Rules are the Court of Protection (Enduring Powers of Attorney) Rules 1986 (Statutory Instrument 1986/127). The Regulations are the Enduring Powers of Attorney (Prescribed Form) Regulations 1990 (Statutory Instrument 1990/1376).

10 **Note to Attorney(s)**
After the power has been registered you should notify the Court of Protection if the donor dies or recovers.

11 **Note to Donor**
Some of these explanatory notes may not apply to the form you are using if it has already been adapted to suit your particular requirements.

YOU CAN CANCEL THIS POWER AT ANY TIME BEFORE IT HAS TO BE REGISTERED

Part B: To be completed by the 'donor' (the person appointing the attorney(s))

Don't sign this form unless you understand what it means

Please read the notes in the margin which follow and which are part of the form itself.

Donor's name and address.	I .... of ....
Donor's date of birth.	born on ....
	appoint ....
See note 1 on the front of this form. If you are appointing only one attorney you should cross out everything between the square brackets. If appointing more than two attorneys please give the additional name(s) on an attached sheet.	of .... • [and .... of ....
Cross out the one which does not apply (see note 1 on the front of this form).	• jointly • jointly and severally]
	to be my attorney(s) for the purpose of the Enduring Powers of Attorney Act 1985
Cross out the one which does not apply (see note 2 on the front of this form). Add any additional powers. If you don't want the attorney(s) to have general power, you must give details here of what authority you are giving the attorney(s).	• with general authority to act on my behalf • with authority to do the following on my behalf:
Cross out the one which does not apply.	in relation to • all my property and affairs: • the following property and affairs:

Part B: continued

Please read the notes in the margin which follow and which are part of the form itself. If there are restrictions or conditions, insert them here; if not, cross out these words if you wish (see note 3 on the front of this form).	• subject to the following restrictions and conditions:
If this form is being signed at your direction: • the person signing must not be an attorney or any witness (to Parts B or C). • you must add a statement that this form has been signed at your direction. • a second witness is necessary (please see below).	I intend that this power shall continue even if I become mentally incapable I have read or have had read to me the notes in Part A which are part of, and explain, this form.
Your signature (or mark).	Signed by me as a deed .... and delivered
Date. Someone must witness your signature.	on ....
Signature of witness.	in the presence of ....
	Full name of witness ....
Your attorney(s) cannot be your witness. It is not advisable for your husband or wife to be your witness.	Address of witness ....
A second witness is only necessary if this form is not being signed by you personally but at your direction (for example, if a physical disability prevents you from signing).	
Signature of second witness.	in the presence of ....
	Full name of witness ....
	Address of witness ....

Part C: To be completed by the attorney(s)

Note: 1. This form may be adapted to provide for execution by a corporation
2. If there is more than one attorney additional sheets in the form as shown below must be added to this Part C

Please read the notes in the margin which follow and which are part of the form itself.	
Don't sign this form before the donor has signed Part B or if, in your opinion, the donor was already mentally incapable at the time of signing Part B.	I understand that I have a duty to apply to the Court for the registration of this form under the Enduring Powers of Attorney Act 1985 when the donor is becoming or has become mentally incapable.
If this form is being signed at your direction: • the person signing must not be an attorney or any witness (to Parts B or C). • you must add a statement that this form has been signed at your direction. • a second witness is necessary (please see below).	I also understand my limited power to use the donor's property to benefit persons other than the donor. I am not a minor.
Signature (or mark) of attorney.	Signed by me as a deed .... and delivered
Date.	on ....
Signature of witness.	in the presence of ....
The attorney must sign the form and his signature must be witnessed. The donor may not be the witness and one attorney may not witness the signature of the other.	Full name of witness .... Address of witness ....
A second witness is only necessary if this form is not being signed by you personally but at your direction (for example, if a physical disability prevents you from signing). Signature of second witness.	in the presence of .... Full name of witness .... Address of witness ....

NOTICE OF INTENTION TO APPLY FOR REGISTRATION EP1

Court of Protection/Public Trust Office

Enduring Powers of Attorney Act 1985

Notice of intention to apply for registration

To ....

of ....

This form may be adapted for use by three or more attorneys.

TAKE NOTICE THAT

I ....

of ....

and I ....

of ....

Give the name and address of the donor.

the attorney(s) of..

....

of ....

intend to apply to the Public Trustee for registration of the enduring power of attorney appointing me (us) attorney(s) and made by the donor on the .... 20........

It will be necessary for you to produce evidence in support of your objection. If evidence is available please send it with your objection, the attorney(s) will be given an opportunity to respond to your objection.

The grounds upon which you can object are limited and are shown at 2 overleaf.

1. If you wish to object to the proposed registration you have 4 weeks from the day on which this notice is given to you to do so in writing. Any objections should be sent to the Public Trustee and should contain the following details:

- your name and address;
- any relationship to the donor;
- if you are not the donor, the name and address of the donor;
- the name and address of the attorney;
- the grounds for objecting to the registration of the enduring power.

Note. The instrument means the enduring power of attorney made by the donor which it is sought to register. The attorney(s) does not have to be a relative. Relatives are not entitled to know of the existence of the enduring power of attorney prior to being given this notice.	2. The grounds on which you may object are: • that the power purported to have been created by the instrument is not valid as an enduring power of attorney; • that the power created by the instrument no longer subsists; • that the application is premature because the donor is not yet becoming mentally incapable; • that fraud or undue pressure was used to induce the donor to make the power; • that the attorney is unsuitable to be the donor's attorney (having regard to all the circumstances and in particular the attorney's relationship to or connection with the donor).
Note. This is addressed only to the donor.	3. You are informed that while the enduring power of attorney remains registered, you will not be able to revoke it until the Court of Protection confirms the revocation.
Note. This notice should be signed by every one of the attorneys who are applying to register the enduring power of attorney.	Signed .... Dated .... Signed .... Dated ....

APPLICATION FOR REGISTRATION EP2

Court of Protection/Public Trust Office No .....

Enduring Powers of Attorney Act 1985

Application for registration

Note. Give the full name and present address of the donor. If the donor's address on the enduring power of attorney is different give that one too.	The donor Name .... Address.. .... Address on the Enduring Power of Attorney (if different) ....
Note. Give the full name(s) and details of the attorney(s). This form may be adapted for use by three or more attorneys.	The attorney(s) Name .... Address.. age .... occupation .... relationship to donor (if any) .... Name .... Address.. age .... occupation .... relationship to donor (if any) ....
The date is the date upon which the donor signed the enduring power of attorney	I (we) the attorney(s) apply to register the enduring power of attorney made by the donor under the above Act on the .... 20.......... the original of which accompanies this application
	I (we) have reason to believe that the donor is or is becoming mentally incapable.
Notice must be personally given. It should be made clear if someone other than the attorney(s) gives the notice.	I (we) have given notice in the prescribed form to the following: • the donor personally at .... on the .... 20.........

• The following relatives of the donor at the address below on the dates given:

If there are no relatives entitled to notice please say so

Names	Relationship	addresses	date

Note. Cross out this section if it does not apply.

• The Co-Attorney(s) ....

at ....

on ....

A remittance for the registration fee accompanies this application

Note. The application should be signed by all the attorneys who are making the application.

I (we) certify that the above information is correct and that to the best of my (our) knowledge and belief I (we) have complied with the provisions of the Enduring Power of Attorney Act 1985 and of all the Rules and Regulations under it.

This must not pre-date the date(s) when the notices were given.

Signed .... Dated ....

Signed .... Dated ....

Address to which correspondence relating to the application is to be sent if different to that of the first-named attorney making this application ....

....

GENERAL FORM OF APPLICATION EP3

Court of Protection/Public Trust Office

Enduring Powers of Attorney Act 1985

In the matter of a power given by

If this application is being made prior to an application for registration the original enduring power of attorney should accompany this application.

.... (a donor)
to .... (attorney)
and .... (attorney)

General form of application

I ....
of ....
and I ....
of ....

Note. Give details of the order or directions that you are seeking

State under which sub-section of the Enduring Powers of Attorney Act 1985 or which rule of the Court of Protection (Enduring Powers of Attorney) Rules 1994 this application is made.

Apply for an order or direction that ....
....
....
....
....
....
....

and for any other directions which are necessary as a result of my/our application.

Note. Give details of the grounds on which you are seeking the order or directions

Evidence in support should accompany this application

The grounds on which I/we make this application are:
....
....
....

Note. The application should be signed by all the applicants or their solicitors.

Signed .... Dated ....
Signed .... Dated ....
Address where notices should be sent
....
....

Appendix IV

Terrence Higgins Trust Living Will

There is reproduced on the following pages, by kind permission of the Terrence Higgins Trust, the latest version of the Form first produced in 1992 by the Terrence Higgins Trust jointly with The Centre of Medical Law and Ethics of King's College London.

LIVING WILL

LIVING WILL

Third Edition

The Terrence Higgins Trust

KING'S College LONDON *Founded* 1829

Note to doctors: this Living Will is not a

Living Will

About Living Wills

Before you fill in your Living Will, please read all these notes carefully.

What is a Living Will?

This Living Will only takes effect if you become unable to tell people your wishes about your medical treatment, so you can no longer take part in decisions about it. You can use this form to do one or both of the following.

- Say in advance what your wishes are about medical treatment. These statements are called *'advance directives'*.
- Appoint someone, called a *'health care proxy'*, to take part in decisions about medical treatment on your behalf.

We have designed this form for people living with HIV or AIDS to use, but anyone can use it.

This Living Will is only about medical treatment. You cannot use it to say what you want to happen to your property after you die, or to make funeral requests. You will need an ordinary will to deal with your property. If you are thinking of making an ordinary will, we recommend that you get professional legal advice first.

In England and Wales an advance *refusal* of treatment is legally binding as long as the following conditions apply.

- You made your refusal when you were mentally capable of making that kind of decision.
- You meant your refusal to apply in the kind of situation which later arose, and you understood the consequences of your decision in that kind of situation.
- It really was your decision, and you did not decide under someone else's influence.

You cannot insist on *receiving* any particular treatment.

The legal status of a health care proxy is uncertain, but we believe that in practice doctors will pay attention to what your proxy says.

We have tried to provide a Living Will form which doctors are willing to act on. The British Medical Association has issued a statement supporting the use of Living Wills.

Discussing your Living Will with other people

A Living Will expresses important and very personal wishes. Please think about them carefully.

The form has been designed for you to fill in yourself, without the help of a lawyer, although you can consult a lawyer if you want to. You do not have to discuss what you plan to say in your Living Will with anybody, but we strongly urge you to talk to a doctor. (It could be any doctor. It does not have to be your own GP.) This is because a doctor will be able to explain what health care options are open to you. If you make any advance directives, discussing them with a doctor will also show that you were fully aware of the consequences of the decision you were taking and that the doctor fully understands what you want in case there is a dispute about your true wishes later. You might also want to discuss your plans with other people, for example, your partner, family or friends, or a nurse, counsellor, or religious adviser.

What happens if you change your mind?

The wishes stated in a Living Will are not final. You can change them at any time while you are still mentally capable of doing so. You do not have to do this in writing, it is enough just to tell your doctor. But if you do change your wishes, it is wise to destroy your Living Will (and all copies of it). You may choose to make a new Living Will on a new form. **Make sure any doctor who is treating you, and the people close to you, know what you have done.**

How to fill in the Living Will form

The following notes are to help you fill in the form. Please fill the form in clearly, using ink or a ballpoint pen.

This Living Will form has two main sections:

- one for advance directives; and
- one for appointing a health care proxy.

If you want to record your wishes about medical treatment, use the advance directives section. If you want to appoint someone else to make decisions about your medical treatment, use the health care proxy section. You can use either one or both sections.

Advance directives

Doctors must take patients' wishes into account. They must not give patients treatment which they do not want to have.

You can use this part of the Living Will form to record your wishes about medical treatment, to make sure that doctors know your wishes if you become unable to tell them yourself.

If you do want to use this part of the form, you do not have to fill in all the sections. Fill in as much or as little of the form as you like. If you do not want to make any advance directives at all, go straight to the part of the form headed 'health care proxy'.

1 – Medical treatment in general

This section lists three possible health conditions, called Case 1, Case 2 and Case 3. For each one you can say what you want to happen, by ticking the box for 'A' or 'B'. If you do not want to choose between 'A' and 'B', leave both boxes blank. If neither box 'A' nor box 'B' sets out your true wishes, you will need to discuss your actual wishes with your doctor. Treat each case separately. You may not want the same thing in all three cases.

In Case 1 (life-threatening condition) you can say what your wishes are if you develop an infection or other illness which cannot be cured and which has become so serious that your life is nearly at an end because of it.

Case 2 (permanent mental impairment) and Case 3 (permanent unconsciousness) cover two situations where your mental faculties are damaged. 'Permanent mental impairment' means a severe mental condition (like dementia). Case 2 applies where you have a severe mental condition, and your physical state then becomes so bad that you could only be kept alive by medical treatment. This might happen because you develop an illness, even if the illness is a minor one, which could be cured but which would threaten your life if it was not treated. Case 3 is where you fall into a permanent coma, or 'persistent vegetative state'.

It is important to realise that choosing box 'A' does not make sure that you will receive any particular treatment. The treatment you receive will depend on what your doctor thinks is reasonable in the circumstances.

Choosing box 'B' is legally binding as long as you meet the conditions (see under 'What is a Living Will?').

Artificial feeding and drinking (feeding and drinking through a tube) count as 'medical treatment', so your wishes will cover these too unless you say otherwise. If you have views about feeding and drinking through a tube, tell your doctor about them, and write them down in the section for particular treatments or tests.

2 – Particular treatments or tests

If you have strong views about particular types of medical treatment or test, you can write them here. For example, you might have views about ventilation (artificial breathing), or feeding through a tube. Please discuss this section with a doctor before you fill it in, as it is important that the doctor who is treating you can easily understand anything you write.

Say clearly if you want to refuse a particular treatment or test. This will help to avoid any dispute later. You cannot insist on receiving any particular treatment, although your wishes will be taken into account.

If this form does not give you the chance to give your views about something, please make sure you explain them to your doctor.

3 - Having a friend or relative with you if your life is in danger

If there is someone you would like to be with you before you die, you can write his or her name, address and phone number in this section so that he or she can be contacted if your life is in danger. **It may not be possible to contact the person you name, or for him or her to reach you in time.**

Tick the small box if you would like the people caring for you to do their best to keep you alive for as long as is reasonable to give the person you name a chance to reach you, **even if this means temporarily disregarding a choice of box 'B' in any of Cases 1, 2 or 3, and also any refusal of particular treatments or tests.**
If you tick this box, any refusal of treatment you have recorded earlier in the form will *not* be put into effect until the medical staff have tried to contact the person you name, and he or she has had a reasonable chance to reach you.

If you do not tick the small box, the wishes you have given earlier in this form will be put into effect even if the person you name has not yet had a chance to be with you.

Health care proxy

You can fill in this part of the form even if you have not made any advance directives earlier in the form.

There may be somebody (for example, your partner, a relative, or a friend) you would like to take part in medical decisions on your behalf if you become unable to do so. If so, write his or her name, address and phone number in this section of the form. This person is known as a 'health care proxy'.

Your health care proxy will be taking on an important responsibility. Please discuss this with the person you have in mind.

You need to make sure that he or she:

- is prepared to be your health care proxy;
- knows your wishes about medical treatment; and
- is prepared to express your wishes about medical treatment on your behalf.

If your proxy does not share your views on medical treatment, it may be difficult for him or her to represent you properly.

If medical staff cannot contact your proxy, they may have to make a decision without involving your proxy.

If you have to go into hospital, you may be asked to say who your 'next-of-kin' is. The term 'next-of-kin' has no defined legal meaning and you can name any person. If you appoint a health care proxy, it may avoid confusion if you name the same person as your 'next-of-kin'.

Your signature and witness

When you have filled in the form, you must date and sign it in front of an independent witness. The witness does not need to read your Living Will. The witness should watch you sign the form and then he or she should also sign it and clearly write his or her name and address in the spaces provided.

The witness should be aged 18 or over, and should not be any of the following people.

- Your husband, wife or partner.
- A relative.
- Anyone who stands to gain anything by your death, for example by inheriting anything from you.
- Anyone you have appointed as a health care proxy, or his or her husband, wife or partner.

Discussing your Living Will with a doctor

We recommend that you discuss your wishes with a doctor before you make your Living Will, but you do not have to. However, you might decide to do so later, after you have signed your Living Will. If you do discuss your Living Will with a doctor at any stage, please write the doctor's name, address and phone number in the space provided.
A different doctor caring for you later may want to confirm your wishes by speaking to the doctor you discussed your Living Will with.

What to do with your Living Will once you have filled it in

Make sure the people close to you (including your health care proxy, if you have one) know you have made a Living Will and where to find it.

If you have to go into hospital, make sure your doctor there knows you have a Living Will and what it says. Ask for a copy of your Living Will to be added to your hospital notes and to the notes of any other doctor who is treating you.

Living Will
Declaration

This is an important document. Before you fill it in, please read the notes which are attached to this form. We recommend that you discuss your Living Will with a doctor, but you do not have to.

Your name and address

Your name:

Your address:

I make this Living Will to record my wishes in case I become unable to communicate, and cannot take part in decisions about my medical care.

If you discuss this Living Will with a doctor before or after you fill it in, please fill in this section.

I have discussed this Living Will with the following doctor.

Doctor's name:

Doctor's address:

Doctor's phone number:

Living Will
Advance Directives

1 – Medical treatment in general

Three possible health conditions are described below.

For each condition, choose 'A' or 'B' by ticking the appropriate box, or leave both boxes blank if you have no preference. The choice between 'A' and 'B' is exactly the same in each case.

Treat each case separately. You do not have to make the same choice for each one.

I declare that my wishes concerning medical treatment are as follows.

Case 1 – Life-threatening condition

Here are my wishes if:

- **I have a physical illness from which there is no likelihood of recovery; *and***
- **the illness is so serious that my life is nearing its end.**

A **I want to be kept alive for as long as is reasonably possible using whatever forms of medical treatment are available.** ☐

B **I do not want to be kept alive by medical treatment. I want medical treatment to be limited to keeping me comfortable and free from pain. I refuse all other medical treatment.** ☐

Case 2 – Permanent mental impairment

Here are my wishes if:

- **my mental functions have become permanently impaired;**
- **the impairment is so severe that I do not understand what is happening to me;**
- **there is no likelihood of improvement; *and***
- **my physical condition then becomes so bad that I would need medical treatment to keep me alive.**

A **I want to be kept alive for as long as is reasonably possible using whatever forms of medical treatment are available.** ☐

B **I do not want to be kept alive by medical treatment. I want medical treatment to be limited to keeping me comfortable and free from pain. I refuse all other medical treatment.** ☐

Case 3 – Permanent unconsciousness

Here are my wishes if:

- **I become permanently unconscious and there is no likelihood I will regain consciousness.**

A **I want to be kept alive for as long as is reasonably possible using whatever forms of medical treatment are available.** ☐

B **I do not want to be kept alive by medical treatment. I want medical treatment to be limited to keeping me comfortable and free from pain. I refuse all other medical treatment.** ☐

Living Will
Advance Directives

2 – Particular treatments or tests

If you have any wishes about particular medical treatments or tests, you can record them here. If you want to refuse a particular treatment or test, you should say so clearly. You should speak to a doctor before you write anything in this space.

I have the following wishes about particular medical treatments or tests.

3 – Having a friend or relative with you if your life is in danger

You can fill in this section if you would like a particular person to be with you if your life is in danger. It may not be possible to contact the person you name, or for him or her to arrive in time.

If my life is in danger, I want the following person to be contacted to give him or her a chance to be with me before I die.

Name:

Address:

Daytime phone number:

Evening phone number:

Tick this box if you fill in a name in this section, and you want to be kept alive for as long as is reasonable to give the person you name a chance to reach you. ☐

If you tick this box, any wishes you have stated above in Section 1 – *Medical treatment in general* and Section 2 - *Particular treatments or tests* may be **temporarily disregarded**. This is explained in the notes with this form.

Living Will
Health Care Proxy

I appoint the following person to take part in decisions about my medical care on my behalf and to represent my views about the decisions if I am unable to do so. I want him or her to be consulted about and involved in those decisions and I want anyone who is caring for me to respect the views he or she expresses on my behalf.

Name:

Address:

Daytime phone number:

Evening phone number:

This Living Will remains effective until I make clear that my wishes have changed.

Signatures

Sign and date the form here in the presence of a witness.

Date:

/ /

Your signature:

The witness must sign here after you have signed the form. The witness should then print his or her name and address in the spaces provided. Please read the notes to this form to see who should not be a witness.

Signature of witness:

Name of witness:

Address of witness:

The Terrence Higgins Trust and the Centre of Medical Law and Ethics, King's College London developed this Living Will form.

The Terrence Higgins Trust

We are a registered charity. We provide practical support, help, counselling and advice for anyone living with or concerned about AIDS and HIV infection.

The Terrence Higgins Trust
52-54 Grays Inn Road
London WC1X 8JU

Administration and advice centre
Phone: 0171 831 0330
Fax: 0171 242 0121

Charity Registration Number: 288527
Company Registration Number: 1778149
Registered in England
A company limited by guarantee

Helpline
0171 242 1010
12 noon to 10pm every day

Legal Line
0171 405 2381
7pm to 9pm on Monday and Wednesday

Our work is mainly supported by voluntary donations.

KING'S College LONDON
Founded 1829

The Centre of Medical Law and Ethics researches in and teaches all aspects of medical law, medical ethics and related public policy.

The Centre of Medical Law and Ethics
King's College London
Strand
London WC2R 2LS

THE QUEEN'S ANNIVERSARY PRIZES
1996

2154 Crystal Mark
Clarity approved by Plain English Campaign

Third edition April 1997

We would like to thank the Lyndhurst Settlement for the financial help they gave us towards producing this form.

LIVING WILL—SHORT FORM

This form is suggested for practitioners who are asked to prepare a simple living will for their clients dealing with the withholding of medical treatment. It merely reflects the present state of the law and does not attempt to appoint a medical treatment proxy. It is based on a form first published in EAGLE in January 1994 and in the *Law Society's Elderly Client Handbook*, having been contributed by Denzil Lush, now the Master of the Court of Protection. It is reproduced here with kind permission of District Judge Gordon Ashton, General Editor of *Butterworths Older Client Law Service* and Master Denzil Lush.

This Living Will

is made on [*date*]

by me [*full name*] of [*full address*] born on [*date of birth*]

I Wish these instructions to be acted upon if two registered medical practitioners are of the opinion that I am no longer capable of making and communicating a treatment decision AND that I am:

- unconscious, and it is unlikely that I shall ever regain consciousness; **or**
- suffering from an incurable or irreversible condition that will result in my death within a relatively short time; **or**
- so severely disabled, physically or mentally, that I shall be totally dependent on others for the rest of my life.

I Refuse any medical or surgical treatment if:

- its burdens and risks outweigh its potential benefits; **or**
- it involves any research or experimentation which is likely to be of little or no therapeutic value to me; **or**
- it will prolong my life or postpone the actual moment of my death with no further benefit to me.

I Consent to being fed orally, and to any treatment that may:

- safeguard my dignity; **or**
- make me more comfortable; **or**
- relieve pain and suffering,

even though such treatment might unintentionally precipitate my death.

If I change the terms of this document I will notify the undermentioned person(s) so every effort should be made to contact (one of) them before relying on it: [*state name(s) together with address and telephone numbers*]

Signed by me [*full name*] *Signature*

in the presence of:

Name [*full name of witness*] *Signature of witness*

Address [*full address of witness*]

Afterword

The legal needs of people with HIV and AIDS

Professor Avrom Sherr
Dr Lorraine Sherr

In this Afterword, we report on what is known about cases currently or previously taken on behalf of people with AIDS or HIV or affected by the disease. Discrimination is often reported in connection with gender, race or sexuality, some of which is actionable discrimination. With HIV infection there is a complex phenomenon of discrimination associated with a viral infection, at times overlaid with the life condition of the very individuals who may be disproportionately affected by the virus and who may have been the subject of primary discrimination for their membership or affiliation to these initial groupings, through sexuality, sex work or usage of drugs. We report here on a particular project which was initially set up to understand the complexities of the discrimination experience as well as exploring redress through law. Charting redress reveals the extent to which the legal system can provide protection from discrimination or can ameliorate mental damage, physical damage or direct (and indirect) suffering associated with HIV-related discrimination. It is also possible that legal redress provides a framework of protection against the fear of discrimination, itself a potentially debilitating experience.

The literature on HIV describes discrimination as 'pervasive and extensive' (van de Ven et al 1996). However, there are few studies which have actually set out to elucidate how pervasive and extensive the phenomenon is, how it affects individuals and what they do about it (Altman 1992, Leach 1995, Neilsen and Young 1994, Tindall and Tillett 1990, Lester et al 1995). The undertones of discrimination are evidenced in practices such as avoidance of people who belong to specific groups, pressure to test people prior to decision-making (such as army recruitment or entry into countries such as the USA), or even the physical isolation (or the call for such isolation) of people infected with the virus. This occurs despite clear medical evidence that infection is not casual and public health is not in any way jeopardised by behaviours other than those directly associated with transmission, notably sexual, mother to child transmission and exchange of body fluids or parts. The condition is often described as one which is stigmatised (Price and Hsu 1992, Kraft and Rise 1995).

Discrimination is a negative event for both the individuals against whom discriminatory actions are aimed and the wider population. Effects include avoidance (van de Ven et al 1996, Osborne 1994), reluctance to initiate or avoid people with HIV, especially in the early years of the epidemic (Herdman and Kippax 1995, Kelly 1987, McGrory et al 1990, Jemmott 1992) and other resources such as housing and employment (Osborn 1994). As a result, people with HIV are said to experience feelings of isolation, may fail to disclose their status to family, friends and even healthcare providers. The indirect effects of such reactions could be social withdrawal or inappropriate medical care—both of which could have negative mental health and physical health consequences.

Few studies have set out and described both the detailed experiences of people with HIV infection in relation to discrimination and their evaluation of attempts to get legal redress as a result of these experiences. The most detailed study (Green 1995) compared the attitudes of the public and the perceptions of HIV positive people. This showed at times differences in the feelings and fears of the HIV positive compared to the actual attitudes expressed by the general population. However this may be a rather academic approach to the notion given that the general population may express tolerant attitudes but display intolerant behaviour. Furthermore the fear of discrimination may be a powerful restricting force for people with HIV, irrespective of actual experiences. It is unclear to what extent such fear corresponds to actual experiences, but the implications of fear still affect the lives of those who perceive real or imagined discriminatory experiences. Within the remit of a European initiative it was felt important to document the exact experience of discrimination of people with HIV, however subtle or extreme, as well as gathering detailed insight into their contact with legal remedy sources and an appraisal of the quality of these. In addition the level of exposure to HIV-related case work among the legal profession needed to be monitored. A range of training and educational initiatives have been introduced to health care professionals across the board in relation to HIV, and the corresponding experience and need among lawyers needed documenting (Sherr et al 1998).

A WHAT WE KNOW ABOUT THIS CLIENT GROUP

Two detailed surveys were carried out under the aegis of the European Funding initiative (Grant number SOC 200862 OSFO2 (95CVVF2–023–0) and in collaboration with the English and Welsh Legal Aid Board). The first initiative provided detailed survey information from a mixed cohort of UK HIV positive individuals gathered from a variety of access points (Sherr et al under submission). The second initiative took the form of a monitoring questionnaire to a large sample of UK legal aid lawyers (Sherr et al 1999). The results of these two surveys provide clear evidence of the extent of the problem, the gaps in legal service provision on the one hand and the experience and needs of the legal service providers on the other.

B CLIENTS WITH HIV

One hundred and eight HIV positive individuals (83.2% male; 16.8% female) attending medical, community or legal services agreed to provide detailed anonymous information. The sample included people from a variety of backgrounds with an age range from 18 to 70 (mean 36.1 years) with 30.6% ethnic minority individuals. The majority were diagnosed as HIV positive and well, with a quarter diagnosed with opportunistic infections. The sample included a variety of social conditions, including home owners, renters and homeless (3.9%), with over a third (35.4%) having experienced HIV-related hospitalisations and 55.6% being unemployed at the time of survey.

The majority of respondents (82.4%) stated that they experienced the fear of discrimination. Disclosure of their status to others was directly affected with only a minute proportion (6.5%) not hesitating in some way with regard to disclosing their status. Over a third (38%) felt their lives were substantially affected by discrimination while an additional 15.7% were mildly affected. Respondents were asked to provide details on who had perpetrated discriminatory acts against them. Unknown individuals accounted for 28%, landlords for 3.7%, healthcare workers 15.7%, family members 7.4%, social services 9.3%, other service providers 8.3% or professionals 15.7%; 45% felt that discrimination was associated with HIV as well as being a gay man or lesbian woman, 12% with HIV and ethnicity, 9% with HIV and drug use.

Experiences of discrimination since diagnosis are frequent, as set out in Table 1.

Table 1 Experiences of discrimination

Since being HIV positive have you experienced:		**% yes***
Subtle acts of discrimination		57.4%
Mild acts of discrimination, hard to quantify but hurtful		56.5%
Obvious acts of discrimination		47.2%
Acts of discrimination that have resulted in:		
(a) hurt feelings	67.6%	
(b) exclusion	49.1%	
(c) loss	42.6%	
(d) physical damage	12.0%	
(e) mental damage	54.6%	
(f) financial damage	40.7%	

* respondents could tick more than one category thus percentages total more than 100.

Fears of discrimination or actual experiences have affected client behaviour. This is set out in Table 2.

Table 2 Effects of discrimination fears on behaviour

Have fears of discrimination affected you undertaking the following:	**% of HIV positive people affected**
Telling family about status	59
Telling friends about status	60
Telling people at work about status	70
Undertaking non-work activities	56
Applying for employment	67
Seeking out any form of healthcare	53

The data shows the pervasiveness of discrimination effects on disclosure, employment, leisure and healthcare seeking. When respondents experienced discrimination, they only sought formal legal advice or took legal action in a minority of cases. Indeed, the most frequently expressed reaction was 'keeping it to myself'. Although many report it to healthcare workers, the absence of good links between professions may limit the referral chain.

Table 3 Reaction to incidents of discrimination by HIV positive people

When you experienced discrimination how did you respond?	**% responding yes**
Told friends/family	50.0%
Kept it to myself	34.3%
Reported it to healthcare workers	31.5%
Sought informal legal advice	25.0%
Sought formal advice	23.1%
Took legal action	11.1%
Went to court on the issue	4.6%

These tables clearly show the wide extent of discrimination experience on which potential legal redress could be based. The effect of discrimination on mental and physical health was described as being severe, moderate or mild. The range of effects are set out in Table 4.

Table 4 Effect of discrimination experiences on mental health

Effect	**% Severe**	**% Moderate**	**% Mild**
Emotional trauma	25.9	26.9	10.2
Secondary physical problems	7.4	20.4	10.2
Deterioration of health	17.6	13.0	13.0
Despair	23.1	19.4	12.0
Fear of recriminations	21.3	21.3	7.4
Reluctance to proceed	16.7	16.7	11.1
Stigma	19.4	14.8	13.9
Depressed	32.4	19.4	11.1
Confidentiality problems	22.2	15.7	8.3
Concern for dependants	12.0	8.3	10.2
Reluctance to seek help	28.1	18.8	12.0
Suicidal	11.1	11.1	14.8

The mental and associated physical wellbeing of people experiencing discrimination seems to be affected to a considerable degree, with many individuals feeling depressed, reporting deterioration of health, emotional trauma and physical problems. Of concern is the suicidal level of worry reported by almost a third.

The small sample may be biased, but if these figures transfer to the total cohort of HIV positive individuals in the UK for example, the legal need is considerable. Given the pervasiveness of the experiences, it was important to log action taken and then evaluate the quality of service and appraisal of this service by the sample. The data suggests an enormous unmet need, with a third keeping the experiences to themselves. Only 23.1% reported having sought formal legal advice and only half that number (11.1%) noted any legal action. Only five (4.6%) had proceed to court on the issue. Legal resources utilised were varied, with the following being approached.

Citizen's Advice Bureaux	12%
Hospital clinics	11%
Specialists provided by clinics (eg housing officer)	5.6%
Social workers	21%
Welfare rights officers	7%
Specialised legal providers	33%
Lawyers (privately at law centres or on legal aid)	14%

Very few of the respondents recorded how they knew their problems could be helped by legal assistance. Only 22.2% sought legal advice on their own initiative, with 5.6% doing so at the suggestion of their clinic and 6.5% at the suggestion of friends or family. Legal outreach was a trigger for a further 6.5%. It was not uncommon for a variety of alternative remedies to be tried prior to legal assistance seeking—including counselling, approaching unions, self confrontation or even approaches to the media. It was not uncommon for individuals to experience multiple rather than single problems.

Respondents were asked to categorise the primary nature of their legal problems. The data revealed a wide spread of issues, covering most areas of law as follows.

Employment	41.4%
Immigration	13.8%
Grievous bodily harm	10.3%
Harassment	6.9%
Child issues	3.4%
Breach of confidentiality	6.9%
Medical treatment	13.8%
Discrimination	3.4%

All clients were asked if they had a 'legal' problem—49.1% believed that they had no legal problem; 19.4% felt discrimination was linked to their legal problem, 18.5% felt it was the main issue and 4.6% reported it as a background issue. It is clear that clients experienced more problems than those for which they sought help. The range is wide and 27 areas of legal problem were mentioned, notably:

Housing	18.5%	Employment	29.6%	Insurance	22.2%
Childbirth	3.7%	Education	6.5%	Health	24.1%
Welfare benefits	18.5%	Migration	13%	Crime	5.6%
Wills & probate	1.9%	Confidentiality	25%	Tort	0.9%
Contract	2.8%	Consumer	3.7%	Finance	18.5%
Family law	0.9%	Civil liberties	7.4%	Discrimination	23.1%
Harassment	13%	Travel	17.6%	Abuse	13.0%
Consent	2.8%	Care	13.9%	Social	22.2%
Prisoners' rights	2.8%	[illegible]	[illegible]		

Detailed data was explored with the 76 respondents who recorded a clear experience of discrimination. Just over a third (35.5%) believed that the experience was not actionable in law, 36.8% felt it was possibly actionable and 27.6% felt it was probably actionable in law. For those who believed it was possibly or probably actionable in law, reasons for not seeking legal help were associated with lack of energy (22%), overwhelming barriers of time in the presence of a fatal illness (17%), expense (19%), exhaustion (22%) and confidentiality worries (20%).

Only 4% of the sample turned to law despite the fact that 82% reported experiences of discrimination. Of the 11 who had entered the legal process, seven recorded that formal proceedings had been taken—six recorded a court or tribunal appointment and one a hearing. For two clients the case proceeded partially, for four it proceeded to settlement, three to court and four did not proceed. Some clients withdrew after starting negotiations.

Twelve respondents gave details of legal initiatives, eight (7.4% of the total sample) had used legal aid assistance, two (1.9% of the whole sample) had been self-funded and two had other sources of funding (such as charity help). All respondents who had any contact with legal services during the HIV or AIDS illness provided appraisal of these services.

Table 5 Appraisal of legal services

Service aspect	**n**	**% Appraising legal service as**				
		Very good	*Good*	*Average*	*Poor*	*Very poor*
Legal services	25	30.8	30.8	19.2	3.8	11.5
Individual lawyer on your case	17	52.9	23.5	5.9	11.8	5.9
Communication over your case	18	27.8	27.8	22.2	11.1	11.1
Sympathy	20	35.0	20.0	5.0	25.0	15.0
Understanding of HIV issues	26	53.8	23.1	3.8	7.1	11.5
The legal system	18	5.6	16.7	16.7	33.3	27.8
The outcome	11	27.3	9.1	9.1	9.1	45.5

The overall ratings of lawyers was positive (good, very good or even average). On balance clients tended to approve of the provider but not of the legal system. Poor or very poor performance ratings are a matter of concern, and the data does show that in each category a notable minority displayed dissatisfaction. Training, input and provision may well allow for improvements and initiatives to meet the needs of this group: 15% found legal services poor, 18% thought their lawyer was poor, over one in four (22%) felt communication was poor and 40% felt the simple basics of sympathy were lacking. Almost one in five (19%) felt lawyers did not understand HIV issues and 61% believed the legal system to be inadequate. Over half also thought the outcome was poor.

This survey pointed out the widespread experience of discrimination and the poor utilisation of legal pathways for redress. The situation was exacerbated by the fact that of the very few who proceeded to law, satisfaction was not unanimous. Clearly experience and expertise building is needed.

C LAWYER PERSPECTIVES

A simultaneous initiative tapped the experience of lawyers and their needs in relation to HIV, discrimination and the law (Sherr et al 1998). A standardised questionnaire was posted out with all Legal Aid payment cheques sent to a sample of 11,000 law providers. The brief survey asked for any lawyers with either dealings in HIV or AIDS or training needs to respond. From the 600 returns received 146 noted at least one client with HIV and provided detailed information (84% solicitors and 16% barristers). Solicitors recorded coming from a range of firms, with a mean number of 7.8 partners (ranging from 0–50). The following table sets out the areas of expertise the lawyers represented.

Area	n	%*
Crime	52	36%
Family	52	36%
Housing	26	18%
General	24	17%
Immigration	23	16%
Litigation	23	16%
Personal injury	23	16%
Property/convey	18	12%
Employment	12	8%
Wills/probate	10	7%
Medical negligence	8	6%
Commercial	8	6%
Company	4	3%
Mental health	5	3%
Welfare benefits	3	2%
Discrimination	3	2%
Debt	2	1%

* respondents could represent more than one area

There is an obviously wide range of expertise consulted across the legal profession. However, those specialising in crime and family work are most prominent in their representation, followed by housing, immigration, litigation and personal injury. The lawyers recorded a mean of 2.2 clients over the year preceding the survey (minimum zero: maximum 30) and a mean of 5.5 clients in previous years (range 0–340). The survey described a total of 303 client contacts in the previous year and a further 700 in past years providing a minimum experience of 1,003 clients in total. This data would suggest a growing need.

Detail of the legal service provision for these clients from the lawyers contacted show an interesting pattern, with revealing contrasts when set against the client data. The usual pattern of case distribution is one with a preponderance of advice with the majority of cases receiving advice and assistance and proceeding to some form of compromise. Case load distribution would

HIV or AIDS cases this pattern was inverted with the majority of cases (69.5%) proceeding to court or tribunal, as set out in the following figures.

Table 6 Nature of service provided

Service provided	n	%
Advice only	189	19.9%
Settled without action	85	8.9%
Abandoned	16	1.7%
Proceed to court/tribunal	662	69.5%

Explanations for this spread may be varied. It may be that the severity of the issues inevitably leads to court and away from advice only. It may be that the nature of the problems lend themselves to this distribution or it may be that legal aid provision associated with specific types of cases is disproportionately represented. This may reveal a hidden difficulty of accessing services for those who do not have automatic rights to legal aid as can be seen by the high proportions of crime (25.5%), immigration (22.6%) and family matters.

Lawyers provided information on the legal category of 460 their HIV related cases. These were:

Area of law	Number of cases (%)
Discrimination direct	18 (4.3%)
Discrimination indirect	24 (5.8%)
Crime	106 (25.5%)
Housing	60 (14.4%)
Employment	14 (3.4%)
Immigration	94 (22.6%)
Family	24 (5.8%)
Other	58 (13.9%)
Medical negligence	18 (4.3%)
Total	**416**

Access problems also become clear when comparing the transmission category of the clients to the national data on transmission categories of those diagnosed with HIV. Essentially, 41.4% of the cases dealt with by the lawyers were associated with haemophilia and only 19.3 and 11% respectively for gay men or ethnic minorities. The actual distribution of HIV tends to show a preponderance of infection concentrated among gay men and ethnic minorities.

The organisation of the legal profession in response to AIDS lags dramatically behind the organisation seen in the medical profession (Holmes 1990, Pick 1996, Gerbert 1988). Many doctors receive special training on HIV-related issues (Sherr 1989), while the majority of lawyers taking cases (81%) had no specialist training at all. Only 9% had referred clients elsewhere (invariably to other legal service providers). This contrasts to the well-established multidisciplinary approach in health which actively involves lawyers and in some instances (such as the Immunity Legal Aid Centre was able to do before joining up with the Terrence Higgins Trust) funds legal services from healthcare budgets. Desire for information was high among the group of lawyers, with 71% expressing a desire to have helpline advice available and 67% requesting specialist training.

D CONCLUSIONS

These two UK-based studies provide a snapshot of legal demand and legal service provision. It is clear that there is a growing need, that there are limitations in terms of access to lawyers and there is a training need for law providers. Discrimination, direct or indirect, is a common experience for people with HIV and it affects their mental health and quality of life. Until societal attitudes change, legal pathways of redress are required. The availability of new combination therapies may provide a renewed energy to pursue their rights and a new motivation to address their human rights. Lawyers have an increasing case load, often confined to areas of law where free legal provision is available and skewed towards cases which proceed to courts or tribunals. There is much more in terms of advice and settlement that the legal profession can offer people with HIV. If advances in discrimination prevention provision in other areas are to be adapted and applied to the rights of people with HIV, the educational and training needs of lawyers ought to be addressed. Hopefully this book will provide a beginning for many lawyers and legal advice workers to take forward issues on behalf of a needy population.

1 Acknowledgements

We would wish to acknowledge the contributions of all the participants as well as the help of the European group and the EC funding initiative (SOC 200862 OSFO2 (95CVVF2-023-0) and SI2.123174 (99CVF4-022 on Discrimination against people with HIV and AIDS—good practice in legal advice and litigation concerning employment, insurance, credit housing education and health care). Special thanks to Lisa Webley, Jonathan Grimshaw OBE, Steve Orchard CBE and Geoffrey Bindman).

2 References

Altman, D 'The most political of diseases' in Timewell, E, Minichiello, V and Plummer, D (eds) *AIDS in Australia* (1992) Prentice Hall, pp 55–72

Crawford, J, Turtle, A and Kippax, S 'Student favoured strategies for AIDS avoidance' *Aus Jnl of Psychology* (1990) 42 pp 123–37

Green, G 'Attitudes towards people with HIV: Are they as stigmatizing as people with HIV perceive them to be?' *Social Science & Medicine* (1995) 41(4) pp 557–68

Gerbert, B, Maguire, B, Badner, V, Greenspan, D, Greenspan, J, Barnes, D, Carlton, R 'Changing dentists' knowledge, attitudes, and behaviors relating to AIDS: a controlled educational intervention' *J Am Dent Assoc* (1988) 116(7) pp 851–4

Herdman, E, and Kippax, S, 'Institutional HIV AIDS-related discrimination' (1995) Sydney HIV AIDS and Society publications

Holmes, C A J 'AIDS education for the podiatric physician. Evaluating program impact' (1990) *Amer Podiat Med Assoc* 80(1) pp 31–5

Jemmott, J, Freleicher, J and Jemmott, L 'Perceived risk of infection and attitudes toward risk groups determinants of nurses behavioural intentions regarding AIDS patients' research' (1992) *Nursing and Health* 15 pp 295–301

Johnston, D, Stall, R, Smith, K 'Reliance by gay men and intravenous drug users on friends and family for AIDS-related care' (1995) *AIDS Care* 7(3) pp 307–19

Kadushin, G, 'Gay men with AIDS and their families of origin: an analysis of social support' (1996) *Health & Social Work* 21(2) pp 141–9

Kelly, J, St Lawrence, J, Smith, S, Hood, H, Cook, D 'Medical students' attitudes towards AIDS and homosexual patients' *Jnl of Medical Education* 62 pp 549–56

Kraft, P and Rise, J 'Prediction of attitudes towards restrictive AIDS policies a structural equation modelling approach' (1995) *Social Sciences and Medicine* 40 pp 711–8

Lester, P, Partridge, J C, Chesney, M A, Cooke, M 'The consequences of a positive prenatal HIV antibody test for women' (1995) *Journal of Acquired Immune Deficiency Syndromes & Human Retrovirology* 10(3) pp 341–9

Neilsen, G and Young, F 'HIV, AIDS advocacy and anti-discrimination legislation: the Australian response' (1994) *Intl Jnl of STD and AIDS* 5 pp 13–17

Noble, J, Kippax, S and Crawford, J 'Some demographic correlates of HIV AIDS related discrimination (1995) *Australian Journal of Social Issues* 30 pp 310–24

Osbone, J E 'Public health, HIV and AIDS' *Textbook of AIDS Medicine* Broder, S, Merigan, T and Bolognesi, D (eds) (1994) Ch 9 pp 133–148

Pick, S, Reyes, J, Alvarez, M, Cohen, S, Craige, J, Troya, A, 'AIDS prevention: training for pharmacy workers in Mexico City' (1996) *AIDS Care* 8(1) pp 55–69

Price, V, and Hsu, M 'Public opinion about AIDS policies the role of misinformation and attitudes towards homosexuals' (1992) *Public Opinion Quarterly* 56 pp 29–52

Sherr, A H *Client Interviewing for Lawyers—An Analysis and Guide* (1986) Sweet & Maxwell

Sherr, A H 'Lawyers and Clients—The First Meeting' (1986) 49 MLR 323

Sherr, L 'The person behind the virus: migration, human factors and some moral and ethical questions' Haour, Knipe, M and Rector, R (1996a) op cit Ch 5 pp 70–85

Sherr, L *Grief and AIDS* (1996b) John Wiley and Son, Chichester

Sherr, L *AIDS as a Gender Issue* (1996c) Taylor and Francis

Sherr, L 'Psychosocial services and providing care for women with HIV infection' in Minkoff, H, Dehovitz, J and Duerr, A (eds) *HIV infection in Women* (1995) Raven Press pp 107–124

Sherr, L 'Women and Power' in Shenker, I (ed) *AIDS Multicultural Issues* (1997) Plenum Press

Sherr, L, Sherr, A H and Orchard, S 'JAMA Controversies: the role of HIV specialists' (1998) JAMA 18 279(11) 834; discussion 835

Sherr, L, Sherr, A H, Peters, B and Webley, L (under submission) 'You don't shout it from the rooftops—discriminatory experiences of people with HIV' *International Journal of Health and Human rights*

Sherr, L 'Summary evaluation of the National AIDS council training unit' (1989) *Counselling Psychology Quarterly*

Sherr, L, Christie, G, Sher, R, Metz, 'J Evaluation of the effectiveness of AIDS training and information courses' (1989) *S Afr Med J* 7 76(7) pp 358–62

Stiff, J, McCormack, M, Zook, E, Stein, T and Henry, R 'Learning about AIDS and HIV transmission in collegiate students' (1990) *Communication Research* 17 pp 743–58

Stipp, H and Kerr, D 'Determinants of public opinion about AIDS' (1989)*Public Opinion Quarterly* 53 pp 98–106

Tindall, B and Tillett, G 'HIV-related discrimination' (1990) *AIDS* 4 Sup 1 pp 251–56

Van de Ven, P, Turtle, A, Kippax, S, Crawford, J and French, J 'Trends in heterosexual tertiary students' knowledge of HIV and intentions to avoid people who might have HIV/AIDS' (1996) *Care* 8(1) pp 43–53

Westerman, P and Davidson, P 'Homophobic attitudes and AIDS-risk behaviour of adolescents' (1993) *Jnl of Adolescent Health* 14 pp 208–213

Index